W9-AEF-984

Jonathan Swift

European University Studies

Europäische Hochschulschriften
Publications Universitaires Européennes

Series XIV
Anglo-Saxon Language and Literature

Reihe XIV   Série XIV
Langue et littérature anglo-saxonnes
Angelsächsische Sprache und Literatur

Band/Vol. 220

PETER LANG
Berne · Frankfurt am Main · New York · Paris

Jean-Paul Forster

JONATHAN SWIFT

The Fictions of the Satirist

PETER LANG
Berne · Frankfurt am Main · New York · Paris

CIP-Titelaufnahme der Deutschen Bibliothek

Forster, Jean-Paul:
Jonathan Swift: the fictions of the satirist/Jean-Paul Forster.
– Bern; Frankfurt am Main; New York; Paris: Lang, 1991
  (European university studies: Anglo-Saxon language and
  literature; Vol. 220)
  ISBN 3-261-04259-1
NE: Europäische Hochschulschriften/14

This book has been published with the help
of a grant from the Swiss Academy of Humanities

ISBN 3-261-04259-1
ISSN 0721-3387

© Peter Lang Publishers, Inc., Berne 1991

Druck: Weihert-Druck GmbH, Darmstadt

Je vois dans les intrigues que nous inventons le moyen privilégié par lequel nous re-figurons notre expérience temporelle confuse, informe, et, à la limite, muette.
Paul Ricoeur

Acknowledgments

A great many colleagues and students, with whom I discussed my ideas, have helped me to write this book. They may be happily ignorant of the fact, but I wish to thank them for their stimulating suggestions. As for my indebtedness to Swift scholars and critics, it is obvious. I am also grateful to Brian Stanton and Paul Hunter for their patient and pertinent comments on the manuscript.

The generous support of the Swiss Academy of Humanities has greatly facilitated the preparation of the book for publication, for which I am equally grateful.

The publisher and the author thank the editor of *SPELL* and Gunter Narr Verlag for permission to reprint extensive portions of an essay that appeared in the series of publications of the Swiss Association of University Teachers of English.

Contents

Abbreviations

PW   *The Prose Writings of Jonathan Swift*, ed. Herbert Davis, 14 volumes. Oxford. Blackwell, [1939 - 1963] 1965.

SPW   *Swift: Poetical Works*, ed. Herbert Davis. London. Oxford University Press, 1967.

Introduction

As time passes and the circumstances that have inspired artists retreat into the distance, to become first the past, and then history, their works lose their topical interest. When the works are texts, and the texts are narrative or dramatic in nature, they inevitably become a source of fables or myths for later ages, no matter how accurately they once reflected their epoch. Satires do not escape this fate, and this is why the most highly valued satirists in world literature are also usually inventors of fictions. What distinguishes them from minor satirists, and from one another, is neither the number nor the nature of the excesses and deviations in human behaviour, social activity, politics, and religion which they write about – these are eternal and constant. Their writings to a large extent endure thanks to their stories or sketches: *these* are memorable, and *these* endow their author's wit and social criticism with its distinctive character. Such is the case of Jonathan Swift.

He is considered to be one of the great satirists of all time, and the popularity of *Gulliver's Travels* is a sure sign that this is no idle claim. People who have never read a line of the celebrated satire know it in a way: have they not heard about the Lilliputians and the giants? Whoever has read Swift can usually recall at will visions of giants lying on their sides and lending an attentive ear to diminutive human creatures, of men extravagantly dressed, or of babies' flesh cooked and dressed in various ways and offered as delicacies to the rich. Yet there is something odd about his reputation: something like a flaw in it. One might say that some readers tend to value his fictions for themselves – in their minds, they have become like dissociated from their satirical bias –, whereas for others Swift stands as a master ironist, rather than a creator of fictions. This is, of course, a gross oversimplification, but the fact remains that influential voices, among literary historians and critics in particular, have regularly disputed Swift's qualities as a man of imagination. Dryden was the first, when he said to him long before he wrote his great works: "Cousin Swift, you will never be a poet." Dr Johnson, who reports this anecdote,[1] is another. Once, in a conversation, he expressed the poor opinion he had of the *Travels*: "When once you have thought of big men and little men," he said, "it is very easy to do all the rest."[2] A third was no less a person than Herder, the German critic, who described Swift as a rational genius.[3] As these quotations suggest, Swift's fictions, for all their wealth, diversity and captivating character, have not received the amount of critical attention to which they were entitled, as the perhaps most attractive aspect in his satires. It might be said that they were more often taken for granted in discussions of the work than studied as a significant element in his satirical art and as of interest in themselves, if such a summary statement may be permitted in describing the general trend in criticism over the past 250 years. As for the few studies of the problem that exist, they mainly deal with one or other of the fictional patterns in one or several works, but little research has been done into the general rôle of the fictional element within the satires and, in particular, into what it contributes to the character of the satirical vision of the writer. The purpose of the present study is to help fill this gap. It proposes a revaluation of a side of Swift's art that has been less thoroughly explored than the others, and at the same time offers a tentative explanation of the way some satires succeed in transcending the critique of an age, to remain alive centuries after they were composed.

The fictions of a satirist are his imaginative reconstructions of his times. The facts to which they refer should not be viewed as "flies in amber": they are not foreign bodies incorporated into a substance of a different, transparent, nature, as strict historical research, and footnotes, might sometimes seem to imply. They are assimilated and transformed by the fiction, and if they remain recognizable, it is because, in each case, the whole of the fiction, and not mere isolated details, contributes to establishing a link with the world of circumstantial reality that is

1 *Lives of the English Poets* [1779 - 1781], quoted from *Jonathan Swift* (Penguin Critical Anthologies), ed. Denis Donoghue, Harmondsworth, Penguin, 1971, p. 78.

2 James Boswell, *The Life of Samuel Johnson*, quoted from *Swift: The Critical Heritage*, ed. Kathleen Williams, London, Routledge and Kegan Paul, 1970, p. 205.

3 *Adrastea* I (1801), *Herders Sämmtliche Werke*, Berlin, Weidmann, 1885, vol. xxiii, pp. 180 - 185. Because Herder fails to appreciate the strength of Swift's imagination, he even goes so far as to suggest that his work will not survive (see pp. 188-189).

referred to. In other words, the fictions of the satirist are, like all fictions, global recreations, by means of specially selected fictional devices, of a reference to the world of the writer's experience.

At the same time, satirical fictions are different from other fictions, and there is every reason to believe that this is because the attitude of satirists towards fiction in general differs from that of other writers. They do not create their own sort of fiction because it proves to be a suitable outlet for personal concerns. They do not elaborate it because it appeals aesthetically to their imagination. For them, such qualities are at most of secondary importance. In satire the value of a fiction depends on whether or not it can be turned to good satirical account. Much less than in other kinds of writings are fictions an end in themselves. Their function is mainly instrumental: a means to an end, which lies outside the fictions themselves. This end is, of course, criticism, which is expressed through ridicule and laughter. Although the satirist may not be seeking fantasy at any cost, and may even be content to remain within the realistic register of fiction writing, his aim is neither truth, nor fidelity to experience, but rather a sort of artificiality, through which the referent is distorted beyond immediate recognition in an attempt to render it objectionable; and it will often be observed that the more fanciful the construction of the reference, the more provocative it is, and the more successfully it turns the world into ridicule. On the other hand, excessive artificiality and fancifulness can become drawbacks, if they are taken too far. With highly fanciful fictions, it is less easy to say exactly what they mean, although it should be admitted that fictions are in any case elusive discourses, and that they are inevitably the most elusive aspect of satire as well. The uneasy compromise existing between a fictional artificiality which distorts facts and an adequate, namely a still recognizable, picture of actual people and events, is the hallmark of successful satirical fictions.

On this head, Swift's satires confront the reader with a problem which is related to that flaw in their reputation alluded to above. The history of their reception shows that, even among those familiar with his work, there have always been some who seem to have been unable, in their reading, to reconcile the two sides of his satires' antithetic orientation, towards an ironical, but precise and recognizable, representation of the referent on the one hand, and towards fanciful fabrication on the other ; either, like the first readers, they have been so engrossed in the writer's criticism of his epoch that they have tended to overlook the other aspect, the way it is presented or, like those who turned *Gulliver's Travels* into a book for children, they have cherished the product of a vivid imagination at the exclusion of everything else.

If, on the whole, the fictions of the satirist themselves have attracted less critical attention than other aspects of his satires and if, consequently, they have been less systematically explored, this is probably due in the first place to their deceptively unsophisticated character: while their elaboration can be quite intricate, they also preserve an unassuming air which, as Dr Johnson's comment quoted above suggests, does not tempt the analyst. This could never have happened with the other aspects of the satires. Every twist of Swift's irony can be – and has been – rationally explained, because they appeal directly to the intellect; every stylistic device can expect to be interpreted convincingly in terms of expressivity, because his style exerts a spell on anyone sensitive to the quality of language; and most persons and events alluded to can find a proper historical identification, because the writer knows how to stir our curiosity: but the nature of the fictions remains outwardly so unpretentious that they tend to be merely taken for granted. That said, it is possible to learn something about them by studying their function as a component in the satires.

This function is to a large extent structural. Analytical philosophy has convincingly argued that structures of experience are that which is most universally communicable. But structures of experience do not find direct expression in what are commonly called the structures of texts, namely the aesthetic order of their presentation. They undergo a dynamic process of refiguration. As I shall try to demonstrate, this refiguration of experience involves, in the case of Swift's satires, the utilization of a selection of patterns which constitute what Hayden White, Louis O. Mink and Paul Ricoeur, developing Aristotle's notion of mythos, would call types of emplotment.[4] Their ordering (*"mise en forme"*) extracts from what is a mere succession or juxtaposition of gestures, actions and

---

4 Hayden White, *Metahistory: The Historical Imagination in Nineteenth-Century Europe*, Baltimore, Johns Hopkins University Press, 1973, pp. 1 - 42; Louis O. Mink, "Philosophical Analysis and Historical Understanding", *Review of Metaphysics* 20: 667 - 698 (1968) and "History and Fiction as Modes of Comprehension", *New Literary History* (1979): 541 - 558. These two writers are mainly concerned with the function of narrative in historical studies. Paul Ricoeur, *Time and Narrative*, vol. i, Chicago, Chicago University Press, 1983, pp. 31 - 87. Ricoeur is concerned with both literature and history.

events "a configuration which organizes [these actions and events] into an intelligible whole, of a sort such that we can always ask what is the 'thought'" of this fiction.[5] Moreover, the study of the fictional refiguration of experience in the satires provides the analyst with an opportunity to address himself to such important questions as where these fictional patterns come from; what their connection is with the time of their utilization; what rôle they play in individual satires, and how they are made to function satirically; how they manage to remain alive, when the world to which they refer is dead and gone; what happens when, as a result of this, a reader favours the fiction, at the expense of the facts referred to, which have lost their topical interest for him; whether, in this case, his reading distorts the delicate balance achieved by the writer and whether it is not, in this, essentially different from that of a contemporary reader; and, finally, whether the fictions of the satirist can help to "ascertain the ontological status of [Swift's] writings between the permanence of true literature and their fleeting topicality as an event"[6] – which remains one of the fundamental problems posed by the work.

It is well-known that early readers of satire – and what we know of Swift's own first readers illustrates this point well – are usually bent on translating the fictions back into the language of facts correctly: what they are interested in is keys for decoding the satirical message. Does this mean that the nature of the reconstruction of contemporary reality into fictional terms escapes their notice completely? Certainly not: the very turn taken by their decoding shows that the general character assumed by the fiction is always present in their minds, and it plays a significant part in their interpretation by performing a guiding rôle. Quite simply, they are too exclusively taken up by the topical interest of the satires to express directly their appreciation of what, in them, affords pleasure. But let there be no mistake about it: the very eagerness with which they embark on the business of explaining every reference is itself evidence that they are not blind to the imaginative qualities of the fictions. With later readers the reaction is different, of course. For them the satires have lost much of their urgency with their topicality, and yet

---

5 Paul Ricoeur, op. cit., p. 65.
6 Johann N. Schmidt, "Swift's Uses of Facts and Fictions: *The Drapier's Letters*", *Proceedings of the First Münster Symposium on Jonathan Swift*, eds Hermann J. Real and Heinz J. Vienken, München, Fink, 1985, p. 252.

they will generally be well aware that they must not completely lose sight of what were the satirist's original targets. Whatever else may separate them, early and late readers have then at least one basic attitude to the text in common: both read a satire, some more and some less deliberately, as though they had, on the one hand, solid facts and, on the other, a partly disguised transposition of them; and as though understanding the satire consisted in appreciating the amount of distortion that had been employed in the reconstruction of circumstantial reality. Consequently, we may consider that distortion, disguise – what was referred to above as the fanciful character and deliberate artificiality of the fiction – and their decoding are inseparable from the satirical deployment of fiction, and that one of the central functions of the fictional emplotments is, as already said, interpretative. If this is the case, it is insufficient to seek to understand a particular satire, simply by trying to retrace the facts and events it refers to. However thrilling it may be for the literary historian to discover that, at a certain point, Gulliver refers to events that took place in 1715 or 1721, or that Swift got this or that idea from a book found in his library, such findings are sadly wanting when the reader tries to appreciate the satirical nature of the comment made by the connection, and to explain what contribution this connection makes to his enjoyment of the satires – for the decoding of a satire is always a pleasurable activity. Similarly, the reading of satirical fictions on their own, as pure fictions, is fraught with dangers and is equally unsatisfactory, since they have not been conceived to be read by themselves, but rather to be instruments to achieve certain ends. In discussions of Swift's satires, insufficient emphasis has been put on the difficulty of reconciling the facts with the fictions, and the decoding activity proper with the pleasure afforded by the recognition of the patterns of emplotments. It is only together that they can produce that renewed understanding of life of which satire, like all "mimetic" representations, offers an example.[7]

Since the fictional patterns in Swift's satires are mostly borrowed from various modes of expression, or semeiotic systems utilized by his contemporaries to interpret their time and voice their reactions to it, as well as to express their beliefs, it seems advisable to begin the present investigation with a study of the way the satirist adapted these modes and

7 Paul Ricoeur, op. cit., p. 42: "This pleasure of recognition . . . presupposes, I think, a prospective concept of truth, according to which to invent is to rediscover." See also pp. 48 - 50.

semeiotic systems to satirical purposes. This was, in fact, the germ of the project of the present study. The presumed validity of such an investigation was quickly confirmed by the realization that later readers had not relied on the same fictional patterns to guide their understanding of the satires as earlier readers had and that, although this change of dominant in their reading had not affected the essence of the satirical meaning, it had unquestionably modified their perception of its nature by lending it a different quality.

Swift's borrowings from contemporary modes of expression are numerous and multifarious, but they can be divided into three categories. Each type corresponds to one of the structural devices that give his satires that special provocative character which is usually associated with his name. The first category is the one that is most strictly indebted to eighteenth-century models. It usually forms the external packaging of the satires and constitutes one of the aspects of the work most frequently analyzed. Although rooted just as deeply in the period of their conception, the other two fictional patterns, which form the core of the satires, are easier to relate to more perennial literary and non-literary modes of expression. They have been the object of much less attention. One often constitutes the inner story or plot contained within the satire, and it uses traditional, not to say perennial, literary motifs. The other enlivens this story or plot with what, for ease of expression, can be summed up as the fictions of the human body. In proposing an exploration of these three fictional patterns, and the way they contribute, singly and together, to the satirist's interpretation of reality, the present study proceeds from the more to the less frequently discussed aspects of the satires, as well as from their rind to their pulp. It also seeks to suggest that there exists a connection between the structural rôle these patterns play, their nature and the appeal they have had for readers of different periods. In this respect, the first of the fictional patterns mentioned must have struck the early readers most forcefully, because of its strong contemporary flavour, whereas its significance would have been far reduced for later readers, who, in contrast, are bound to have been more deeply impressed by the more enduring vision offered by the internal patterns.

Everyone knows that Swift was a prolific writer, whose satires account for less than a third of his output. Hence a study of his satirical fictions leaves much untackled. At the same time, such a study proposes a new distinction between the fictional writings on the one hand, and the non-fictional writings on the other, instead of adhering to the traditional divisions. This approach leaves out much of the poetry, which is not satirical, as well as the polemical, didactic, historical and auto-biographical pieces, because these do not have recourse to fictional devices, or, when they do, like the polemical pieces, they are content to deploy more or less consistent masks, in order to conceal the writer's true identity. In the satires, on the other hand, fictionalizing always goes beyond this assuming of masks. Whether in prose or verse, satires make a sustained and pronounced utilization of fiction. Thus the distinction between the satires and the other works is a practical one, imposed by the subject matter, but it is also much more: it is inscribed in the work itself, and draws attention to certain differences and particularities of the two arts of satire and polemic, otherwise so closely related in the case of Swift. The distinction used here not only does not coincide, but it intersects with the usual one made between Swift's prose and his poetry, which is often reflected in separate editions of his collected works and separate studies. In fact, it even goes so far as to question the validity of the latter, in that it fails to account for the substantial amount of verse written in the same spirit as the satirical prose. In this respect, it proposes another way of looking at the writer's work, more in keeping with his practice as a satirist and a polemicist and with the literary presuppositions on which it is based. Finally, the distinction between satirical and non-satirical writings, and the restriction of the field of investigation to the former, is further justified for a subsidiary reason: the increasing number of studies which have been devoted to other aspects of Swift's work in recent times have not caused any substantial revision of the view that he is first and foremost a satirist, and there is every reason to believe that his reputation as a major writer will continue to rest securely on his satires. On this point, it is interesting to note that his polemical and didactic writings, which form his second body of works in order of importance, have never been able to vie with the satires for interest and popularity, however brilliantly executed some of them are. This is undoubtedly due in the main to their being written with a view to answering limited and rapidly outdated issues. But, considering that most of his satires were similarly inspired by immediate and practical problems, it is impossible to escape the impression that the superior attraction of the satires is directly connected with their more extensive use of fiction.

The following analysis does not intend to offer the reader of Swift the kind of new-at-all-cost interpretation of his works which seems to be fashionable with some reviewers at present. As already said, its aim is to give a better account of the way in which an understanding of his individual satires is affected by the fictional patterns, which are also the source of the reader's pleasure. In this respect, it will more frequently confirm those interpretations that have imposed themselves as the most seminal – these are often due to both the perceptive readings of earlier writers and those of modern scholars – than break new interpretative ground, and it will more often draw attention to the expressive richness of the satires than to the limits of their criticism of life, to their insights than to their blindness. But this is only as it should be in a study concerned with the quality of the reading experience and the universality of the writer's vision.

The variety of the fictional patterns identified here and the variations in their treatments are considerable, and some readers will perhaps feel that, considering the great unevenness of Swift's satirical output, it might have been preferable to follow the usual practice in Swiftian studies, and offer a closer analysis of one, maybe two, major works, hence leaving aside the texts of secondary importance. This solution was rejected because, all things considered, the advantages of a larger spectrum for illustrative demonstration was seen to outweigh the drawbacks. It is not simply that even trifling pieces are devoid neither of charm nor of subtlety in themselves, but rather that the more rudimentary structure of some minor pieces sheds useful light on the complex strategies of the major satires. As for the danger of giving too much importance to the minor pieces, and conveying the impression that they are greater works than they are, this was felt to be negligible. The superiority of *Gulliver's Travels* and *A Tale of a Tub*, with *A Modest Proposal* running a comfortable third, is too obvious, in terms of perfection and scope of execution, for their excellence to pass unnoticed in the discussion. Finally, a general study of fictional patterns, although limited to the satires, does, up to a point, meet the complaint of those who have professed dissatisfaction lately with the excessive slicing up of the Swiftian domain:[8] there have been invaluable studies on *A Tale*, the *Intelligencer* papers, the political tracts, and separate articles on

---

8 Carole Fabricant, *Swift's Landscape*, Baltimore, Johns Hopkins University Press, 1982, p. 8.

individual books of *Gulliver's Travels* or on this or that aspect of Swift's ideas, to list but a few examples, but little effort has been made recently to view his art as a writer on a larger scale. And yet, in the present case, general need not be synonymous with exhaustive. In a study devoted to the revaluation of such an elusive quality as the universal appeal of Swift's fictions, and the gusto with which his satires are written, it was judged preferable to retain the tentative character of the essay. The essay is also the form best suited to gather, for the benefit of the non-specialist, the scattered elements of a reflexion on this significant aspect of his art. They are often found in the form of mere hints in the secondary literature on the satirist, and it was felt that a general and simple account, which could become a companion to studies of other aspects of the satirical work, such as irony, style, or rhetoric, would be welcome.

It is somewhat unfashionable nowadays to devote a book-length study to a single writer. But Swift is not any writer. His works are texts of historical importance, which mark a turning point in literary history. There is only to remember how many of his satires are overtly critical of the dominant ideas of his time and oppose their moral and imaginative mistrust – not to say scepticism – to some of its theoretical abstractions. In this they can be said to have directly and indirectly contributed to setting a pattern for much imaginative writing of the Enlightenment. Besides, at a moment when the long-term historical phenomena of the eighteenth century and their reflections in the literature of the period are the object of renewed attention, it is not inappropriate to divert some of this attention back to its influential works, in order to rediscover them as texts rather than pretexts.

If the orientation of the present study has been influenced by the recent philosophical and linguistic interest in the way language constructs its references to circumstantial reality, and if the critical tools have been provided by other recent critical trends, direct reference to them has been avoided, as they should be in a study using literary pragmatics in order to evaluate how a message is received. The only critical concepts employed are a few well-worn ideas. From a pragmatic approach, a text is first of all a "symbolic" representation of the world by means of which a man organizes his experience while standing aloof from it. A text is also an event: the fulfilling of an intention, of which it is the only "material" mark, and a gesture addressing others. In so far as the material object, the text, is the only complete expression of an intention which inevitably changed as it developed and found its literary form, it is on this object that the analyst must found the work of literary evaluation in the first place. This work of evaluation usually follows three main lines: it brings forth the text's numerous symbolic configurations which give rise to the variety of its interpretations; it analyzes the traces left in the organization of the discourse by the practical strategies which led to its production, in order to understand the nature of the gesture; and it studies those aspects of the text's reception which explain how the signs that constitute it reflect their referents. In other words, the pragmatic approach tries to get at a text's meanings by considering how the symbolic and the practical intersect to produce them.[9] Furthermore, however greatly or little indebted to modern critical trends, any study focusing on a satirist's fictions, and on the way he reconstructs reality by means of vivid inventions, is bound to part company with modern critical practice on one major point. We live in a cultural environment which has become increasingly abstract, a universe of signposts and mathematical encoding and decoding. Criticism has followed suit, when it has not been in the lead itself. Drawing attention to what is most concrete and alive for the imagination in Swift's work, even in an analysis of structures and patterns, forces the critic to follow more traditional paths, lest he should fail in his task of bringing the reader's mind back to what distinguishes literature, and the arts in general, from all other languages: their hold on the totality of human experience, both intellectual and physical.[10]

9 Nelson Goodman, *Ways of Worldmaking*, Indianapolis, Hackett, 1978; Ian Hacking, *Representing and Intervening:Introductory Topics in the Philosophy of Natural Science*, Cambridge, Cambridge University Press, 1983.
10 The present study aims at a reappraisal of the imaginative density of individual works, and not of the density of the perception and psychological life of the man behind the work as in Carole Fabricant's remarkable *Swift's Landscape*.

Chapter 1

The Satirical Use of Framing Fictions[1]

Swift's satires are often loosely described as blending different genres with one another: allegory, parody, mock encomium in *A Tale of a Tub*, or travel book, imaginary voyage, utopia and autobiography in *Gulliver's Travels*. At the same time, it is obvious that Swift did not so much follow classical models as borrow the least literary forms of his time, immortalizing its ephemeral writings, while mocking its achievements. That the professed conservative and presumed champion of the "Ancients" in the quarrel between "Ancients" and "Moderns" should so resolutely have chosen to play the "Modern" and express his views in the least traditional and most fugitively fashionable genres of Queen Anne's reign is just one of a number of contradictions for which Swift's work is famous. The utilization of contemporary genres and the combination of disparate elements warrant investigation as one of the crucial, though little studied strategies used by the author to produce the corrosive effect of satire.

More directly than any other literary genre, satire usually refers, as already said, to a situation outside the text and insists that the reference be considered as part and parcel of the economy of the text. This reference often takes the form of an "isomorphic" representation of circumstantial reality. With Swift, the problem of referentiality is more complex and more fundamental. The satirizing of the contemporary world takes place at different levels, usually involving transpositions rather than "isomorphism". But it begins with the choice of a form of publication or genre as part of a complex structure.

In his satires Swift parodies the forms and genres that he follows. However his use of parody is different from that of his contemporary and friend Alexander Pope. In his mock epics, the latter aims, through the use of a deliberately debased form, to suggest the remoteness of modern life from the classical ideals celebrated by the great epic poets. At the

---

1 Some of the material of this chapter was presented at a symposium on "The Structure of Texts" in 1985 and is reprinted here by permission of the editors of *SPELL 3* (Tübingen, Gunter Narr Verlag, 1987).

same time, the echo of classical models serves to heighten the distinction of the work and to give it permanence. The attitude manifested by this handling of form, which is common to much Augustan satire, is conservative and nostalgic. Swift's parodies ignore the possibilities of the classical parallels and do not evidence the usual type of indirectness and claim to immortality. They are straightforward imitations of the *discourses* of contemporary journalism, science – or natural philosophy, as it was then called –, and literary criticism.[2] Whatever may be said of Swift's political and religious ideas, there is no trace of conservatism and nostalgia here.

Much has been made of his use of masks or *personae*.[3] Central as it is to his fiction making, Swift's impersonations of various types of scribblers is, however, subordinated to a wider strategy. This appears clearly from cases in which there is no readily identifiable *persona* in the satirical fiction and the fiction is hardly less vivid for it. Usually it is more proper to speak of Swift as simply "striking a pose" rather than wearing a mask.[4] Even where an individualized *persona* becomes

2 In literary studies, the concept of mimesis usually refers to a discourse imitating an action and a narrative or dramatic type of emplotment. This type of imitation is here called "isomorphic" to distinguish it from another device, Swift's mimicking of writers addressing their public, for which the words "mimesis" and "mimetic" have been retained in their usual meaning. The present chapter is concerned with formal and generic parody. For Swift's parodies of styles, see Martin Price, *Swift's Rhetorical Art: A Study in Structure and Meaning*, New Haven, Yale University Press, 1953, and Ronald Paulson, *Theme and Structure in Swift's "Tale of a Tub"*, New Haven, Yale University Press, 1960. Generic and stylistic parodies are, of course, closely related.

3 It is worth noting that, for Swift's contemporaries, the use of masks and personae in literature in general, and satire in particular, was also a real and much debated theoretical issue, as it had been for Latin writers: on the question, see Howard D. Weinbrot, *Eighteenth-Century Satire: Essays on Text and Context from Dryden to Peter Pindar*, Cambridge, Cambridge University Press, 1988, pp. 34 - 43. Closer to us, since William B. Ewald's *The Masks of Jonathan Swift* (Oxford, Blackwell, 1954), the debate on this aspect of Swift's art has focused on two issues principally: the consistency of his impersonations and the degree of his involvement in the satirical portrayals.

4 Gardner Stout ("Speaker and Satiric Vision in Swift's *Tale of a Tub*", *Eighteenth-Century Studies* 2: 183 , 1969), who, on this point follows Irvin Ehrenpreis ("Personae", *Restoration and Eighteenth-Century Literature*, ed. Carroll Camden, Chicago, Chicago University Press, 1963, pp. 25 - 37), rejects the notion of masks altogether. Herbert Davis remarks in *Jonathan Swift: Essays on his Satire and*

identifiable, it is in the first place an emanation of the playful imitation of a discourse, and only subsidiarily an actor in a story or drama. Close attention to the form or genre borrowed by the satire shows that discourse has priority over *persona*.

For two reasons, discourse is an apt concept to describe Swift's satires and, in particular, their framework, which is the object of the present chapter. On the one hand, the framework, however discreet, is always argumentative or explanatory, in contradistinction to narrative or dramatic structures. On the other hand, the term refers to a new conception of language that emerged at the end of the seventeenth century and aimed at representing the world and experience in such a way as to give a faithful verbal picture of them, and with a view, likewise, to their verbal analysis, what Michel Foucault has called a representation of representation.[5] Other studies on the attitude of the eighteenth century towards language confirm that Swift shared such a conception.[6] His mimicking of typical genres and forms of publication has the aforesaid purpose described by Foucault. It presents them as the molds in which specific concerns find their natural expression, in other words as types of discourses or ways in which certain groups of people – one is tempted to say pressure groups – think and speak of certain subjects: religion, politics, science or madness. The importance taken by the mimicking of contemporary genres indirectly lends support to Swift's own contention that his parodies do not primarily intend to ridicule people, "John, Peter, Thomas and so forth", as he once put it in a letter about *Gulliver's Travels*.[7] It also helps to place the debate upon his use of masks in a wider perspective. But, above all, it should make us see the imitation as a move to isolate samples from diverse discourses to hold them up for inspection and criticism.

Other Studies (New York, Oxford University Press, 1964, pp. 9, 13 - 14) that Swift's impersonations are not sustained enough to give the impression of real persons.

5 *Les Mots et les choses*, Paris, Gallimard, 1966, chapters 3 - 4.
6 Murray Cohen, *Sensible Words: Linguistic Practice in England, 1640 - 1785*, Baltimore, Johns Hopkins University Press, 1977. Robert Martin Adams, *Strains of Discord: Studies in Literary Openness*, Ithaca, Cornell University Press, 1958, p. 161. Everett Zimmerman, *Swift's Narrative Satires: Author and Authority*, Ithaca, Cornell University Press, 1983, pp. 168 - 178.
7 *The Correspondence of Jonathan Swift*, ed. Harold Williams, Oxford, Clarendon, 1963, vol. iii, p. 103.

To be immediately identifiable, the individual sample of fashionable discourse must present the typical characteristics of the genre in a pure and/or concentrated form: hence the necessity of some degree of caricature or, at least, purity of design. So the parodic quality that results from underlining typical features achieves two things: it introduces the distancing that makes a critical evaluation possible, and it draws something like a magic circle around the sample, which reveals it as a fake. The magic circle is the starting point of the fictionalizing process. Swift makes it sufficiently visible for the fictitious to be easily distinguished from the real thing. He does so mainly by a device that criticism calls *framing*. By including – framing – one type of discourse within another, he presents the phenomenon of communication as complex and the relationship between text or original intention, and reader or reception, as problematic.

The sense of this metaphor, which is commonly used in the discussion of narrative fiction and has even been adopted by the social sciences,[8] has been obscured by recent suggestions that all literature is "framed" discourse and that it is enough to find the word "novel" or "poem" on a title page for the content of the volume to become divorced from the usual communicative function of language.[9] Such is not the meaning given to the metaphor here. What is more traditionally referred to by framing in literature is the inclusion of a central narrative within another one, which introduces it and places it in a perspective aiming at favouring a particular interpretation, while preventing a divorce between the three elements, literature, textuality and life. "The Rime of the Ancient Mariner" and *Heart of Darkness* offer this kind of structure. Naturally, in Swift's satires, the nature and particularly the aims of framing are somewhat different from what they are in Coleridge and Conrad. In fact, much of what is described below as framing might just as well have been designated by the word "peritext". This "threshold" to the text, as Gérard Genette calls it, which comprehends the features "by which the text becomes a publication and offers itself as such to its readers, and more generally to the public," has also been described as "an

8 Ervin Goffman, *Frame Analysis: An Essay on the Organization of Experience*, New York, Harper and Row, 1974.
9 Patricia Waugh, *Metafiction: The Theory and Practice of Self-Conscious Fiction*, London, Methuen, 1984, p. 28. The two acceptations of "framing" are not totally unrelated, however, as what follows will show.

undefined zone between the inside and the outside of a publication".[10] It is to some extent this grey zone of "transition", where a "transaction" between the text and its readers takes place, that the following pages investigate, because Swift makes imaginative use of it, in order to create a mock-serious effect or an effect of parody. However, the notion of peritext is not quite adequate when discussing the structure of his satires. It fails to take into account the central rôle that a dedication or preface can play when they serve to underscore the satirical effect, a rôle out of all proportion with their habitual peripheral connection to the text itself in other writings. For this reason they can no longer be considered as merely belonging to the para-text of the work they accompany. Furthermore, certain peritextual features will occasionally be found to be inseparable from what are in fact portions of the text and, in this case, peritext and these portions of the text form together a comprehensive fiction which serves to introduce either another fiction of a different nature, or another level of fiction. They also constitute what the reader identifies as a sort of packaging, in the form of a pretence of serious publication, which is reminiscent of the Chinese-box character of narrative framing. Because the notion of framing is more comprehensive than that of peritext and because it offers the further advantage of suggesting that, in Swift, the device is fictional in essence, it has been preferred to the other term. Now, within the global notion of framing, it will be necessary to distinguish between editorial framing, when only peritextual elements are utilized fictionally, and framing discourse, when some aspect of the text contributes to the effect along with the peritext.

Framing as defined here, and particularly editorial framing in the shape of a pretence that the central narrative is a document discovered at some later date, which finds its way to the printer's thanks to the interest of an intermediary, was a common feature in the early novel and throughout the eighteenth century. It seems to have had a particular appeal for writers at the time when Swift was writing.[11] It took various

10 Gérard Genette, *Seuils*, Paris, Seuil, 1987, pp. 7, 8. Genette defines the "peritext" as a part of the "paratext", which includes everything a writer may say or write about one of his works in the course of his life. The "peritext" includes only those aspects which are published along with the text but cannot be said to belong to it: title, preface, dedication and epigraph (ibid., pp. 10 - 11).

11 The influence of Swift on the novel has attracted more attention than the connection of his satires with the early contemporary novels: see Ian Watt, *The Rise of the Novel*, London, Chatto and Windus, 1957, and Ronald Paulson, *Satire and*

forms, some quite elementary. A novel sometimes merely purported to be the editing of private papers, memoirs or letters. If no full account was given of the provenance, the title page at least vouchsafed its authenticity and hinted at the eventful history of the manuscript or its author. Defoe's *Journal of the Plague Years* is subtitled: "Written by a Citizen who continued all the while in London. Never made public before." Before Defoe, Aphra Behn had utilized a complete framing discourse in *Oroonoko* (1678) and hints of editorial framing in four other romances. In the latter she contented herself with inserting into the text incidental remarks like "as near as I can remember" or "I have seen him pass the streets".[12] Both sorts of framing underlined the fact that there was some direct connection between real life and the fiction. In short, the framing claimed for the artefact the status of a truthful document. It pretended to give the public not something novel or new, as is often understood today, but news of the world.

A similar kind of staging characterizes Swift's satires, as well as those of a direct contemporary, Mary de la Rivière Manley, the author of *The Secret History of Queen Zarah* (1705) and *The New Atlantis* (1709).

the Novel in Eighteenth-Century England, New Haven, Yale University Press, 1967. Everett Zimmerman, op. cit., p. 14, has recently pointed out that "Swift's major satires analyze the context in which the novel arose, engaging the hermeneutical and epistemological concerns that are implicit in the new form." The most comprehensive study of this historical background and of its epistemological concerns is Michael McKeon's *The Origins of the English Novel 1600 - 1740* (Baltimore, Johns Hopkins University Press, 1987), which describes in great details "the complex development of the romance genre, its resolution into 'romance' and 'historical' elements" (p. 63) under the influence first of a concern with historicity and quantifiable facts and then of an increasing scepticism towards the possibility of achieving historical authenticity by means of empiricism. McKeon argues that this epistemological revolution eventually led to an absolute dichotomy between "true history" and "romance" being replaced by the more supple "distinction between the fact of being history, and the quality of being history-like"(p. 121), which made the birth of the novel proper possible. According to him, Swift and his contemporaries lived at a critical moment in the debate between empiricism and scepticism, and this affected their ideas in a decisive manner. McKeon even enlists *Gulliver's Travels* among the intermediary forms of "generically uncertain character" which led to the development of the novel (p. 341).

12 *The Works of Aphra Behn*, ed. Montague Summers, New York, B. Bloom, 1967, vol. V, pp. 3, 98.

The fact that the device, uncommon in satire, was used in all kinds of different works over the same years is remarkable enough to be worth mentioning. In Swift's and in Mrs Manley's satires, as in Defoe's realistic romances, framing may be roughly equated with the editing of purportedly true pieces of writing. There the similarities between them end, however. Swift does not write exactly the same kind of narrative or allegedly documentary fictions as the early novelists, or Mary Manley, even when his satires do take a narrative turn. It is well-known that satires usually promise one thing and end up offering another. Swift's parodies of forms of publications, genres, and more generally discourses, do precisely this. They pretend to have a serious and immediate purpose that other narrative fictions have not. Their declared intention is to inform readers on pressing issues, to discuss these issues, to take a stand on them, or even to contribute to the advancement of learning, but they do not fulfil their promises to the letter. They are editing tricks which promise information but frame fanciful tales or made up stories. Consequently, the framing in Swift plays a different rôle from that in the novel, in Mrs Manley's satires, or in utopias, where it authenticates the fiction.

The problem and the critical tools being presented, there remains to consider the material to which these tools are to be applied. The number of forms and genres handled by Swift in his satires is impressive. Seldom are more than two pieces found of the same type in the collected works. Some are ambitious. Others have been described as trifles and are seldom referred to. On the whole they form a unique collection of the genres current at the end of the seventeenth and at the beginning of the eighteenth century. *A Tale of a Tub* proposes an apparently allegorical Christian tale.[13] The allegory is presented in such a way as to ridicule at the same time the mannerisms of scholars, their collation of recondite sources, their digressive interpolations, their displays of erudition, and the way they have of praising themselves and their work in their prefaces and introductions.[14] It is best viewed as a combination of several types of parodies. *The Battle of the Books*, one of the few satires to use an easily

13 PW vol. i.
14 Miriam K. Starkman, *Swift's Satire on Learning in "A Tale of a Tub"*, Princeton, Princeton University Press, 1950, pp. 97, 129.

identifiable literary pattern, that of the mock epic, has been described as an allegory within an allegory and, indeed, narrates the battle fought in a library by the works of the "Ancients", the Greek and Latin authors and their allies on one side, and the "Moderns", the writers who reject the example of the "Ancients", on the other side. But the mock epic is not in verse, as it should be, and it is framed in such a way that the reader only becomes aware of this dimension in the second half of the text. *The Battle* begins like an eighteenth-century disquisition on the moral causes of wars:

Whoever examines with due Circumspection into the *Annual Records* of *Time*, will find it remarked, that *War is the Child of Pride*, and *Pride the Daughter of Riches ...*   (PW vol. i, p. 141)

Then the narrative is interrupted to make room for an animal fable representing a dispute between a spider and a bee. The fable is used to illustrate another aspect of the controversy between "Ancients" and "Moderns". As a result, the epic "Account" of the battle strikes a very different note from that of Pope's *Rape of the Lock* or *The Dunciad*. *Meditation upon a Broomstick* mocks a favourite genre with churchmen: the meditation.[15] *The Mechanical Operation of the Spirit*, an essay about the human propensity to confuse true spiritual inspiration with merely physical disorders, is entitled a "discourse". However, the "discourse" begins in the more current and leisurely style of an epistolary exchange:

For T.H. *Esquire*, at his Chambers in the Academy of the *Beaux Esprits* in *New-Holland*.

Sir,
It is now a good while since I have had in my Head something, not only very material, but absolutely necessary to my Health, that the World should be informed in.
                                                                                    (Ibid., p. 171)

Oddly, the essay is in a way included in the letter:

And now, Sir, having dispatch'd what I had to say of Forms, or of Business, let me intreat, you will suffer me to proceed upon my Subject; and to pardon me, if I make no farther Use of the Epistolary Stile, till I come to conclude.

15 PW vol.i.

30

SECTION I.

Tis recorded of *Mahomet*, that upon a Visit he was going to pay in *Paradise*, he had an Offer of several Vehicles to conduct him upwards; as fiery Chariots, wing'd Horses, and celestial Sedans; but he refused them all, and would be born to Heaven upon nothing but his *Ass*. Now, this Inclination of *Mahomet*, as singular as it seems, hath been since taken up by a great Number of devout *Christians*; and doubtless, with very good Reason. (Ibid., pp. 172 - 173)

This procedure was frequent and, by an amusing irony, it was used less than a year after the publication of *The Mechanical Operation* by one of the very enemies that Swift had pilloried in his *Tale of a Tub* for such an absence of critical discrimination.[16] A *Tritical Essay upon the Faculties of the Mind* is a mock psychological, or, in eighteenth-century language, physiological essay.[17] But, the product of an erratic mind, it dwells above all on the erroneous views held by some philosophers, instead of treating the topic announced by the title.

These fictional satires are in a sense the more literary ones in the corpus. They are all early pieces, written between 1690 and 1710 at the latest. Those that were to follow extend the range to embrace, apart from the genres used by men of letters and natural philosophers, journalistic, political, and more humble and popular, even plebeian, kinds of writings. They show Swift moving towards less and less literary concerns. The nucleus of *The Bickerstaff Papers* (1708 - 1709) is the imitation of an almanac and its core is both public polemics and the story of the life and death of a repentant forger of lies. *A Complete Collection of Genteel and Ingenious Conversation* (begun in 1704 and completed in 1732) satirizes manuals of good manners and includes model conversations in the form of a satirical comedy.[18] *Directions to Servants*, for which Swift gathered material throughout his literary career, but which he left unfinished at his death, is another conduct book.[19] Composed in the manner of Castiglione's *The Courtier* and of Machiavelli's *The Prince*,[20]

16 William Wotton, *A Defense of the Reflections upon Ancient and Modern Learning, In Answer to the Objections of Sir William Temple and Others. With Observations upon "The Tale of a Tub"*, London, Goodwind, 1705. The "Observations" are presented in the form of a letter "To Anthony Hammond, Esq."
17 PW vol.i.
18 PW vol.iv.
19 PW vol.xiii.
20 David Nokes, *Raillery and Rage: A Study of Eighteenth-Century Satire*, Brighton, Harvester, 1987, p. 189.

it contains an ironical account of all kinds of misbehaviour that servants may be found guilty of in their various employments. Further satires borrow the form of news items or reports. *A New Journey to Paris* (1711), subtitled "Together with some Secret Transactions between the Fr. . .h K. . .g, and an Eng. . . Gentleman, by the Sieur du Baudrier, Translated from the French", is a pretended report of secret negociations between the English government and the King of France. It was meant to amplify the rumours that had leaked about such negociations.[21] *A Hue and Cry after Dismal* (1712) is reportedly the account of a visit made in all secrecy to the French town of Dunkirk by a member of the opposition to Her Majesty's government, after the town had been delivered to the English forces as a result of a peace treaty that had brought Marlborough's wars to an end.[22] *The Last Speech and Dying Words of Ebenezor Elliston*, written on the occasion of the execution of the said robber on 2nd May 1722, is to all evidence a proclamation of guilt and betrayal by the celebrated criminal but, what is interesting, is that it is contained in a sort of prose broadside ballad which itself conceals an attack against similar sentimental confessions. Such ballads belonged to an old tradition and were something like the first equivalent of the modern popular gutter newspaper.[23] Sentimental confessions were a favourite topic with this type of unofficial journalism.

Swift often chose the disguise of private letters accidentally or intentionally made public to deal with political and official matters. *A Letter from the Pretender to a Whig Lord* (1712) and *A Letter of Thanks from Lord Wharton* (1712) are meant to be taken as two compromising pieces from a secret correspondence between supposed enemies.[24] *The Story of the Injured Lady. Written by herself. In a Letter to her Friend, with his Answer* (1746) is different.[25] It offers, in the style of a private exchange of letters, an allegorical tale of the relationships between England, Scotland and Ireland. The latter is the injured lady of the tale, whom England had first courted, but now neglects in favour of a far less attractive lady, Scotland. Between private and open letters on the

---

21 PW vol. iii, pp. xxxi - xxxii. For the title, see p. 207.
22 PW vol. vi.
23 Hyder Rollins, ed., *A Pepsyan Garland: Black Letter Broadside Ballads of the Years 1595 - 1639*, Cambridge Mass., Harvard University Press, 1971, p. xi. For Swift's text, see PW vol. ix.
24 PW vol. vi.
25 PW vol. ix.

one hand and petitions and public protests on the other, the distinction is often slight. "Mrs Harris's Petition" (1701), is a private petition. It is in verse and the recrimination of a faithful servant whose savings have been stolen.[26] Another, *The Humble Petition of the Footmen of Dublin* (1732) is in prose and a more formal public call to the authorities to protect their profession against unscrupulous people who try to pass themselves off as real footmen for seditious motives.[27] *An Examination of Certain Abuses, Corruptions and Enormities in the City of Dublin* (1732) is an individual, but similarly formal, protest and warning to the authorities of the city to beware of the hawker's cries, which, according to the author of the protest, are used by enemies of the government to criticize its policy and rally the malcontents.[28] Mention must finally be made of two of Swift's major works, *Gulliver's Travels* (1726), the travel account of a supposed ship surgeon,[29] and *A Modest Proposal* (1729), a fake proposal for a radical solution to the problem of poverty in Ireland.[30]

To these satires can be added some of Swift's verse: lampoons in the form of fables like "The Fable of Midas", or mock elegies like "A Satirical Elegy on the Death of a late Famous General" and the "Verses on the Death of Dr Swift", or mock pastorals like "A Description of the Morning" and "A Description of a City Shower".[31] It must indeed be borne in mind that lampoons, songs, broadsides and other verses were frequently circulated like news and pamphlets at the time,[32] and that Swift was an adept at all these forms. Most of the pieces mentioned here, unequal as they are qualitatively speaking, have this in common, that they are not exactly what their forms lead the reader to expect.

The variety of the forms handled by Swift still commands the admiration of any reader who goes to the trouble of looking beyond the best-known works. Swift is a parodist of genius. He pushes the art of imitation further than any novelist of his time. There is no genre,

---

26 SPW, pp. 49 - 52.

27 PW vol. xii.

28 Ibid.

29 PW vol. xi.

30 PW vol. xii. Clive T. Probyn, in *Jonathan Swift: The Contemporary Background* (Manchester, Manchester University Press, 1978), offers a number of hints as to the possible models of Swift's satires.

31 SPW, pp. 100 - 102, 228 - 229, 496 - 513, 86, and 91 - 93.

32 Lennard J. Davis, *Factual Fiction: The Origins of the English Novel*, New York, Columbia University Press, 1983, pp. 42 - 70.

however humble and non-literary, that he cannot turn to advantage. This variety undoubtedly accounts for the fact that his satires have more often been studied individually, or in a biographical perspective, than in their formal relation with one another. In general the forms he chooses for his framing devices are the same he handles in the other important aspect of his production, the polemical writings:[33] prefaces, forewords, advertisements to readers, digressions, letters, pamphlets, apologies, petitions, manuals, proposals, songs, satirical elegies, lampoons and broadsides. The result is that it is sometimes difficult to distinguish between satirical fictions and polemics, the more so as his polemical writings also occasionally use fictional disguises, as *The Drapier's Letters* do. To mention but one example, there are good reasons for considering *Mr C[olli]ns's Discourse of Free-Thinking* (1713), a public letter, apology, and popularizing "Abstract", which praises free-thinking to run it down, as both polemics and parodic fiction.[34] It is presented as an essay written by an admirer of the original *Discourse*, but it is neither possible nor perhaps judicious to place it in one category rather than the other. No clear line is drawn between the two kinds of writings by Swift himself. Every gradation is possible. What is certain, on the other hand, is that his satirical fictions are never offered to the reader as literature, as the work of a highbrow man of letters like Pope, but as contributions to a vast public debate of ideas on politics, religion, superstition, education, social life and relationships, as well as literature. Their forms, down to the use of disguises, which was a common feature of all journalistic writing and was meant to protect the critical writer from governmental pressures, are those typical of this public debate. By Pope's standards, and on the basis of the criterion of genre, Swift's satirical fictions can

33 The distinction drawn here between satirical fiction and polemics assumes that satire is distinct from polemics. Not all critics of satire and Swift agree on this point. Edward W. Rosenheim (*Swift and the Satirist's Art*, Chicago, Chicago University Press, 1963), Sheldon Sacks (*Fiction and the Shape of Belief: A Study of Henry Fielding, with Glances at Swift, Johnson and Richardson*, Berkeley, University of California, 1964) and James A.W. Rembert (*Swift and the Dialectical Tradition*, London, Macmillan, 1988) consider Swift's art as mainly a rhetorical strategy to ridicule external objects and even a mere extension of the art of polemics. John R. Clark (*Form and Frenzy in Swift's "Tale of a Tub"*, Ithaca, Cornell University Press, 1970) and Ronald Paulson (*Fictions of Satire*, Baltimore, Johns Hopkins University Press, 1967) prefer to stress the "specifically ... fictional construct" (Paulson, p. 9), as does the following argument.
34 PW vol. iv.

34

mostly be classed as low and answering practical purposes: he prefers the broadside to the epistle, the travel book, the proposal or the conduct book to the mock epic.

The fake, the satirical pretence, and the real thing, the polemical writings, are outwardly so closely akin that, frequently, only the degree of fictionalization resulting from the coupling of a framing device with a framed fiction, and their different finalities mark off the former from the latter. A study of framing is then doubly useful: it explains on the one hand the specific nature of the satirical fictions and on the other the very different appeal that *A Modest Proposal* or *The Bickerstaff Papers* make, compared with *The Conduct of the Allies* or *The Drapier's Letters*.

II

Considering the variety of the satirical fictions and of the forms used, it would be illusory to try to reduce them all to the same pattern and to look for traces of framing in each. In fact, most of the satirical verse had better be regarded as unframed narrative, descriptive or dramatic fictions, and likewise a prose account such as *The Court and Emperor of Japan*.[35] This restriction aside, the major works and a large proportion of minor pieces can be said to use framing in one way or another. This type of double structuring of texts, so characteristically Swiftian, is even sometimes found in works written by other writers, but at Swift's instigation or with his assistance. Mrs Manley's *A Modest Enquiry into the Reasons of the Joy Expressed by a Certain Sett of People, upon the Spreading of a Report of Her Majesty's Death* is a case in point.[36] There is as much variety in the nature of the framings as there is in the genres parodied. In some cases the framing is minimal and consists only in a peritextual signal, external to the text. In others, it becomes a fiction on its own, containing another fiction and forming a wrapping.

At one end of the spectrum, there are the specimens of conspicuous textual framing or framing discourse, in which the framing threatens to swallow up the framed fiction or allows it only the ghost of an existence. *An Examination of Certain Abuses* and *A Modest Proposal* are so full

35 PW vol. v.
36 PW vol. viii, pp. 183 - 197. See also the introduction, p. xvi.

of their supposed authors' presence and concerns in their different ways as to leave little room for the development of the fictional message they contain, as will be seen in the next chapter. For some readers, *The Bickerstaff Papers* are the story of an astrologer's death, but structurally they contain much else: they consist of a whole sequence of emphatically polemical pieces and belong to the same category as the two afore-mentioned works.

Evidently it is *A Tale of a Tub* which presents the most elaborate case of framing ever attempted by Swift. It offers in a concentrated form all that he considered to be typical mannerism in the rhetoric of the "Moderns" and all the methods used by hack writers with little talent to make up for their lack of imagination and attract public notice. It ridicules the formlessness of so many of their works. Leaving aside the long "Apology", in which Swift later found it necessary to defend the *Tale* against its detractors, because it is not part of the fiction, the reader has to get through no less than seven pieces of introductory material, four declared digressive chapters and a fifth unannounced one, to which must be added a number of footnotes, before he comes to the end of the tale of the three brothers, which the alleged author is supposed to be merely editing. Every type of peritext could be said to be represented in the work. First comes, for want of a list of actual publications, a note on the purported writer's still unprinted – and probably unwritten – works.[37] Follows a first dedicatory epistle, "To the Right Honourable, John Lord Sommers", a semi-fictitious letter. It is supposedly penned by the book-seller – in other words, the publisher – but addressed to a real historical figure and introduces the impersonation of the alleged author. The reference that the bookseller makes to the Grubstreet writers he "employs" on occasion suggests that he provides hacks with work and has become one of the promoters of a real industry of modern writing (PW vol. i, p. 14). His dedication to an important personage was considered a sure way of getting some kind of attention from the public and, perhaps, his protection and eventually his favour. The bookseller then provides a short note, "The Bookseller to the Reader", explaining how the manuscript came into his hands and what led to the belated publication. The note illustrates the practices of the time:

---

[37] As this study focuses on the satirist's art of pretence, the qualifiers "purported" and "alleged" have been preferred to the usual "putative".

But, I have been lately alarm'd with Intelligence of a surreptitious Copy, which a certain great Wit had new polish'd and refin'd, or as our present Writers express themselves, *fitted to the Humor of the Age* . . . (PW vol. i, p. 17)

Both the dedication and note are true to the general character of such pieces. In sharp contrast to what follows, their style and development are sober. They also evidence a sense of humour, which conveys the impression that the bookseller is, albeit a promoter of modern writing, a practical joker like Swift himself.

Then comes the hack's own dedicatory epistle. Like the list of unpublished works, it testifies to his ambition and vanity. It is in a quite different vein from the bookseller's dedication and note. It is addressed to Prince Posterity and praises modern writing and writers, both so numerous and ephemeral, "hurryed so hastily off the Scene, that they escape our Memory" almost at once after achieving publication (ibid., p. 21). At the same time as it explains the writer's intention, "The Preface" enlarges further upon the merit and exuberance of modern writing, considered to excel all those of other periods in every respect. Finally, instead of introducing the tale, the framed fiction, "The Introduction" once again defends modern writing in general, and the present project in particular, against possible detractors:

But to return. I am assured from the Reader's Candor, that the brief Specimen I have given, will easily clear all the rest of our Society's Productions from an Aspersion grown, as it is manifest, out of Envy and Ignorance . . . (Ibid., p. 43)

Bookseller and author insist that they have consulted hundreds of models before composing their respective introductory pieces. They also discuss their models, so that each item is an exposition of contemporary practice, at the same time as it serves to flatter the reader and boost the project:

But, to return. I am sufficiently instructed in the Principal Duty of a Preface, if my Genius were capable of arriving at it. Thrice have I forced my Imagination to make the *Tour* of my Invention, and thrice it has returned empty; the latter having been wholly drained by the following Treatise. Not so, my more successful Brethren the *Moderns*, who will by no means let slip a Preface or Dedication, without some notable distinguishing Stroke, to surprize the Reader at the Entry, and kindle a Wonderful Expectation of what is to ensue. Such was that of a most ingenious Poet, who solliciting his Brain for something new, compared himself to the *Hangman*, and his Patron to the *Patient*: This was *Insigne, recens, indictum ore alio*.

(Ibid., pp. 25 - 26)

The dedications and prefaces are offered in turn as models and recipes: a sort of handbook for the perfect little hack,[38] as later *Polite Conversation* will claim to be a guide to conversation. Compared with the bookseller's dedication to Lord Somers, the hack's pieces however look more like caricatures than models. In them, as in the "digressions" that follow, Swift improves on the satirical technique of the seventeenth century, that of John Eachard's *Some Observations upon the Answer to an Enquiry* (London, 1671) and of Andrew Marvell's *Rehearsal Transposed* (London, 1672; Part ii, 1673), which consisted in borrowing directly from the text of the victim and turning its metaphors upside down to create a parody.[39] Swift's technique differs from theirs in the sense that his parody is collective and not individual, so that it is more generic than stylistic. There is no better proof than these pieces in *A Tale* that he is mainly concerned with utilizing contemporary genres to satirical purposes, whilst his style remains inimitably his own. The satirist also uses parody as metacommentary. With it he attacks the unavowed motivations behind the fashionable vindications and inconsistent arguments of his victims. His aim is a general parody of the uses to which such kinds of writings as those he imitates are put. The juxtaposition of the bookseller's critical and humorous dedication with the hack's pompous and uncritical "Dedication to Prince Posterity" is highly suggestive in this respect. As for the hack's preface and introduction, they are not even allowed to fulfil their main functions: they do not give the slightest inkling of what the "tale" itself may be about.

If the reader believes that he can enjoy a pleasant, linear, narrative framed fiction after overcoming the obstacle of these six introductions, he is soon disappointed. The heavy peritext only constitutes the first part of the framing. Hardly has the story of the three brothers and their father's will started than digressions begin to interrupt its flow. They return to the concerns with modern writing of the introductions. Within the narrative sections themselves, the hack's pen is prone to wander into

---

38 Developing an idea from W.B. Ewald, Ronald Paulson was the first of many to designate the narrator of *A Tale* the "Grub Street Hack" or just "the Hack" in *Theme and Structure in Swift's "Tale of a Tub"* (pp. 28, 29).

39 Paulson, ibid., chapter 1, and pp. 36 - 45. According to A.C. Elias (*Swift at Moorpark: Problems in Biography and Criticism*, Philadelphia, University of Pennsylvania Press, 1982, pp. 77 - 94, 155 - 195), Swift seems to have perfected this satirical technique when he was Temple's secretary and to have first practised it at the old statesman's expense.

still other digressions inspired by the narrative,[40] like that about the worship of tailors after only two pages of story-telling. At times the tale seems forgotten for good. Section x, entitled "A Tale of a Tub", promises a resumption of the narrative, but it is only half-way through Section xi that the story of the three brothers is brought to its conclusion.

Finally, there is the critical apparatus of one hundred and thirty odd footnotes added to the fifth edition of *A Tale of a Tub* in 1710, five years after it was first brought out. This addition is a touch of genius. As three fourth of them concern the story of the three brothers, to which they form a sort of authorized "key", the footnotes can really be said to have turned *A Tale* into what "The Introduction" meant it to be from the first: the scholarly edition of an old document. The 1710 edition makes it clear that the notes have been provided neither by the bookseller nor by the purported author himself. They are presented as the work of three annotators. One footnote is supposedly by an old writer of commentaries, the French Lambin (1516 - 1572; see *Tale*, p. 44). Twenty-eight are borrowed from one of the very "Moderns" that Swift's satire attacks by name, William Wotton; and the rest are given as the work of an anonymous commentator, who sometimes accepts Wotton's reading of what the latter considers as an allegory, sometimes disagrees with him and sometimes elucidates details that Wotton had ignored. Wotton's comments are quoted literally from his attack on *A Tale, Observations upon a "Tale of a Tub"*.[41] The other footnotes are composed in the same literal-minded spirit, translating every suggestive detail that the author identifies as allegorical into a plain reference to religion. On the contrary of the marginal notes already found in the first edition, which were becoming out of date, footnotes were coming strongly into fashion at the time, and those in *A Tale* can be said to be what holds the different kinds of parody together, giving the satire a semblance of editorial coherence. Together with the bookseller's dedication, they also form the type of parody which Swift was to favour in the rest of his satirical work: parody as faithful, in contradistinction to caricatural or exaggerated, parody.

Introductions, digressions and footnotes by other pens, swell the meagre framed fiction of the tale to a publication twice the size of the

---

40 Mary de la Rivière Manley's *Secret History of Queen Zarah* (London, 1705, pp. 96-132), which appeared one year after *A Tale* offers a splendid illustration of precisely the type of digression that Swift ridicules in his satire. She had not yet understood the lesson.

41 See above, note 16, p. 31.

latter. By amplifying the framing structure in such a way that the text the hack is supposed simply to edit looks of secondary importance, Swift not only caricatures a new type of scholarship, as said above, but he also underlines the supposed author's sense of his own importance as a "Modern" and of his need for self-advertizing. He makes his presence, and the imitation of contemporary practices, so intrusive that the parodic fiction of modern writing appears as the central constituent in the hotch-potch. The relevance of the *Tale* to eighteenth-century views is emphasized, and its reading is modified. Instead of the historical and allegorical dimensions of the central story of the three brothers, it is the contemporary quality of their persons and lives, and the reference to the alleged author's present, that compel recognition in the first place.

This kind of heavy framing is however not always desirable. Swift avoids it when his main purpose is not to satirize the nature of modern writing. In *Gulliver's Travels* the framing structure is nevertheless quite complex again. Apart from the three peritextual items prefacing the memoirs – an "Advertisement", "A Letter from Capt. Gulliver, To his Cousin Sympson", and "The Publisher to the Reader" – it also includes those parts of the travel account itself which, within the text, introduce and conclude each of the "voyages". Otherwise the resulting framing discourse is kept within bounds and tailored so as not to interfere with the fourfold framed fiction. It is worth noting in this connection that it is on the individual portions of the framing included in each of the four books, namely the four accounts of the outward voyages and returns to England, that the *Travels* rely more particularly in order to establish their spurious claim as authentic travel book. The expanses of water that Gulliver crosses between his European world and the continents he discovers are the scene of realistically conceived adventures of shipwrecks and rescues which contrast with his incursions into fairyland. The case for distinguishing between the parts composed in the mode of realism and those composed in the mode of fantasy being put forward, it is necessary to add that the *Travels* as a whole make efficient use of what fascinated readers in travel books. Like them, Gulliver's account associates strange and familiar objects and scenes. Like them, it uses the simple and vivid imagery of everyday life to describe the new and unknown countries visited. As a result, early readers of the *Travels* found that "the strange assumed perforce the guise of the familiar, and familiar terms took on enchanting connotations through their involuntary commerce with the strange",[42] as they did in all travel literature. But, as Swift is writing a satire, he dissociates in part what travel books combine. He underlines the discrepancy between the two components, the strange and the familiar, and with them forms two separate worlds: the everyday world of England and its sailors described in his framing discourse and the strange one of his framed fictions. Between them ambiguous connections exist, or develop, which are the salt of the satire.

In the cases mentioned so far, the framing constitutes a complete fiction in itself. It is the parody of a discourse, and from this discourse there sometimes emerges the personality of a purported author. At the other end of the spectrum are found cases of minimal framing or editorial framing, which one hesitates to call fictional and which simply anchor the parody in the literary and intellectual debate of the time. Sometimes all the framing consists in a title, a subtitle, the lay-out of the printed text, or some other component of the peritext which creates the fiction of a certain context. Sometimes even, it is only present by implication, in the margins of the text, as when the material support of the item, the mode of publication, could be said to be all the framing there is. Basically, however, the purpose of the editorial framing remains the same everywhere, whatever the form it takes: it can be said to correspond to an imaginative use of context and to play the usual function of such devices, which is to prepare the reader to receive the message in a certain way. *A Hue and Cry after Dismal* and several of the songs or poems – "The Fable of Midas", which contains a satirical portrait of the Duke of Marlborough is one of them – were distributed as half-sheets, printed on one side, and fulfilled a function similar to that of special newspaper editions today.[43] The half-sheet presented them as news or comments on some important news. As for the two poems, "A Description of the Morning" and "A Description of a City Shower", they may have appeared framed to their first readers, who discovered them in *The Tatler* and no doubt saw in them true instances of poetic reportage on city life, something like the equivalent of today's magazine photographs.[44] Such instances of

42 The words are those of J.L. Lowes writing about Coleridge's sources in *The Road to Xanadu* (London, Constable, 1927, p. 313).
43 See PW vol. vi, p. 210. Herbert Davis's text of "The Fable of Midas" is "Printed from the original Half-Sheet, London, 1712" (SPW, p. 100).
44 That the two poems are not mere reportage, mere "impressionistic photomontage", as Pat Rogers puts it (p. 252), is a commonplace of criticism, but no critic has ever

framing come close to the pretence of serious editing found in the novel of the age.

Editing some writing of a particular kind will usually imply that the editor takes its contents seriously and has given it what he believes to be appropriate diffusion as news, pamphlet or declaration. If the attitude implied by the editing and the genre of the writing, or its place of appearance, does not match the nature of the contents, of the framed fiction, the disjunction draws attention to itself, and this is sufficient to trace around the satirical fiction the magical circle that frames it and shows it to be a fake. Whether in the case of heavy or minimal framing, it is always the nature of the framed fiction and the relationship it bears to the framing device that makes the satirical intent clear. Even where the framing device does not look much of a fiction in itself, it is one in so far as it pretends to be what it is not and cannot be, something true and authentic.

III

As a structuring device, framing looks both inward towards the organization of the individual works and outward towards the world outside the texts. As such it is the articulation of a complex relationship, only a few of whose traits are relevant to Swift's satirical fictionalizing. To begin with the internal aspect of the work, it is a commonplace of criticism that its structure is in its broad outlines dictated by the conventions of genre, which are themselves, as has been said above, connected with the nature of the discourse. The more elementary the genre, the more invariable the plan of the work. As readers of newspapers know, there are not several ways of reporting news. In *A Hue and Cry after Dismal* the subtitle already gives the essential clue, like the

denied their "realistic" foundation. On the "realistic" background, see Pat Rogers, *Grub Street: Studies in a Subculture*, London, Methuen, 1972, pp. 249 - 253. This is how F.W. Bateson sums up the issue in *English Poetry: A Critical Introduction* (London, Longmans, Green & Co., 1950, pp. 175 - 180). Speaking of the first poem, which appeared in *The Tatler* on 28. April 1709, he writes that it "had camouflaged itself behind the parody of a recognized literary form" but that "as such . . . it cannot have been likely to have attracted the attention of the City merchants, who were Philistines almost to a man." (p. 180). The second poem appeared in Octobre 1710.

boldface type at the beginning of a modern article: "Being a full and true Account, how a *Whig* Lord was taken at *Dunkirk*, in the Habit of a Chimney-sweeper, and carryed before General *Hill*" (PW vol. vi, p. 139).[45] Then comes a brief reminder of the general political situation that led to the event:

We have an old Saying, *That it is better to play at small Game than to stand out:* And it seems, the Whigs practice accordingly, there being nothing so little or so base, that they will not attempt, to recover their Power. (Ibid.)

After which, the story of the arrest is given with all the details desired: "On Wednesday Morning the 9th Instant, we are certainly informed, that Collonell Killegrew (who went to France with General Hill) walking in Dunkirk Streets met a tall Chimney-Sweeper with his Brooms and Poles ..." (ibid., p. 139). Needless to say, not a word of the anecdote is true. Swift enjoyed creating fully developed little fictions like this one, or that of *A New Journey to Paris*, as a relaxation from his serious work as a Tory pamphleteer. Another simple structure dictated by the nature of the genre is that of *Directions to Servants*. After a chapter on the rules of conduct applying to all servants, whatever their positions, it deals in turn with each employment from butler and cook to coachman and governess.

In a similar way, once it is realized that *A Tale of a Tub* satirizes the editing practices of a new generation of scholars,[46] whom Swift accuses of boosting their reputation by publishing the stories or writings of others, instead of doing original work, its structure becomes clear.[47] The

---

45 Udo Fries calls this part the "summary" of the article in "Summaries in Newspapers: A Textlinguistic Investigation", *The Structure of Texts*, ed. Udo Fries (SPELL 3), Tübingen, Gunter Narr, 1987, pp. 47 - 63. This study suggests that there has been a remarkable stability in the genre since the seventeenth century.

46 Jay Arnold Levine ("The Design of *A Tale of a Tub*", *ELH: A Journal of English Literary History* 33: 206, 1966) and Paul J. Korshin ("Swift and Typological Narrative in *A Tale of a Tub*", *Harvard English Studies* 1: 67 - 91, 1970) identify the scholarship as that of a typical critic of Scripture. Herbert Davis (op. cit., pp. 117 - 118) is enclined to favour Dryden's translation of *The Works of Virgil* (1697) as Swift's model. The disagreement confirms that Swift satirizes not one type of scholarship, but general practices.

47 E. Zimmerman (op. cit., p. 40) writes: "The text [of the framed tale] is presented as a reconstructed work of a conjectural author." See also Hugh Kenner, *The Stoic Comedians*, Berkeley, University of California, 1974, pp. 37 - 42.

bookseller's note corresponds to our modern dust jacket notices; a preface, an introduction and notes are in the order of what any reader has come to expect of a good scholarly edition, and the digressions would be today relegated to the end of the volume and be called appendices. Swift seems to have anticipated the modern practice when he invites "the judicious Reader" to assign a fitter place to his digressions: "I do here empower him to remove [them] into any other Corner he please" (PW vol. i, p. 94). The multiplying of introductory material and its peculiar nature evidence Swift's intention to caricature the practice and show that he would have been delighted with certain modern editions which lapse into the same excess. The structure of *Gulliver's Travels* is equally straightforward and in keeping with conventions. Gulliver introduces the story of his four incursions into strange countries with a brief account of his person, quality and life. Each voyage begins and ends with a glimpse of his life in England or aboard Western ships. His account is not uniformly narrative. The long discursive passages that intersperse the otherwise chronological sequence departure - adventure - discovery - return are ordinarily expected in the genre of the memoirs.[48] The patterning is only more insistent than in true travel books, being repeated four times. Swift adopts conventions and follows them faithfully. There is no search for renewal or sophistication on this head, nor does one expect any, as the structure must remain a reminder to the end that a discourse is being utilized to satiric ends. Generic transparency plays a capital rôle.

Because the framing devices are structured in such a way as to produce recognizable imitations of current literary and non-literary genres, they also contribute to anchor the fictions in the literary, political or religious context of the time. On this point, the rôle of framing fictions is different from that in the novel of the period. In the eighteenth-century novel, it claims for the framed fiction the status of an authentic document. It is not the claim which is problematic, but the relationship of the framed fiction to the circumstantial reality of the time. As the next

---

48 Northrop Frye, *Anatomy of Criticism*, Princeton, Princeton University Press, [1957] 1973, p. 307. Dirk Friederich Passmann offers the most thorough and up-to-date assessment of Swift's indebtedness to the tradition of travel accounts and investigation of his readers' "horizon of expectations" in *"Full of Improbable Lies": "Gulliver's Travels" und die Reiseliteratur vor 1726* (Frankfort, Peter Lang, 1987).

chapter will confirm, the fantasy of Swift's framed fictions and the unreliability of some of their purported authors prevent the reader's taking the fictional satire for anything but a hoax. But, at first sight, things look different. It is as though the framing fiction, the genre of the piece, or at least its material support, were in part dictated by the circumstances occasioning the purported author's gesture, and as though Swift wanted his fictitious discourses to pass off for real contributions to the intellectual debate of the period. He shows his purported authors to be directly involved in its activities, acting in a socio-political context and reacting to it, as he himself was doing as a friend and later political opponent of Addison and Steele.

In historical terms, it is possible to describe the intellectual debate that was raging during the last years of Queen Anne's reign as a real literary and journalistic war. The phenomenon was rendered, if anything, more virulent owing to the emergence of a pre-modern press and newspaper system catering for a public hungry for social, political and international news. News were not only read, they were avidly commented in coffee-houses and other similar meeting-places. The rivalry between the two political parties, Tories and Whigs, both bidding for the favour of the electorate to get control of political affairs, added its tension to the passionate climate. All the channels of information were used for propaganda purposes, so that little information filtered that was not distorted. Everything printed had a tendency to turn to polemics.[49] Nor was this all. At the beginning of Swift's career the literary quarrel between admirers of the ancient authors and those advocating the supremacy of the modern writers was resumed. Partly overlapping with it, another quarrel broke out between the theologians and natural philosophers about the nature of religion. The crisis found the churches divided against each other and often more concerned with wordly problems than the threat of free-thinking. Anglicans and Dissenters disagreed about the political rights to which the different protestant sects were entitled, and within the Anglican church itself there existed an endemic conflict between the higher clergy, jealous of its prerogatives, and the lower clergy. Swift's time was

---

49 In *Swift's Tory Politics* (London, Duckworth, 1983, p. 2) F.P. Lock describes the period, and particularly the years 1710 - 1714, as "unequalled before the reign of George III for the volume and virulence of its paper controversies." He adds that authors could count on "an audience of about 80,000 regular readers of political news and comment" (ibid.).

one of heated debate in every field. The spread of cheap publications, cheap to print and sell, coupled with the progressive disappearance of patronage, moreover favoured the development of a new class of independent men of letters, particularly free-lance writers with a very average education, collectively referred to as "Grubstreet".[50] They looked to the political parties to give them work and were in constant fear of censorship. But the literary and journalistic war was not restricted to this new class of writers. It was widely open to anyone who wished and could afford the cost of printing a sheet with an open letter or ballad, or a pamphlet, when no bookseller would assume responsibility for the publication.

Swift's satirical fictions not only look like, but they are contributions to this multiple warfare. It must be remembered that print had a legitimizing effect[51] when it was used as a medium to inform the public. There was a general trust in whatever news or factual account was printed, which writers soon felt tempted to exploit. The fashion seems to have originated in France and, from there, spread to England. At any rate, numerous fake personal memoirs of public figures who had failed to record their experiences were thus palmed off onto an avid and credulous public. One of these volumes of memoirs, Sandras de Courtilz's *Mémoires du comte de Rochefort*, translated into English in 1696, was so cleverly contrived that Defoe was completely taken in. He did not realize that it was a fake and took it as a true model for his own fake biographies, *Moll Flanders* and *Captain Singleton*.[52] The case of Defoe ought to be sufficient illustration of this power of authentication of print. However different they were, Swift's fictions must have benefited from the same implicit trust. They must have seemed just as irresistibly convincing. Readers must have thought at first that they were dealing with true journalistic or polemical writings. *A New Journey to Paris* and *A Hue and Cry*, which claimed to be news, must have been thought to disclose to the public something that was happening behind the political scene. A half-sheet about a man nicknamed Midas was a political manifesto of a sort, even if entitled a fable. *An Examination of Certain*

50 For a complete study of their background, see Pat Roger's study *Grub Street*.
51 Lennard J. Davis, op. cit., p. 148. On the problem of the historicity of news, see MacKeon, op. cit., pp. 47 - 64.
52 Michael M. Boardman, *Defoe and the Uses of Narrative*, New Brunswick, Rutgers University Press, 1983, p. 15.

Abuses and *The Humble Petition of the Footmen of Dublin* expressed identifiable grievances. When Wagstaff proposes his models for better conversation, he is really anxious, as Swift was, to improve its deplorable level in society, even though he does so in a silly way and with great presumption. In *A Modest Proposal* the projector is not only bent upon earning the gratitude of the whole country:

whoever could find out a fair, cheap, and easy Method of making these Children sound and useful Members of the Commonwealth, would deserve so well of the Publick, as to have his Statue set up for a Preserver of the Nation.

(PW vol. xii, p. 109)

He is concerned with a real problem, of which everyone in Ireland is conscious. What leads him to advertize his scheme is the laudable and humanitarian intention to save thousands of people from poverty. Swift underlines the fact that the projector's proposal for an economic solution is one among many other similar proposals. His purported writer, he says, had "maturely weighed" these other projects for many years, "and found them grosly mistaken in their Computation" (ibid., p. 110). As such, his *Proposal* could not fail to interest the public.

The purported authors mentioned so far join the social, political, economic and cultural debate of the time as professionals of the pen, or at least regular participants, which Gulliver and the anonymous author of *Directions to Servants* are not. They are amateurs and remain on the periphery of contemporary polemics. *Directions to Servants* is supposedly written by a customs-house clerk, who describes himself as a former footman. He addresses his former brother footmen with some nostalgia in the chapter he devotes to them:

I have a true Veneration for your Office, because I had once the Honour to be one of your Order, which I foolishly left by demeaning myself with accepting an Employment in the Custom-house. (PW vol. xiii, p. 34)

As for Gulliver, as everyone knows, he is a ship surgeon and navigator turned memorialist late in life. Gulliver's contribution to the intellectual debate of the eighteenth century is of special interest for literary history. Not only is he the best known of Swift's purported authors, but he is also one of the least involved in the passionate polemics of the time. And yet there is a faint flavour of it in his *Travels*, too.

Like other contemporary travellers, in fact, Gulliver primarily wants to inform readers and enlarge their horizons. His memoirs are also a memoir. He writes as a natural philosopher and anthropologist. The significance of this aspect of his *Travels* is brought into relief by a comparison with *Robinson Crusoe*, Defoe's celebrated story, which literary historians have long made it a practice to present together with Swift's no less famous masterpiece. It so happens that both books are fakes which capitalized on a vogue for travel accounts about remote countries, that both can be said to be shaped by the requirements and fashion of the genre as it existed then, and that they remain, after 250 years, two of the most popular works of their time and the only examples of its travel literature that have not been forgotten by the general public. Yet there are important differences between them. Not only is Defoe's fake meant to be taken seriously, whereas Swift ultimately expects his readers to detect the literary fabrication and to view it as a satirical device but, even when they are considered as two specimens of travels books, they must be admitted to have distinct characters. The figure of Robinson is more central to Defoe's realistic romance than Gulliver is to Swift's satire. Of the two, Crusoe's story is also less typical as a travel account on one crucial point: the reader is more involved in the way the hero overcomes difficulties and in what he does with his life than interested in what he can report on the lands where his fate strands him. *Robinson Crusoe* is an adventure story and exemplary autobiography, and Robinson is an adventurer. Gulliver is a traveller and visitor of places. He significantly entitles his memoir *Travels into Several Remote Nations of the World*, a title which is more explicit than the traditional one and sounds more like those of other contemporary travel books.

In fact, a more perfect illustration of the travel literature of the time could hardly be imagined. Besides being more thrilling and deliciously entertaining than most authentic travel books, Gulliver's memoir presents a vivid picture of navigation at the beginning of the eighteenth century in its three distinct aspects: trading, adventure and exploration. It is about the rivalry between colonial powers, competition between trading companies and, more generally, power struggle everywhere in the world; it is also about survival in remote areas of the globe, contacts with new nations, undreamt-of cultures, and about learning to communicate with them. It offers some quite detailed accounts of what most struck the visitor about the way of life, social and political organization, arts and crafts or architecture of these peoples. In his *Travels* Gulliver boasts of having discovered new continents and islands inhabited by strange races – but races hardly queerer than the more credulous people were still ready to expect, according to the old tradition of travel literature, and he wants to interest his countrymen in them. He follows – or tries to follow – the recommendations of the Royal Society for faithful reports of what he observes, and only secondarily of what he experiences.

Topical descriptions are lengthy. When something unusual happens, the narrative retains its honest "objectivity", and all events are accorded the same importance: none is apparently selected for particular attention or with a view to heightening the narrative interest. The space allotted to each may vary, because the period of time over which they develop may be shorter or longer, but the plain style and the focusing on concrete details tone down the dramatic note that here and there creeps into the text. Even in such a critical situation as that in which Gulliver finds himself in Chapter 7, when the King of Lilliput is about to impeach him for high treason, the narrative is content to relate the manner in which he is warned, the substance of the charges against him, and the way in which he forestalls the carrying out of the sentence that threatens him (PW vol. xii, pp. 67 - 74). Gulliver also tells what happens to himself mainly as relevant information about the people he describes. When the Brobdingnagian reaper finds him in the cornfield where he is hidden, Gulliver writes dispassionately:

And therefore when he was again about to move, I screamed as loud as Fear could make me. Whereupon the huge Creature trod short, and looking round about under him for some time, at last espied me as I lay on the Ground. He considered a while with the Caution of one who endeavours to lay hold on a small dangerous Animal in such a Manner that it shall not be able to scratch or bite him; as I my self have sometimes done with a *Weasel* in *England*. At length he ventured to take me up behind by the middle between his Fore-finger and Thumb, and brought me within three Yards of his Eyes, that he might behold my Shape more perfectly.   (Ibid., p. 87)

In this passage there are evident reasons for giving such a full account of the giant's reactions. In the general perspective of the whole satire, it prepares the reader for the later description of man as a grovelling insect. However, the satirical move is far from obvious at this point in the story. On the other hand, it is clear that the quotation focuses on the giant's size and reaction of prudence more insistently than on Gulliver's fear as soon as the stranger enters the scene, which is what one would expect from an observant traveller describing people very different from himself.

Likewise, on the level of the travelling experience, Gulliver's references to Europe are not so much to be taken as referring to himself, but simply as underlining similarities and differences between the reality he and his readers are familiar with and the different, "alleged", reality he explores, in the same way as the biologist of the time had learnt to proceed in the description of animals of the same kind but different species.

For Gulliver, one of the central interests of his *Travels* is geographical whereas, for Crusoe, it could be said to be the moral lesson of his adventures. Gulliver attaches great importance to this aspect of his memoir. It matters more to him than the fact of having claimed a few more territories for the Crown of England. With the feigned modesty of the amateur who has made a discovery, he would have the reader believe that he even has some pretentions as a cartographer, and it is here that a polemical note can be detected. In the following quotation concerning the Land of the Houyhnhnms, Gulliver specifically refers to a Dutch cartographer, who was to die only a few years later:

This confirmed me in the Opinion I have long entertained, that the *Maps* and *Charts* place this Country at least three Degrees more to the *East* than it really is; which Thought I communicated many Years ago to my worthy Friend, Mr Herman Moll. . .

(Ibid., p. 284)

Gulliver situates the island of Lilliput and Blefuscu north-west or north-east of Australia and Tasmania, and that of the Houyhnhnms, reached after his ship had been blown off course on its way from the Cape of Good Hope to Madagascar, somewhere west of the most south-western point of Australia, in the Indian Ocean, unless it is a little further east, considering that, in Chapter 11 of the fourth part, he leaves the clever horses in his canoe of stitched Yahoo skins, and soon after reaches the southern coast of Tasmania. As for Brobdingnag and the islands of Lapu-ta, Balnibarbi and Luggnagg, the first is situated east of China and north-west of North America, of which it might be a larger peninsula, like a sort of more southern Alaska, and the others lie somewhere between Japan and America, in the middle of the Pacific Ocean, which is broad enough in these latitudes to accommodate a few more islands.[53] Swift

53 For a discussion of the geography in *Gulliver's Travels*, see Arthur E. Case, *Four Essays on "Gulliver's Travels"*, Princeton, Princeton University Press, 1945, pp. 50 - 61 and, above all, Passmann, op. cit., pp. 235 - 266. Whatever contradictions may exist between the maps provided by the editor and Swift's text, contemporary readers are unlikely to have been much troubled by the discrepancies and the

was careful to locate his new territories in little known waters or in areas where the Dutch made it difficult for anyone to trade but themselves, so that information was scarce. What emerges from all this is that Gulliver claims to have made significant contributions to the knowledge of the eighteenth century in two important fields, namely cartography and natural science, while at the same time helping to enlarge England's possessions overseas.

The geographical and topographical dimension of *Gulliver's Travels,* as well as its alleged intellectual contribution to the debate of ideas, cannot be sufficiently stressed. Interest in the nature of Swift's irony and use of narrators should not obscure this essential aspect of the narrative, so typical of the period when it was written. It appears clearly from what precedes that the *Travels* were composed in such a way as to meet certain precise expectations on the part of the at the time numerous readers of travel literature. Gulliver's account did not seem simply intended to satisfy a general curiosity about the world, its vastness, of which a new awareness was developing, and the diversity of life on the earth. The profusion of geographical markers, dates and nautical terms at the beginning of the relation of each voyage gave the reader to understand that one of the author's more ambitious aims was to offer detailed factual, even quantifiable, information about his travels, and the account of Lilliput, Brobdingnag, Laputa and Houyhnhnmland which followed showed that this was no idle promise on his part.

It is impossible not to notice that we have here another vivid illustration of the manner in which the faithful imitation of a genre, especially in connection with the framing discourse, paves the way for the satirical developments that are to follow. The very same factual and quantifiable information which, at the beginning of each book, raises the reader's expectation of truthfulness and accuracy, must inevitably draw their attention to everything that is extravagantly out of proportion or outlandish when they come across similar data later on with respect to Gulliver's discoveries. For the early readers, this cannot but have put them on the scent of the literary fabrication, as it made them realize that "Gulliver" was putting their credulity to the test. Compared to *Robinson Crusoe,* the *Travels* is then formally the more faithful to the conven-

lack of accuracy: their standards of factual precision were different from those of today's readers of detective stories, who, according to Agatha Christie are very exacting in this respect (*The Clock*, Glasgow, Fontana, 1986, p. 34).

tions of travel literature, and yet it is the more conspicuous lie. Swift spares the reader no surprise. The manipulation of the generic conventions of travel literature to satirical ends furthermore brings out the fact that the geography of the *Travels* forms one of the non-negligible satirical dimensions. What Gulliver sees as his participation in the geographical debate of his age does not simply serve to anchor the satire of the *Travels* in the contemporary reality. It is also connected with, and draws attention to, Swift's symbolic use of space.

The similarities and differences with *Robinson Crusoe* are here again striking. In both travel accounts, geographical features come to represent the human activities they accommodate and acquire moral connotations in the process. On the other hand, Swift's islands, peninsulas and seas are the opposite of Defoe's. His islands and continents are thickly populated by communities that have their specific problems. His seas are passing-through places between these populated lands. They are not just dangerous because of their tempests, as they usually are in adventure stories: but they are also obstacles that trade and progress must eliminate. On Swift's oceans sailors get lost in unchartered waters and discover new lands. Oceans spell distances and separation, as noted above, and distances allow for differences between races and cultures, as well as between climates and types of vegetation or fauna. Sometimes they bring remote nations into contact with one another. Swift can even claim to be more conscious than most travellers were in his time of representing seas at a turning point in history: they had so far been protective barriers, which had safeguarded the natural innocence of some populations – the Houynhnhnms –, ensured the stability of other societies – the Brobding-nagians –, or, at least, forced certain political regimes to keep their deficiencies to themselves – the Laputans; but, becoming passing-through places, oceans were suddenly promoted to the status of links between nations and threatened to favour the spreading of European evils to the rest of the world, rather than being the occasion of a beneficial lesson for Western man. Each of Gulliver's four adventures makes this abundantly clear. On leaving Blefuscu, Swift's ship surgeon, whose attitude on this occasion is typical of Western merchant travellers and explorers, has to be prevented by a responsible and humane monarch from pocketing a few specimens of the tiny inhabitants, whom he wishes to exhibit to his countrymen on his return to England, as was frequently done by other explorers with other sorts of "savages". Later, this same typical Western merchant traveller is ready to offer gunpowder to the Brobdingnagians, who had been spared this treacherous invention. At the end of his adventures, he is finally unable to share with his contemporaries the wisdom he might have learnt from the Houyhnhnms or the Struldbruggs. According to the satirist, contacts between nations bring more trouble than benefit to mankind.

In *Gulliver's Travels* the geographical dimension holds such a central place that Swift can even be said to have transposed historical into geographical events. It is common knowledge that the *Travels* refer to his own recent past, what happened at the end of Queen Anne's reign, and during Walpole's later Whig government. In the satire these events become part of a report on the geography of the unknown islands of Lilliput and Blefuscu and on their inhabitants, as can be seen in the story of Gulliver's capture of the Blefuscudian fleet, which represents "the dismantling of the naval base of Dunkirk under the Treaty of Utrecht (1713)" and of his being created a Nardac in recompense for his great service to the state, which clearly recalls that Queen Anne had rewarded Lord Oxford and Bolingbroke for similar services in 1711 and 1712.[54] Imaginatively, it is to exploration of remote countries and civilizations that the reader is invited, in the company of a new-style traveller, briefed by the Royal Academy, who expected facts from him and not "Panegyricks of the amenities of the place": "In our designed *Natural History* we have more need of severe, full and punctuall Truth, than of Romances or Panegyricks."[55] As, furthermore, this new-style traveller shows the usual resilience of his class and, until well into the fourth book, is little changed by the events he reports, it would seem inconsequent to attempt to enquire too deeply into his personality and psychology, except in so far as it relates to the "truth" of his memoir as a traveller's document.

There is, of course, the ending which poses a problem. Because the company of the clever horses, the Houyhnhnms, seems to affect Gulliver lastingly (i.e. until the publication of the *Travels* and the later prefatory letter), critics have sometimes felt that this amounted to a change of per-

---

54 Swift handles freely the chronology of the attested historical events he refers to. See Paul Turner's notes to Part one, chapter 5, in his edition of *Gulliver's Travels* (Oxford, Oxford University Press, 1971, p. 317). It seems appropriate to stress this geographical dimension after two critics, Hermann J. Real and Heinz J. Vienken, have proposed the notion of a Gulliver as first time traveller in literature: "The Structure of *Gulliver's Travels*", *First Münster Symposium*, p. 203.

55 *Philosophical Transactions* 11, (London, 1676), p. 552.

sonality that rendered the whole retrospective narrative problematic. It need not be the case. His personality does not change basically. His pessimistic view of what men make of their gifts is present from the beginning, from the description of Lilliput society. Each voyage leaves a deep impression on him, but only for a time. It always wears off before the next. The fourth voyage being the last, however, Gulliver seems to remain a little longer under its impressions, but a return to a normal life is explicitly announced: "I began last Week to permit my Wife to sit at Dinner with me . . ." (ibid., p. 295). Furthermore his depression is proportionate to the exhilarating experience of his life among the clever horses. A narrow escape brings relief, but a thrilling experience leaves nostalgia. Gulliver is a traveller, endowed with the correct zest for discoveries and degree of responsiveness, who has besides a passion for world maps. It is mainly when overlooking the fact that the *Travels* are composed according to the rules of the art of travel literature that problems of interpretation concerning the rôle of its narrator arise. At the level of the travel account that forms the framing fiction, *Gulliver's Travels* has a geographic and anthropological interest, even if it is only a fake one, and Gulliver appears to be, on the whole and at first sight, a satisfactory eyewitness of what he reports: honest, sincere and modest. His personality is much less obtrusive than that of the hack in *A Tale* or Wagstaff in *Polite Conversation*, as a traveller's should, and usually is, in that kind of writing.

It has been necessary to insist on the way the parodies anchor the fictions in the literary, political and religious context of their time, and on their power of authentication, because it is an aspect of the framing fictions to which modern readers are not likely to respond in the same way as earlier ones did. But it must not be forgotten that, for Swift, it was only a trick. The deception was not meant to last. Readers were soon forced to question the "legitimation of print".[56] They did not remain long trapped in the illusion of the fiction. As they began to realize that what they were reading was a counterfeit, a joke, their whole idea of the intellectual and political debate of the time became tainted by analogy. What had looked serious warfare was shown to be what could be designated by the metaphor of a game, and this metaphor turns reality

---

56 Lennard J. Davis, op. cit., p. 148.

into an implicit fiction.[57] At the same time as they anchor a fiction in circumstantial reality, the framing fictions fictionalize reality. They create an alternative reality, part facts part fiction, a sort of revised version of the contemporary world. When Swift invented events, or facts, or a supposed author taking a stand on a question, he was conscious of doing something different from polemicking. Imagination took over, the limited objectives of polemics were abandoned and some human activities were caricatured and aped as activities, or as ludicrous and pointless agitation.

There remains to describe the game, its actors and its fictionalizing of reality. The people playing the game, the purported authors of the satirical fictions, are the same kind of people as the real writers who took part in real polemics in those years. They range from amateurs to professional journalists and pamphleteers, from footmen to lords, and from new-model free-lance writers to worthy citizens. Shadowy figures or well-identified ones, they are hacks, projectors, ship surgeons, almanac writers, bishops or servants. Some find themselves accidentally involved in the fray, and others plunge voluntarily into it.[58] They are sometimes presented as rushing more impetuously into the intellectual and political debate and bandying their arguments and counter-arguments with more vigour and passion than the issues warrant, which can give them the air of being more stooges than real people. Whenever a purported author conveys the feeling that his reputation is at stake, the satirical fiction suggests that the game is fiercely competitive. It is finally to be noted that a plurality of pens is usually an essential feature of the literary game, which must be collective to be fully entertaining. *A Tale of a Tub* is the product of several pens and alludes to many others. The more the merrier, its author-editor insists. Each piece of introductory material has

---

57 I use the metaphor in a different sense from Peter Steele (*Jonathan Swift: Preacher and Jester*, Oxford, Clarendon, 1978, p. 143) who, in a biographical perspective, speaks of Swift as a "*magister ludi*" conducting a game. In *Intricate Laughter in the Satire of Swift and Pope* (London, Macmillan, 1986, p. 148), Allan Ingram similarly notes that, for Swift, the activity of playing governs both "public and private behaviour." My use of the notion of game refers, not to the creator's spirit, but to the fiction he creates and the way it is apprehended by the reader.

58 In *The Fictions of Satire* (p. 136), Ronald Paulson remarks that, with Swift, "the dramatic implications of the situation . . . take precedence over the rhetorical" as soon as there is an identifiable purported author. In many cases, the caricatural utilization of genres and forms suffices to achieve this effect.

necessitated "perusing some hundreds of Prefaces" or dedications (PW vol. i, p. 27; see also p. 14). They also refer to the "Levies of Wits", all "formidable Enquirers" that have inspired the hack (ibid., p. 24). *Gulliver's Travels* is Gulliver's account, published and prefaced by his cousin Sympson. In a letter prefixed to a later edition, Gulliver complains to his cousin about an "Interpolator". This interpolator, also referred to in the "Advertisement", as "a Person since deceased, on whose Judgment the Publisher relyed to make any Alterations that might be thought necessary" (PW vol. xi, p. 3) is accused of having tampered with Gulliver's text. In his letter, Gulliver also claims to be the cousin of William Dampier (1652 - 1715), pirate, explorer and author of two true travel books, *A New Voyage Round the World* (1697) and *A Voyage to New Holland* (1703) (ibid., p. 5). *A Modest Proposal* not only presupposes the existence of other proposals, it also refers to a friend of the author, a merchant, who has given him a good idea (PW vol. xii, p. 111).

By far the most ambitious and complex attempt to inscribe a fiction in the circumstantial reality of the period, and to fictionalize reality through it, resulted in *The Bickerstaff Papers*. On Swift's side, the *Papers* (PW vol. ii) consist of a series of five publications, a whole polemic, allegedly by several hands once more. They form a practical joke at the expense of an almanac writer, John Partridge. The game was to stir up a polemic over the seriousness of almanac writers and "the credulity of the vulgar, and that idle itch of peeping into futurities," as a contemporary put it (ibid., p. 196). Another contemporary, perhaps the poet Nicholas Rowe, described the hoax as a plan "to murder a Man by Way of Prophecy" (ibid., p. 223).[59] It ran over a period of several months and was so successful that not only was Partridge forced to defend himself, but other writers joined in the fray unprompted, helping to blur the distinction between fact and fiction. The *Papers* develop like a comedy in three acts.

Act I. In February 1708 a certain Isaac Bickerstaff, who introduced himself as a serious student of astrology, which almanac writers, he contended, were not, offered the public a counter-almanac. His first prediction for the following months concerned the death of a popular astrologer, the same Partridge. The date given was 29th March, a little more than a month away. Some readers at once detected a *bite*. As for the fools and gulls, "he has them fast for some time", someone commented

59 The author puts these words in Partridge's own mouth.

(ibid., p. 195). In the meantime the astrologer Partridge could not resist rising to the bait and publishing a reply.[60] Act II. 29th March came and went. On the following day an account appeared reporting Partridge's alleged death on the day predicted. The author of this account was not Bickerstaff. He described himself as an acquaintance of the almanac writer and, in his "Letter to a Person of Honour", not only narrated the manner of the astrologer's death, but also attacked Bickerstaff for failing to determine the exact time of the death in question. There was, he argued, as much as four hours' difference (ibid., p. 155). For good measure, there also appeared, presumably on the same day, an anonymous "Elegy on Mr Partridge, the Almanack-maker, who died on the 29th of this Instant March, 1708" (SPW, pp. 67 - 70). It was printed on a separate half-sheet. Unable to foretell the time of his own death, Partridge was discredited. He had been killed metaphorically. Act III. When, in the second half of the same year, the living Partridge ventured to publish his predictions for 1709, protesting that he was still alive and kicking, Bickerstaff was ready to pounce on him and deal him a second metaphorical blow. In a proud and solemn "Vindication", he accused Partridge of not playing fair, of having dealings with the devil as, quite obviously, he was dead and consequently could not publish a new almanac without recourse to the most devilish witchcraft. Such practice, he went on, impeded "the Progress of his own Art" for selfish reasons (ibid., p. 161). Bickerstaff also defended himself against the accusation of failing to determine the exact moment of the astrologer's death the previous spring. To crown the whole, Swift forged a supposedly ancient prophecy, "A Famous Prediction of Merlin" (SPW, pp. 70 - 73), which concluded the polemic. This mock prophecy is in verse, with an accompanying prose commentary turned in such a way as to be a concealed compliment to Marlborough and offer a prediction of a successful campaign. The comedy ends with the defeat of the villain and of the obstructing forces, unscrupulous astrology and superstitions, and with the victory of the genial character, Bickerstaff. Partridge is literally "vaporized" and superstition ridiculed. With this fiction of a polemical debate inscribed in real life, the fictitious character ends up having more presence and reality than the real people taking part in it. After such a promising start, Bickerstaff was guaranteed a brilliant literary career, as everyone knows.

60 PW vol. ii, Appendix B, pp. 201 - 207. See also the introduction to vol. ii, p. xii.

Swift used the same tactics again and again on a more limited time scale. His hoax of 1722 upon the criminal Ebenezor Elliston also made quite a stir.[61] He even repeated the tactics for strictly polemical purposes in *The Drapier's Letters*. In it the mask of the draper is only a thin disguise for the Dean of St. Patrick's, and the polemic is no longer a game but deadly serious. On the structural level, this is made clear by the fact that, in their case, the form adopted is not a device framing an irrelevant fiction. The letters are what they claim to be: open letters to the Irish people, encouraging them to boycott the use of the worthless coinage that the London government wanted to impose on them.

The Bickerstaff Papers inscribe preposterous predictions and events in the contemporary world of the eighteenth century, the *Travels* a fanciful, but likely, geography on the globe, and *A Hue and Cry* or *A New Journey to Paris* invented events in the history of the peace negociations with France. Considered in this light, Swift's prefixing of Gulliver's letter to his cousin Sympson in later editions of the *Travels*, which amounts to an extension of the peritext and, more significantly, of the discursive editorial framing, does not appear to be so much intended to conceal his authorship and to protect him, as is still occasionally argued. Gulliver's protest against the way his travelling account had been published and come to be read allegorically was meant rather to anchor the story more firmly in the context of the literary game of the time, at a moment when it had become increasingly clear anyway that *Gulliver's Travels* was pure satirical fiction.[62] It shows Swift enjoying the game as a game.

---

61 George P. Mayhew gives an account of this other hoax in "Jonathan Swift's Hoax of 1722 upon Ebenezor Elliston", *Fair Liberty was All his Cry*, ed. A. Norman Jeffares, London, Macmillan, 1967, pp. 290 - 310.

62 The question as to whether early readers could see through the fiction is still much disputed. Dirk F. Passmann (op. cit.) suggests throughout his study that Swift's contemporaries read "Gulliver" and Dampier in the same way, and in the same way as they read Purchas. To this can be objected that there were other readers who were never deceived by the pretence, such as the Duchess of Marlborough, and that the relation between knowledge and belief had changed considerably since Hakluyt and Purchas, seventy years before, owing to the new empiricism, its emphasis on measuring and quantifying reality – Gulliver measures and quantifies it in a way which made it clear that he was lying. The new empiricism and the sceptical reaction that followed it suggest that readers were no longer so credulous as to accept as authentic any kind of wonder reported in travel books.

Much earlier already, he and his friends had been delighted with reports of people who had taken the book for a true report. Arburthnot mentions the master of a ship who asserted that he was acquainted with Gulliver, "but that the printer had Mistaken, that he lived in Wapping, and not in Rotherhith", and a letter to Pope alludes to a bishop who protested that "that Book was full of improbable lies".[63] For those in the know, the game was the more enjoyable for being taken seriously by some readers, and for the fiction passing for the reality, at least for a while.[64]

In their relationship to the context of circumstantial reality the framing fictions have been seen to express two opposed, even contradictory aims. On the one hand they fictionalize reality, and on the other hand they claim for themselves the status of facts and real events. Either way the structuring of the satires blurs the distinction between real life and fiction and lends them an ambivalent character. To what end? In so far as the fictionalizing of reality turns contemporary polemics, reports and the public taking of stands by private individuals into a mere game – this is an interesting instance of what criticism today calls "troping" of reality –, it casts doubt on the seriousness and honesty of many intellectual, scholarly and journalistic activities: it belittles the efforts of several writers, ridicules the low level of the debate itself, and questions the validity of current views. The use of framing fictions thus contributes a crucial element to the satirical strategy. The parody of a genre is prolonged beyond the text, so as to become a parody of the intellectual activities of the time. If, in a novel of Aphra Behn and Defoe, or the satires of Mary Manley, the editorial framing mediates between facts and fiction and guarantees a factual fiction, in Swift's satires the framing fictions do not become factual. On the contrary, his satires may more properly be described as fictional gestures and events, in that, in them, a fictitious writer, writing about his fictitious experience, publishes a materially real, credible and printed contribution to the contemporary debate of ideas. When the fictitious authors imitate their contemporaries and compose news reports, pamphlets, petitions, prefaces, digressions, notes, proposals or travel books, they give no guarantee but of their

---

63 *Swift: The Critical Heritage*, pp. 62, 64.
64 On this point, see Hermann J. Real and Heinz J. Vienken, *Jonathan Swift: "Gulliver's Travels"* (Münich, Fink, 1984), p. 24.

fictionality, and it is fiction that steps into reality.[65] Instead of a literary realism offered as an extension of the commonsense world, Swift's satirical fictions suggest that the commonsense world is more properly seen as a continuation of the fictitious. The fictionalizing force is such, as has been seen with *The Bickerstaff Papers*, that historical figures whose example is directly called upon are metamorphosed into fictional types. This fate is incurred not only by Partridge, but by a well-known scholar of the period, William Wotton, in *A Tale of a Tub*, and by the other historical figures that put in an appearance in other satires. The fictionalizing of reality that occurs when the framing fiction suggests the image of the literary and journalistic game and an active participation in it produces various types of dramatic emplotments, which may be said to supply the fictional plots that have eluded critics.[66] Only here the plot is to be looked for outside the text, in its imaginative extension. The framing device contextualizes the fiction, at the same time as it fictionalizes the context, to make a fictional participation in the drama of real life possible. The game also turns life into a great comedy, and this not only in *The Bickerstaff Papers*, where the pattern is most explicit, but in all the satirical fictions. That this is so is not a total surprise when it is remembered that satire was still commonly believed by contemporary satirists and critics to have its roots in drama and the playing of comic rôles.

There remains one point of the fictionalizing of reality to consider. The caricature of discourses or fictitious utilization of journalistic, polemical or "scientific" publications does not only create the fiction of the literary game and produce comedy. In so far as each discourse or publication is a credible contribution to actual polemics from a pretended author, it is supposed to express an individual or a collective view, as well as an interpretation of facts. It constitutes a subjective statement. Even Gulliver's apparently detached report of plain facts is marred by limitations, his own as a person and those of the kind of discourse, with

---

65 One type of fiction, that of Defoe and Aphra Behn, in this sense reflects what McKeon describes as the epistemology of a naive empiricism coloured with a shade of scepticism, and the other type, Swift's, illustrates the attitude of extreme scepticism, which leads to "solipsistic subjectivity" (op. cit., p. 87).

66 A notable example is John R. Clark (op. cit.), who looks for a fictional plot in various abstract patterns of the *Tale*: the conflict between knave and fool and the Icarian flight of madness, among others, which account more for the choice of the tropes than the sense of dramatic unity.

its dry style, that he has chosen to report his experience. The significance of what he describes often eludes him. With his love of fictions, Swift comes close to a conception of reality as the construction of a mind. This conception is also Lockean.[67] The pieces without identifiable authorial figures, like *A New Journey to Paris*, or "A Description of a City Shower", which appear more truly factual and objective than Bickerstaff's benevolent polemicking or Wagstaff's eccentric bid for fame, are not really as reliable as they look either, owing to their generic biases. For the satirist, no interpretation of facts can be completely objective, owing to general prejudices, wrong-headedness, narrow partisanship, blinding passion and stupidity on the one hand, and the limitations of the discourses in which they find expression on the other hand. In this respect, one of the purposes of satire's complex structure – the fact will appear more clearly with the study of the framed fictions – is to expose the distortions, and the image of the game is a way of disparaging their reprehensible aspects. Man lives in a world not of facts but of conflicting views, and it is his subjectivity that also invades reality along with the dramatic metaphor of the game.

At the point where people and activities are digested into the fiction, a watershed is reached. The movement is reversed, and the fictionalizing of reality yields to a process that is best described, to oppose it to the other tendency, as the factualization of fiction. It is not just that each framing fiction ends up being an event and gesture inscribed into circumstantial reality. The fiction sifts and assimilates, not only contemporary figures as mentioned above, but also a large number of factual details about everyday life, so that the substance of the framing fiction appears as though contaminated by the contemporary background. The fictitious authors make repeated references to their supposed life, their profession, and the life of the age. These references are usually brief and form many Hogarthian vignettes in the text. They are not intended to give the reader a sense of the individuality of the purported author. They do not build up a coherent vision of life as in a novel. Their rôle is only to create the

---

67 Robert Martin Adams (op. cit. , p. 161) argues that philosophy fell into psychology "as into an ambush". He continues: "Setting out to dispute a substantive matter, [Locke] and his friends quickly found themselves at a complete stand, unable to determine anything until they had come to an agreement concerning human understanding". As for Swift, he fell into the same trap, "and never succeeded in getting out of it, perhaps because he never wanted to." This last statement is at least true of his purported authors as fictitious figures in a game.

impression that the voice of the fictitious author is that of a real person acting in real circumstances. These Hogarthian vignettes[68] sometimes appear purely incidental, like the following one from the bookseller's dedication "To the Right Honourable, John Lord Sommers" at the beginning of *A Tale of a Tub*:

But, it unluckily fell out, that none of the Authors I employ, understood *Latin* (tho' I have them often in pay, to translate out of that Language) I was therefore compelled to have recourse to the Curate of our Parish, who Englished it thus, *Let it be given to the Worthiest*; And his Comment was, that the Author meant, his Work should be dedicated to the sublimest Genius of the Age, for Wit, Learning, Judgment, Eloquence and Wisdom. I call'd at a Poet's Chamber (who works for my Shop) in an Alley hard by, shewed him the Translation, and desired his Opinion, who it was that the Author could mean; He told me, after some Consideration, that Vanity was a Thing he abhorr'd; but by the Description, he thought Himself to be the Person aimed at; And, at the same time, he very kindly offer'd his own Assistance *gratis*, towards penning a Dedication to Himself. I desired him, however, to give a second Guess; Why then, said he, It must be I, or my Lord *Sommers*. From thence I went to several other Wits of my Acquaintance, with no small Hazard and Weariness to my Person, from a prodigious Number of dark, winding Stairs; But found them all in the same Story, both of your Lordship and themselves. Now, your Lordship is to understand, that this Proceeding was not of my own Invention; For, I have somewhere heard, it is a Maxim, that those, to whom every Body allows the second Place, have an undoubted Title to the First. (PW vol. i, p. 14)

The next illustration functions as a simile. Allowances being made for Swift's animus against the Scots, the picture need not apply to Edinburgh in particular, but it is as accurate a picture of city life as "A Description of a City Shower". Much worse was reported of other cities like London,

---

68 The kinship with Hogarth has often been noted. Swift himself mentions him appreciatively in a poem of 1736, "A Character, Panegyric, and Description of the Legion Club" (SPW, p. 607, ll. 219 - 222):
How I want thee, humorous *Hogart*?
Thou I hear, a pleasant Rogue art;
Were but you and I acquainted,
Every Monster should be painted . . .
Drawings from Hogarth have been used to illustrate the covers of Swift's individual works. Peter Steele (op. cit., p. 103) insists on the disturbing quality of the satirist's vignettes, their fusion of knowingness and desire to shock. I should like to stress their visual and dramatic quality.

Dublin or Marseilles.[69] To do their work, the purported author of *A Tale* says, critics must proceed in

> their common perusal of Books, singling out the Errors and Defects, the Nauseous, the Fulsome, the Dull, and the Impertinent, with the Caution of a Man that walks thro' *Edenborough* Streets in a Morning, who is indeed as careful as he can, to watch diligently, and spy out the Filth in his Way, not that he is curious to observe the Colour and Complexion of the Ordure, or take its Dimensions, much less to be padling in, or tasting it: but only with a Design to come out as cleanly as he may.
>
> (Ibid., p. 56)

To this method of completing the anchoring of a satire and of the fictitious author's gesture more firmly in the contemporary reality, the reader owes the short account that Gulliver gives of his parentage and education at the beginning of his *Travels*, as well as a number of allusions to his family life between the voyages. The Wagstaff of *Polite Conversation* and the conversations he collects come more fully alive when he describes himself going about the fashionable world with his "large Table-Book" in his pocket (PW vol. iv, p. 100), like a modern would-be social scientist or anthropologist with tape recorder and camera.

Walter Scott, who, as a novelist, knew the ins and outs of the trade of fiction writing, describes Swift as possessing, "in the most extensive degree, the art of verisimilitude". He notes how much of this effect derives from the clever use of such factual details:

> Small and detached facts form the foreground of a narrative when told by an eye-witness. They are the subjects which immediately press upon his attention, and have, with respect to him as an individual, an importance, which they are far from bearing to the general scene in which he is engaged . . . But to a distant spectator all these minute incidents are lost and blended in the general current of events; and it requires the discrimination of Swift, or of De Foe, to select, in a fictitious narrative, such an enumeration of minute incidents as might strike the beholder of a real fact, especially such a one as has not been taught, by an enlarged mind and education, to generalize his observations.[70]

69 Pat Rogers, op. cit., pp. 141 - 143, & passim; Carole Fabricant, op. cit., pp. 24 - 33; and John Lough, *France Observed in the Seventeenth Century by British Travellers*, Stockfield, Oriel Press, 1985.
70 *Memoirs of Jonathan Swift* (1814), quoted from *Swift: The Critical Heritage*, pp. 299 - 300.

The Hogarthian vignettes considerably reinforce the reader's impression that the satire is relevant to the world outside the text. They are vivid little tableaux and have the ring of authenticity about them. They make the fabrication of the document and the fictitious author look true. They have a visual quality which enables Swift to heighten his staging effect and to make the fictitious authors' gestures look dramatic like that of a character in a play.

IV

Both when they fictionalize reality and when they pass themselves off as genuine contributions to the contemporary debate of ideas, Swift's framing fictions fulfil a more ambitious and complex function than is the case in the novel of the age. The satirist is not content to exploit the news / novel ambiguity like Defoe and to offer the public an allegedly truthful document. He uses his framing fictions like weapons. Whereas Addison and Steele attempted with their essays to raise the periodical newspaper above polemics and to turn their undertaking into literature in the modern sense of the word, Swift seemed, by comparison and for all his scorn of contemporary practices, ever ready to plunge into polemics. It is on precisely this point that his satirical strategy, with its recourse to the framing device, parts company with that of other satirists. These will generally hold up their distorting mirrors to nature at a distance. The framing fictions give Swift's satires the thrust of polemical writings. The reader has the impression of dealing directly with a message which makes a claim on his sympathy and approval. This, satirists normally avoid. His tactics is similar to that of a certain popular press, in which the writer does not so much express what he thinks and wants to tell his readers, as what his readers think and want to be reassured about, in other words what they want to read and approve of. French linguistics speaks of the reader as a "co-enunciator" in this case.[71] Swift's mouth-pieces, his "enunciators" do exactly this. They engage their readers in a sort of magazine dialogue of a low common denominator. They do not come down to the level of their readers: they put themselves in their

71 Sophie Fisher and Eliséo Véron, "Théorie de l'énonciation et discours sociaux", *Etudes de Lettres* 4: 71 - 92 (1986), and more generally the ideas of Antoine Culioli.

place.[72] The anonymous friend of Mr Collins who has prepared an "Abstract for the Use of the Poor" of the latter's *Discourse of Free-Thinking* is perfectly explicit as to this intention in his prefatory letter to Mr Collins himself:

> By these Reflections I was brought to think, that the most ingenious Author of the Discourse upon *Free Thinking*, in a Letter to *Somebody, Esq*; although he hath used less reserve than any of his Predecessors, might yet have been more free and open. I considered, that several *Well-willers* to *Infidelity* might be discouraged by a shew of Logick, and multiplicity of Quotations, scattered through his Book, which to Understandings of that Size might carry an appearance of something like *Book-learning*, and consequently fright them from reading for their Improvement: I could see no Reason why these great Discoveries should be hid from our Youth of Quality, who frequent *White's* and *Tom's*; why they should not be adapted to the Capacities of the *Kit-Cat* and *Hannover* Clubs, who might *then* be able to read lectures on them to their several *Toasts* . . .   (PW vol. iv, pp. 27 - 28)

Some of the very names of Swift's purported authors betray the connivance between enunciator and co-enunciator or reader. Two could even be said to apply to the rôle in which the co-enunciator is cast as well as to that of the enunciator himself: are not Gull-iver's memoirs aimed at the gullible reader, and Bicker-staff's *Papers* at the reader who enjoys witty "bickering"? Simultaneously the names mark the ironical distance between the puppets of the game and the puppet master.

In Swift's fictions, the reader is called upon to take sides. The satirist manipulates his response so as to provoke a new awareness about the implications of the problem or attitude presented in the fiction. When he completes the framing fiction in *Gulliver's Travels* and adds to the Faulkner edition (1735) an "Advertisement" and a letter from Gulliver to his cousin Sympson, who was the alleged author of the preface to the original edition (1726), Swift's aim is not merely to make the travel account look more genuine and to add to the enjoyment of the game. It is also to confirm that his intention is to provoke a reaction. The starting point is always that the writing should excite curiosity, interest or passion. Then several ways are open. Either the appeal to the reader's sympathy and approval is meant to be answered positively as in *The*

---

72 In so far as they identify themselves with their readers and voice their opinions, they are "middlemen" and "popularizers" of other men's ideas in a very special sense. See Ronald Paulson's discussion of the point with reference to a *Tale*, op. cit., p. 148.

Bickerstaff Papers and *A Hue and Cry*, and the complicity between alleged author and reader leads to their sharing the joke at someone else's expense contained in the framing fiction; or the reader grants his sympathy, but not his approval, as in the petitions, so that the satire is directed both at the alleged author, who becomes the target of Swift's sense of humour, and at the framed fiction, the strictly satirical component; or the claim on the reader's sympathy and approval becomes so embarrassing that the reader is led to reject all collusion with the polemical stance expressed in the framing discourse as in *A Modest Proposal*, but sometimes not before he has been tempted first to embrace it, as in the *Travels*. Sometimes the reader is manoeuvred into giving an impossible assent and feels then taken to task.[73] *Gulliver's Travels* qua travel book takes him to task for , among other things, not discriminating between true reports, good stories and sensational news, as do *A Hue and Cry* and *A New Journey to Paris*. They also satirize the thirst after news and their indiscriminate consumption. *A Modest Proposal* attacks the well-meaning but callous response of Walpole's government and of the Irish upper classes to the problem of poverty and exploitation of Ireland. In fact, it would be a great mistake to ignore this aggressive side of the satires, even where the tone of the purported author is not polemical. As for *A Tale of a Tub*, *Meditation upon a Broomstick* and *The Bickerstaff Papers*, they have been seen to ridicule the public's blindness to uselessly fussy scholarship, pretentious ignorance, cheap moralizing and false predictions, as well as its gullibility. The framing fictions work like shock tactics to prevent a distant and, consequently, indifferent response. Swift has little sympathy for the stance of the privileged observer, the Addisonian "Man of Polite Imagination".[74] Light or ferocious, the lightness or ferociousness of the satire is directed at the general reader, a member of the public, fond of what certain kinds of writings or genres offer him. This is true even where there seems to be a

---

73 The last two cases have been more often discussed than the others. In 1959, Henry Sams described in "Swift's Satire in the Second Person" (ELH: *Journal of English Literary History* 26: 36)- 44) the way in which the satirist manipulates the reader, first provoking his assent, before breaking the "tacit alliance" between him and the putative author. More recently, Claude Rawson (*Gulliver and the Gentle Reader*, London, Routledge and Kegan Paul, 1973, pp. 35 - 36) and David Nokes (op. cit., p. 179) have emphasized the point. What is usually ignored is that the tactics varies and that the effect depends to a large extent on the nature of the fiction, rather than on the rhetoric.

74 See Carole Fabricant, op. cit., pp. 73 - 76.

particular addressee, as in the case of the astrologer Partridge: after all, his almanacs had a large audience. The function of the framing fictions is to avoid at all cost the satirical fictions remaining looking-glasses in which people would recognize everyone's face but their own, as *The Battle of the Books* puts it (PW vol. i, p. 140). With Swift the satirist is no "littérateur", but a polemicist still, or more exactly a preacher still; also a fighter, an activist wielding power.[75] Satire is action, even when it proposes fictions to the public, or rather because its framing fictions are devised as dramatic staging devices. Satire cannot change the world overnight. Nor can sermons for that matter. With Swift, ferociousness becomes direct.

To stress the fact that Swift gives his satirical fictions the thrust of polemical writings is not the same as to say that satire is just another form of polemics for him. The distinction made in the course of the previous discussion is not simply an analytical move used to bring out one of the singular qualities of his satires: the importance of their fictitious side. By overemphasizing the way they take the reader to task personally, one may even run the risk of reducing Swift to the status of "a kind of local activist" and of considering his works as mere "*reactive*" gestures, and "events".[76] Unquestionably, there is in this view a timely reminder that Swift's satirical fictions are deeply rooted in their time. However, the description is unsatisfactory. For one thing, it fails to account for the influence of his work and for the lasting fascination of *Gulliver's Travels* and *A Modest Proposal* – the latter in particular, which deals with a subject that has lost some of its topicality, at least within the Western World, though it might still be read as a comment on the way rich countries treat developing countries. To take notice of the rôle played by the framing devices in the creation of the fakes helps to understand that the distinction between the satires, whose whole textual organization is controlled by fiction, and the polemical writings, in which dialectic, the art of disputing and confounding an opponent,[77] is the predominant factor, is more than one of convenience or degree in the sharpness and directness of the attack. It shows it to correspond to a

---

75 Herbert Davis (op. cit., p. 220) is struck by the fact, as is Edward Said (see note below), and he connects this quality with the conciseness of his style.

76 This is what Edward W. Said does in *The World, the Text, and the Critic* (London, Faber, 1984, pp. 77, 78, 58).

77 James A. W. Rembert, op. cit., pp. 101 - 180.

different intention. The polemical stance has to be considered as part of the larger fiction of the literary and journalistic game. It is itself a fiction. At the same time as the reader is scolded for serious shortcomings, he is also made aware that he has just become a little too much involved in what is for once only a game, which he is free to quit whenever he wishes. This can only be done in a game.[78] The polemical intent is subordinated to the satirical, the satirical intent merges into fictionalizing, and it is well known that games and fictions alone have a lasting appeal, independent of historical contingencies.

Reducing the satirical fictions to polemics would also amount to dismissing the imaginative element, and in particular here the Hogarthian vignettes and the staging effects as purely decorative, which they are not. Swift's satirical art is an art of parody, but also a visionary and dramatic art. It creates ever "new situations, persons, or books", turns the flawed thinking of the enemy he attacks into "orderly self-defeating logical and virtuosic analysis".[79] But it above all makes fun of the style of all sorts of writings that were competing in his time to satisfy, and sometimes pander to, a new thirst for information, discussion and education. Swift does not ridicule only the issues in the controversies of the age. He does, for the flood of popular writings of his time, much the same as Cervantes had done for the vogue of the mediaeval romance. Confronted with a flood of new forms of publications, rather than the sclerosis of one traditional genre, he does not reject or ignore them, but has a close look at each of them. At the same time, because his satirical fictions turn the imitation of these writings into a game, the reader today is still in a position to participate in what looks to him like an educational literary game. Such an impression is most acute when reading *A Tale of Tub*, and it is little wonder that this work should be a favourite with many a literary critic.[80] Throughout the work, the style and organization of the

78 Johan Huizinga writes in *Homo Ludens: A Study of the Play Element in Culture* (London, Routledge and Kegan Paul, 1959, p. 38): "We found that one of the most important characteristics of play was its spacial separation from ordinary life. A closed space is marked out for it, either materially or ideally hedged off from the everyday surroundings. Inside this space the play proceeds, inside it the rules obtain."

79 Edward Said, op. cit., pp. 78, 67. This view has become a commonplace of Swiftian criticism.

80 Ricardo Quintana values *A Tale* above the *Travels* in *The Mind and Art of Jonathan Swift*, London, Oxford University Press, 1936, p. 327.

satires are recognizably Swift's own. His use of generic mimesis, which, far from individualizing each purported author, associates him with a mob of other pens and underlines the collective character of the intellectual and literary debate, generalizes his criticism of the period: it focuses on trends in literary, social, economic and political discourse and behaviour and warns readers against their frequent sophistry.

Mimesis is one of the foundations of the representational arts, painting, sculpture and literature, but it would be erroneous to conceive of it as having been the same sort of imitation of everyday reality throughout history. Different periods have had different conceptions. The parodic devices with which Swift frames his satires bear the stamp of his time and its conception of language as the medium of all knowledge. Mention was made at the beginning of this study of the fact that discourse had become so important because it could represent thought or nature. Discourse, as representation of what is, was analytical knowledge, founded on a perception of differences and similarities. In all the sciences, says Foucault, it aimed at a systematic description of the real conceived as a "spreading out" – he uses the word "étalement" – of the visible or observable.[81] In the systematic description of things and beings, what became essential was to divide – "découper" – all the evidence into distinguishable and yet related categories, which alone could give a complete picture of the object of study by means of classification. This conception of knowledge is interesting because it helps to understand why Swift's mimesis, like most Augustan mimesis, is one of genres and why their satires are usually parodic. First of all, parody, as opposed to "isomorphic" description, is an obvious and elementary type of representation of representation when it comes to dealing with discourse as the "spreading out" of thought and as an object of analysis, although a very different one from those that Foucault had in mind, because it is not directly analytical. However, the caricatural aspect offers the next best thing: a sort of anatomy of the discourse, as a prelude to its classification. As for the division into genres, it is so important in the literary theory of the classical age precisely because it corresponds to the need to establish categories in literature as a field of study. The genres are the kinds of writings that criticism is to analyze in terms of similarities and differences to arrive at a systematic classification and description of their functions, and at a comprehensive view of literature. Such a study could

81 Op. cit., p. 280.

only favour self-consciousness in the use of genres in general, and it is little wonder if, as a result, the practice of parody of genres became as natural as the use itself of genres in their specificity.[82] It led writers on the path of what post-modernist criticism in this century calls meta-fiction. With their exaggerated outlines, parodies became in an eminent sense the "spreading out" of other discourses, "redoubled representations – representations whose rôle is to designate representations, to analyze them, to compose and deconstruct them, to make, with the system of their identities and differences, appear in them the general principle of an order."[83] They became the analysis of the way genres carry out an intention. That they often do so negatively, by proposing examples of disorder and malfunctioning, does not change their purpose and nature.

Parodic mimesis in Swift reflects the same urge to represent the sub-jective representations of the mind as Richardson's use of letters in his novels. But it also plays the part of, and announces, Fielding's and Sterne's explicit references to the technical conventions that they make use of in *Tom Jones* and *Tristram Shandy*, to draw attention to their arbitrary character. Nor is it necessary for this that the parody reveal its critical intention at first sight. The ridiculing of a certain type of discourse usually appears in full light only after the framing fiction has betrayed its serious purpose in an irrelevant framed fiction, as will be seen below. The editorial framing device or the framing discourse serve to raise expectations that Swift disappoints. This procedure sharpens the reader's consciousness of what is going on in the fiction. Once he realizes that *A Hue and Cry* is not news but a joke, or that *A Modest Proposal* does not propose a new solution to the problem of poverty in Ireland, he becomes more aware that printed documents cannot simply be trusted because they look factual and sound serious, or because their arguments have an inner logic of their own. This consciousness enables him to take his distance from the mimesis and to see it as doubling and reflecting other representations, in other writings, only approximately equivalent to it. It offers a strange meta-criticism, not of the nature of discourses as in meta-fiction, however, but of the doubtful uses to which they are frequently put by authors and readers.

---

82 It could even be said to have had as much a stabilizing effect in defining and fix-ing the specificity of each genre, as a subversive effect, as McKeon (op. cit.) argues in the limited instance of the romance and of the novel.
83 Foucault, op. cit., p. 233.

As often noted, criticism today is fond of spatial metaphors. Framing is one. It suggests an enclosed surface, and frames are themselves surfaces of a sort, more often than just lines: they enclose a surface between two lines. The metaphoric meaning, the vehicle of the metaphor, twice points to the notion of enclosure. In Swift's satires the space enclosed by the framing of a satire tends to be the space of an exclusion. Framing a satire becomes a drama: a blacklisting, or proscription, of what does not come up to the decent standards that a classical age, or just decency and commonsense, ought to promote. The notion of enclosure is interesting because it once again recalls Foucault: more particularly here his notion of confinement of people exhibiting irregular behaviour.[84] Foucault nowhere mentions Swift, though, in his time, the satirist may have been the writer who was the most conscious of the social dynamics of confinement and exclusion. On the level of Gulliver's autobiographical confession, his story is that of a man who momentarily shuts himself out of society, because he cannot mend it, and who becomes for a time a prisoner of his memories, with the result that he appears unbalanced at the end of his account of his travels and condemns himself. In the framing fiction of *A Tale*, Swift's most systematic attempt to deal with various aberrant behaviours and enclose them in a fiction, he has his fictitious author propose that certain inmates of Bedlam be paradoxically let out of their confinement and used by the state in different capacities. Such a proposal is in keeping with the intent to fictionalize reality: it vizualizes its invasion by fiction, which the hack's framing fiction dramatizes and constitutes a *mise en abyme* of the work. But it also shows that the choice of genre and the typical character of the discourse can become ways of placing a class of writing, of topics, or of people on a blacklist. The ridicule of the parody becomes in itself denunciatory: a condemnation in the virulent cases and a means of depreciation in the milder ones.

It is obvious from what precedes that the question of whether Swift is a traditionalist or a Tory writer is irrelevant from a creative perspective. Even when the initial germ of his satires is an attachment to certain inherited values, the fact that the satirical intent is effected by, and finds expression in, parodies of fashionable genres that show the prevalent discourses of the age to be problematic makes the fictions more radical than conservative. Imitation is invention. The satirical framing fictions open

84 *Histoire de la folie à l'âge classique*, Paris, Gallimard, 1972.

the way for a new generation of writings: for novels more aware of their fictitious character, and often more humorous or satirical as a result; for the "conte philosophique", which *Gulliver's Travels* and *A Tale of a Tub* prefigure in their different ways; and finally for a prospective examination of more reliable kinds of discourse, or of their better use.

Chapter 2

From the Framing to the Framed Fictions

Swift's art of parody and his rhetoric of caricature are the most often discussed aspects of his satirical fictions. There is hardly a study of his work that does not touch upon the question. His importance as a literary figure has even led some to see the development of the genre in the eighteenth century in terms of this specific contribution to it. From Dryden onwards, the argument goes, satire moved away from an exposition of facts in the direction of a dramatic imitation of the enemy.[1] To limit one's attention to this novel side of Swift's better-known satirical fictions, their imitation of current genres, is doubly unfortunate. It prevents a recognition on the one hand of their two-fold nature and on the other of what remains traditional in his portrayal of human follies. It is true, and this has already been said, that not all Swift's satires exhibit a complex structure. One or two, like *Mr. C[olli]ns's Discourse*, seem to consist only in a discourse similar to those of the framing devices described above. They could be said to be framing fictions with the framed constituent left out. A larger number, including most of the verse satires, remain faithful to the tradition of the simple satirical tale found in Dryden's *Absalom and Architopel*. They will be seen to resemble the framed fictions of the complex satires. And there is finally the group of complex satires, which includes Swift's main works. In them a framing device encloses, or unexpectedly develops into, a framed tale. Each strategy had its use for the satirist, and to fail to appreciate this has led many a critical argument into difficulties. In particular, there has been a vain search for a unifying factor in the complex satires.[2] But the problem

---

1 Ronald Paulson, *The Fictions of Satire*, pp. 70, 72, 98. Martin Price, *Swift's Rhetorical Art*, pp. 62-63.

2 In *The Plot of Satire* (New Haven, Yale University Press, 1965, pp. 97, 100, 102, 120), Alvin B. Kernan concludes that Swift's satires have no plot to speak of beyond a general device to drive a wedge between reality and appearance. In their essay "The Structure of *Gulliver's Travels*" (*First Münster Symposium*, pp. 199 - 202), Hermann J. Real and Heinz J. Vienken sum up the debate concerning the particular case of the *Travels*.

of a unifying factor does not arise when framing and framed constituents are allowed distinct characters as well as distinct plots.

The framed fictions are different from the framing fictions in every respect. They substitute traditional narrative and dramatic isomorphic modes of representation to the mimicry of the framing fictions. More important still, they make no claim to verisimilitude. They do not attempt to deceive the reader with a pretence that the satire is not satire but something else. They have an imaginative quality that contrasts with the realistic trappings of the framing fictions, and it is this aspect of Swift's satires which has more particularly reminded readers of the great comic writers such as Lucian and Rabelais. Considering that his work owes no mean share of its popularity to this fanciful character, one cannot but be surprised that it should have received only glancing attention. Critics are usually content to refer to it as his "fantastic realism", the "crazy" aspect of his reconstructions, his "nightmare fantastication", his "immense comic embroidery", or the "inventiveness of his humour."[3] The treatment of the plots in the framed fictions has not fared better, though the contrast with the framing fictions is patent here again. If the latter belong to the class of argumentative or informative discourses and the framed fictions present either narrative or dramatic features, there can be no question of their sharing a common concept of plot in the circumstances. No less vaguely than for their nature, studies of this aspect of Swift's satires speak of its tendency to use, apart from "sententious proverbs" and "quotable maxims", "miniature dramas", compressed fables and "series of vignettes".[4] Seldom are these narrative and dramatic patterns studied in relation to the general structure of the satires.[5] With respect to individual works, mention has been made of a "fable" or "allegory" in *A Tale of a Tub*, and of the "extravagant fairy tale", or of

---

3 Ricardo Quintana, op. cit., p. 319. Martin Price, op.cit., p. 50. C.J. Rawson, op. cit., p. 34. John Middleton Murry, *Jonathan Swift: A Critical Biography,* London, Cape, 1954, p. 72. Herbert Davis, op. cit., p. 201.

4 Marie-Claire Randolph, "The Structural Design of Formal Verse Satire", *Philological Quarterly* 21: 368 - 384 (1942). See also John M. Bullitt, *Jonathan Swift and the Anatomy of Satire*, Cambridge, Mass., Harvard University Press, 1953, pp. 86 - 87, and H.W. Irving, "Boccalini and Swift", *Eighteenth-Century Studies* 7: 143 - 160 (1973).

5 One exception is Edward W. Rosenheim (op. cit., pp. 17 - 18, 133 - 134), who sees in Swift's capacity to create fictions his true claim to originality.

the "kind of imagination and fancy in which children's tales abound", as a special feature of *Gulliver's Travels*: nothing more.[6]

Another way of not dealing with the imaginative aspect of the framed fictions is to see it as allegorical and consequently transparent. The similarities between allegory and satire are well-known. Among other things they have a predilection for fantasy, precisely. But Swift's tales and stories are much more than allegories, or at least not allegories in any restricted sense. The characters that people them are no mere personified abstractions, polarizing the moral, philosophical and religious conflicts of the world. The characters' actions do not generate a double chain of discourse and narrative in such a way that their gestures and the events systematically point to ideas. In contradistinction to true allegorical writers, who delete details that are not significant, Swift has been said above to multiply them in places, in order to lend his satires a novelistic feel of things impinging on the alleged writer's mind and to anchor them in contemporary reality. For these reasons, it is wrong to by-pass the fanciful element, as is often done, in a haste to get at Swift's criticism of life, in other words at an immediate translation of the imaginative into historical and sociological terms.

The end of the seventeenth century and the beginning of the eighteenth was not only the age of the discovery of a new sort of literary realism, based on empirical premises. It concurrently showed a dawning interest in folktales and a renewed taste for fables, mythological stories and romances. This development is in many respects puzzling. It coincided with an important change in the European way of analyzing man's experience and his world. It led to the view that tales, fables and myths were imaginary stories and artificial fictions, only remotely connected with observable facts and recorded events. Fifty years earlier such stories had still been accepted as true to facts, but Swift and his contemporaries had come to consider them as inventions and lies. Natural philosophers had progressively brought everyone round to their conviction that it was necessary to "separate the knowledge of *Nature*, from the colours of *Rhetorick*, the devices of *Fancy*, or the delightful deceit of *Fables*."[7] The seventeenth century had learnt to distinguish

---

6 John R. Clark, op. cit., p. 162. Walter Scott, see *Swift: The Critical Heritage*, p. 294; Angus Ross, *Swift: "Gulliver's Travels"*, London, Arnold, 1968, p. 11.

7 Thomas Sprat, *The History of the Royal Society of London*, London, J. Martyn and J. Allestry, 1667, p. 62.

between observation and fiction and to unravel truth from myth, not only in the natural sciences and history, but also in literature. There a division had appeared between the writers of fables and of realistic accounts. On the one hand, there were writers who, like Racine, Pope, La Fontaine, Gay, Perrault, or the Lessing of the tale of the three rings in *Nathan der Weise*, were inspired by myths, fables and tales. They knew that these could no longer be read literally but must be reinterpreted to meet the expectations of their time. On the other hand, an increasing number of works dealt with everyday and contemporary life, like Lessing's *Minna von Barnhelm*, La Bruyère's *Caractères*, Saint Simon's *Mémoires*, Defoe's stories and Addison's essays. In his satirical fictions Swift disregards the distinction. He combines what had come to be seen as separate literary modes. His framing fictions tend towards realism, and his framed fictions look towards fables and tales, so that his satires participate in both trends.[8] In so far as his contemporaries had accepted the divorce between them as inevitable, his attempt to recombine the two antithetical modes is significant. It must also have looked confusing. In fact, Swift was quite conscious of breaking what had become a rule – or was quickly hardening into one – and of yoking together mutually exclusive types of writing. He does so to exploit the discrepancy between them. One of the primary rôles of the discrepancy between the frivolity of the framed fictions and their allegedly serious wrapping is, as hinted in the previous chapter, to betray the parody in the representation of

8 On the epistemological causes of the phenomenon and their religious, political and "scientific" ramifications, see Michael McKeon's widely-documented study (op. cit., chapters 1, 2, 4, 5). The differentiation between "romance" and "true history" which, he argues, developed during the seventeenth century and led to the birth of the novel is one aspect of the more general split which I am referring to here and which occurred at the time between a literature whose inspiration was directed towards historicity or factuality and one whose inspiration was directed towards myths and fables. The range of genres in which Swift detects a fantastic, or at least "lying", bias is wide, as will be seen below: besides romances themselves, and such derived forms as secret histories and memoirs, it includes allegories, ballads, fables, folktales and the optimistic pattern of comedy, which cannot be all subsumed under the general concept of romance. It must be repeated here (see above pp. 69-70) that he wrote in an age which attempted to redefine the specificity of each genre, and that it was this redefinition which led him, as it did others, to innovate either by combining existing modes, or by reforming others, or by bringing little esteemed ones out of neglect.

current literary and journalistic discourses. It undermines the claim to seriousness of the whole piece and helps to draw the circle round the sample of discourse that identifies it as a fake.[9] In other words, it makes the rhetorical pose transparent and prevents such accidents as befell Defoe with *The Shortest Way with Dissenters*, whose irony went undetected.

The framed constituent of the fiction forms a strange body of writing in the verisimilar wrapping of the framing device. From the first, it asserts its un-realistic character. There is, of course, nothing exceptional in the device. The hiatus between the kind of publication that the framing fiction claims to be and what it does offer is the form that Swift gives to a common strategy in satire. The personal stamp lies in the nature of the framed component and in the fact that the combination of "literary mimicry" with an "alien subject" is essentially structural and tends to keep them more or less separate, so that they retain their own identity, instead of fusing.[10] On the contrary of other satirists and of most theorists, Swift realized that he could draw more varied and effective satirical effects from structurally flawed than from formally coherent parodies. As a result his satires achieve the singular effect, described above, of pieces of writing with an irrelevant content, which turn the presumed authors' activity into ludicrous parodies of intellectual activity.

Because Swift never writes twice on the same subject in the same manner, his fantasy finds several outlets and his "fantastic realism" varies from case to case. Here again, variety is one of the great characteristics of his work. What remains constant is that his "embroidery" is all the opposite of factual, in the sense of true to circumstantial reality. He does not offer faithful descriptions of events, even when he seems to. His creative method does not rely on selection of facts historically attested or credible. It works through a process of transpositions. His framed fictions transport the reader into artificial, invented and imaginary worlds, the worlds of fables, popular myths, legends, or simply made up stories and comedies such as literature likes to propose. Three types of narrative and dramatic plots or, more generally, transpositions can be distinguished, two of which are occasionally found to combine in the same piece. They lend Swift's satirical fictions the

---

9 See above, pp. 26, 42.
10 C.D. Kirimidjan, "The Aesthetics of Parody", *JAAC: Journal of Aesthetics and Art Criticism* 28: 232 (1969).

appearance or just the flavour of folktales, conspiracy stories or comedies of manners.

It is worth noting that, in Swift, the narrative impulse and the taste for anecdotes and fables is not only exhibited in the framed fictions. It pervades his whole output and is as deeply engrained as the impulse to mimic people and discourses. The way similes and extended metaphors, in the framing discourses or polemical writings, sprout into anecdotes and Hogarthian scenes has already been mentioned.[11] Besides satirical and polemical writings are interspersed with allusions to fables and myths. The tendency did not abate with the years, as Dr Johnson's comments on the superiority of *A Tale of a Tub* over the rest of the work might suggest.[12] In a single *Intelligencer* paper, dating from 1728, are found no less than five striking and unexpected narrative similes, some anecdotal, others reminiscent of fables or proverbs. The Irish authorities' attitude to the monetary situation of the country is likened first to that of a man who would "be impatient about a *Cut-Finger*, when he is struck with the *Plague*" (PW vol. xii, p. 55) and then to that of a person who "dare not so much as complain of the *Tooth-ach*" (ibid., p. 58). The high price of corn reminds the author of the situation of besieged towns in which "*Rats*, and *Cats*, and dead *Horses*, have been often bought for *Gold*" (ibid., p. 59). Irish emigrants to America are shown to react like someone in a fever, who turns in his bed "without any Hope of Ease", or like someone who "leap[s] down a Precipice, to avoid an Enemy just at his Back" (ibid., p. 61). In the other Irish tracts of the same years 1728 - 1733 can be found allusions to such fables as the hen that lays golden eggs (ibid., p. 12), the dunghill that raises "a huge Mushroom of short Duration" (ibid., p. 53), the world in the moon (ibid., p. 67), the frog that burst by overeating (ibid., p. 133), the frogs' fright "upon a Report, that the Sun was going to marry" (ibid., p. 199). They also contain mentions of Rabelais (ibid., 22), Agesilaus, Socrates, Caesar Augustus and Scipio – the last four names being found in the same paragraph (ibid., p. 161).

Swift's taste for concrete imagery of a narrative nature, as opposed to pictorial tropes, is a characteristic of all his work. Besides these narrative traits, it must be remembered that Swift rewrote or composed a number

11 Herbert Davis's selection of quotations from Swift in his chapter entitled "Comedy" (op. cit.) shows that the writer was prompt to imagine little comic scenes or dramas and that he even maintained the tone of comedy in his correspondence with Stella (ibid., p. 70).

12 *Lives of the English Poets*. See *Swift: The Critical Heritage*, pp. 202 - 203.

of verse fables and tales: "A Fable of the Widow and her Cat" and "The Fable of Midas" (1712), "The Dog and the Thief" (1726), the two versions of "Baucis and Philemon" (1706 and 1709), and many others.[13] His writings exhibit an instinctive awareness that a narrative "describes and explains at once"[14] and that, because of their many-sidedness, narrative or dramatic traits are much more thorough explicators of human attitudes and actions than arguments. As a result, his arguments have a tendency to turn into stories, into attested or invented events or scenes. Difficult problems are given concrete experiential explanations, and complicated issues practical applications to the life of the individual. This is how, halfway through an informal essay on the value of a good school and college education for the sons of the nobility who wish to play a rôle worthy of their rank in the affairs of the kingdom, the reader suddenly comes upon a brief scene. Swift has just put forward the idea that some knowledge of Greek and Latin would stand young gentlemen in better stead than learning only "to dance, fence, speak French". Instead of arguing the point, as the reader might expect him to do in the context, he passes on directly to its illustration. The little anecdote shows a specimen of the breed of ill-educated gentlemen, an army officer precisely, impudently intruding upon a conversation between two educated strangers. It is told in such a way that the officer reveals the full extent of his narrow-mindedness, stupidity and arrogance, makes a fool of himself and, in typical Swiftian fashion, condemns himself with his own words:

I remember in those Times, an admired Original of that Vocation [the army], sitting in a Coffee-House near two Gentlemen, whereof one was of the Clergy, who were engaged in some Discourse that savoured of Learning; this Officer thought fit to interpose; and professing to deliver the Sentiments of his Fraternity, as well as his own, (and probably did so of too many among them) turning to the Clergy-Man, spoke in the following Manner. *D–n me, Doctor, say what you will, the Army is the only school for Gentlemen. Do you think my Lord* Marlborough *beat the* French *with* Greek *and* Latin. *D–n me, a Scholar when he comes into good Company, what is he but an Ass? D–n me, I would be glad, by G–d, to see any of your Scholars with his Nouns, and his Verbs, and his Philosophy, and Trigonometry, what a Figure he would make at a Siege or Blockade, or reconoitring —D– me,* &c. After which he

13 SPW, pp. 98 - 100, 100 - 102, 310, 61 - 66, 77 - 82.
14 A.C. Danto, *Analytical Philosophy of History*, Cambridge, Cambridge University Press, 1965, p. 141.

proceeded with a Volley of Military Terms, less significant, sounding worse, and harder to be understood than any that were ever coined by Commentators upon *Aristotle.* (*The Intelligencer* no ix, ibid., p. 49)

Such a passage might well have found its way into a satire. The tales, fables and comic scenes that form the core of the framed fictions in the complex satirical fictions are indeed of the same type as those that illustrate the arguments of the polemical discourses and inspire the fables found in the unframed satires. As in the unframed fictions, they are again used on a large scale as structuring patterns.

The first chapter has emphasized the close relationship between framing and framed fictions and given to understand that the scope of their respective developments varies in inverse proportion. Where the framing device is hardly more than a discreet signal in the margin of the text, the framed fiction can be expected to receive ample development, whereas it will put in a fleeting appearance when the framing is heavy. It is not only the scope of the framed fictions' development that varies from case to case, but also its nature and the way in which it is integrated within the satire. As already said, Swift does not always rely on the structural opposition between text and peritext to create his satirical effects, but on a looser notion of packaging and irrelevant content. Hence the framed fictions may take the shape either of separate units or of a new level of fiction woven into the basic one of the framing discourse, whose character it then alters. As allowances must be made for every nuance, the distinction between framing and framed fictions must be granted to become occasionally elusive. But always a perceptible hiatus remains, which amuses, shocks or embarrasses the reader.

At one end of the spectrum, where the framing fiction threatens to swallow the framed constituent, the latter achieves the ghost of an existence, usually in the form of a second level of fictional elaboration. As will be seen further on, this can find expression in a veiled or implicit reference as in *A Modest Proposal*, where a tale of ogres can be deciphered in transparency; or it can take the form of a fragmentary narrative as in *The Bickerstaff Papers, A Letter from the Pretender to a Whig Lord*, or *The Humble Petition of the Footmen of Dublin*. In *The Mechanical Operation of the Spirit, A Tritical Essay* and *Meditation upon a Broomstick*, there are no more than a few isolated motifs or narrative traits woven into the texture of the argument of the discourse. *Directions to Servants* alternates rules of conduct and farcical illutrations. In *A Tale of a Tub*, on the other hand, the folktale of the three brothers struggles a little more successfully to survive the digressive bend of the hack editor, and by fits and starts is brought to a satisfactory conclusion. It is also kept separate from the discursive framing and fully justifies the present distinction between framing and framed constituents. In *A Complete Collection of Genteel and Ingenious Conversations* and *Gulliver's Travels*, framing and framed fictions have been seen to be about equal in importance and correspond to distinct parts of the works. In the former, a substantial preface introduces the collection of conversations itself. In the *Travels*, the structuring is more complex. The framed fiction does not interrupt the travel account that frames it: it only marks the introduction of a second level of fictional elaboration, and a symbolic expanse of sea divides the world Gulliver and the reader are familiar with from those fabulous lands he explores.

Another kind of balance is achieved with the kind of fiction designated here as the conspiracy story. The framing fiction of the purported author's gesture of protest, denunciation or simply news report interpenetrates with a sombre tale of plotting and corruption, which constitutes the framed fiction. There again, the framed fiction corresponds in most cases to the development of a second level of fictional elaboration. Such are the cases of "Mrs Harris's Petition", *A Hue and Cry after Dismal* and *A New Journey to Paris*. In them a protest or a piece of journalistic information turns into a vivid tableau or story of underhand dealings, and the tendency is for the framing fiction of authentic publication to play the secondary rôle of a mere material support for the framed tale. At the end of the spectrum where the framing is only editorial and consists in the choice of a style and form, or even in the mere material support for the publication, the framed fiction becomes the dominant constituent and its narrative or comedy holds the front of the stage. This is the case in *The Story of the Injured Lady. In a Letter to her Friend, with his Answer*, the "Fable of Midas", the two poems "A Description of the Morning" and "A Description of a City Shower", "A Satirical Elegy on a Late Famous General", the prose broadside entitled *The Last Speech and Dying Words of Ebenezor Elliston*, and the odd *Battle of the Books*, which only begins as a moral disquisition, but almost at once turns into a first tale, that of the attempt of the "Moderns" to dislodge the "Ancients" from the top of Parnassus, then into a second story, the already mentioned fable of the spider and the bee, and finally into a third, the mock-epic battle fought by the books of a library. At this end of the spectrum, the difference between a framed fiction and the unframed fables and tales in prose or verse becomes slight. In this connection, it is interesting to mention the prose story *The Court and Emperor of Japan* (1728). It describes the England of Walpole as though it were a remote country in the far East. It is written in the manner of Montesquieu's *Lettres Persanes* (1721), or, closer to Swift, in that of George Lyttelton's *Letters from a Persian in England to a Friend at Ispahan*, of which a copy was found in the satirist's library.[15] It may have been left unframed only because it never found its way into separate publication.

The technical necessity for the satire to have a content that belies the intention expressed by its external form, and a personal taste for fables, tales and anecdotes, do not explain everything. When Swift's framed fictions follow La Fontaine, Pope, Gay and Perrault, as his framing fictions do Defoe and Addison, one more reason for the choice needs mentioning. "Docere cum delectatione" was still an Augustan catchword. Swift is aware that a picture of everyday life may be dressed to advantage in the disguises of folktales, myths, animal fables and pleasant comic scenes. The popularity that his work enjoyed almost at once, and continues to enjoy, has proved him right.[16] When Swift describes the dissentions between "the whole *Babel*" of Protestant sects as a football game (PW vol. xii, pp. 288 - 289), or when he presents the dispute between Lutherans, Calvinists and Anglicans as a folktale of three brothers quarrelling over their father's will, he wants to entertain the reader. For his framed fictions, he draws on resources with the widest popular appeal, resources which make the journalistic and literary game of the parodies as refreshing as possible. Part of the pleasure derives from the nature of the transpositions, part of it from the surprise afforded by the discrepancy between framing and framed fictions, and part of it from the frivolity of the "fantastication". Finally, by combining the imitation of popular genres current at the time with fables and folktales, rather than with the great myths of Greece and Rome, Swift maintains

15 I am aware that Swift's edition is dated 1735. See Hermann J. Real and Heinz J. Vienken, "A Catalogue of an Exhibition of Imprints from Swift's Library", *First Münster Symposium*, pp. 372 - 373.

16 It was Edward Stone, in "Swift and the Horses: Misanthropy or Comedy?", *Modern Language Quarterly* 10: 367 - 376 (1949), who first contended that the contemporaries were delighted with the comedy of the *Travels* and that the accusation of misanthropy only came later.

the same popular tone and anti-highbrow bias throughout. Classical references to Greek and Roman myths and history there are, but they are kept mostly out of sight or remain discreet. With the variety of forms, this popular quality is the other conspicuous characteristic of his satirical fictions.

II

The folklore colouring is the most easily recognizable, important and fascinating of the three ingredients that lend their character to the framed fictions. It takes various forms: folktale, fable, or popular myth. Swift's best-known satirical fictions exhibit it, and, in their case, there is no doubt that they owe to it their popularity with a large public. It is not possible to trace back folklore components in a story as is done with a writer's echoing of his predecessors. This type of indebtedness is bound to be more diffuse.[17] Swift's imagination ranges freely over available resources and combines their several features in what can sometimes seem a happy-go-lucky way.

To begin with those pieces where the folklore ingredients or colouring is a discreet second level of fictional elaboration, it is present in *A Discourse concerning the Mechanical Operation of the Spirit*. Its central essay, itself enclosed in an informal letter, promises a tale of how Mahomet rode up to Heaven on an ass, though he had been offered other vehicles "to conduct him upwards; as fiery Chariots, wing'd Horses, and celestial Sedans" (PW vol. i, p. 172). The same folklore ingredient is noticeable in *A Tritical Essay upon the Faculties of the Mind*, another discourse which never treats the promised subject, but teases the reader with a succession of allusions to the myth of Ixion, the Biblical story of Nebuchanezzar and, above all, the fable of the monkey that uses the cat's claws to draw the chestnuts out of the fire (ibid., p. 247). The choice of a broomstick, a witch's inseparable mount, as a suitable emblem of man's

---

17 Nor is the dry listing of Stith Thompson's *Motive Index of Folk Literature* (Copenhagen, Rosenkilde and Bagger, 1955) very helpful in the detection of what are often not so much "the facts of fantasy" as a quality of inspiration. In an unpublished doctoral dissertation from the University of Paris, *Jonathan Swift: Les sources irlandaises de la satire dans "Gulliver's Travels"* (1957), Eileen Mac Carvill detects precise childhood memories of Irish tales in Swift.

condition in the mock-serious religious meditation to which it gave its title also comes from folklore. That the Earl of Nottingham in the fake news report *A Hue and Cry* is described as spying on the activities of the Tory general in Dunkirk dressed as "a tall Chimney-Sweeper with his Brooms and Poles, and Bunch of Holly upon his Shoulders" (PW vol. vi, p. 139) is no accident either. Not only is the black disguise suggested by the Tory renegade's nickname of Dismal, but it is also used to turn his disaffection, a bad omen for the party, into a traditional symbol of good luck. The kinship between the jolly rogues of broadside ballads like "The Rake and Rambling Boy"[18] and the Ebenezor Elliston of the prose broadside, *The Last Speech and Dying Words* (PW vol ix, pp. 35 - 41), can be taken as another instance of this deliberate utilization of folklore patterns. As for the similarity between the plight of the heroine in the epistolary exchange entitled *The Story of the Injured Lady* and that of the Cinderellas of fairy tales, it is obvious (ibid., pp. 1 - 9). In all these pieces the use of the folklore ingredients may be discreet, but it is explicitly referred to. Only once, in *A Modest Proposal*, does it remain veiled. Apart from a hint at "a very knowing *American* of my Acquaintance in *London*", who seems to have tasted human flesh like the savages in *Robinson Crusoe* (PW vol. xii, p. 111), there is no apparent allusion to popular beliefs. Yet who can deny that the Irish landlords to whom the projector recommends the consumption of infant flesh to relieve the poverty of the poor in the country are not just anthropophagi from remote countries, but reminiscent of the ogres of legends such as "Hop o' my Thumb" or "Mollie Whuppie"?[19] Even though the proposal is written from the viewpoint of the ogre rather than his young victims, the same shudder runs down the reader's spine when he reads:

the *Carcase of a good fat Child* [. . .], as I have said, will make four Dishes of excellent nutritive Meat, when he [the landlord] hath only some particular Friend, or his own Family, to dine with him.   (Ibid., p. 112)

In "Hop o' my Thumb" or "Mollie Whuppie" the ogre is a single individual, who gives way to his craving for human flesh in strict privacy, behind closed doors. Neither his wife nor his daughters are admitted to

18 *Broadside Ballads*, Laws L. 12.
19 "Hop o' my Thumb", Perrault's "Petit Poucet", was translated by Robert Samber (1729?), but other versions of the folktale existed in the British Isles before this translation. One has a girl heroine, Mollie Whuppie precisely.

the banquet. In Swift's satire the ogre publicly parades his taste and encourages others to act on his suggestion. From a purely private and secret affair, cruelty becomes a shameful social phenomenon on a large scale, and the sense of horror is the greater for it.

The framed fictions of *A Tale of a Tub*, *Gulliver's Travels* and *The Battle of the Books* make far more extensive use of folklore colouring: that of folktales in the first case, of fairy tales in the second, and of animal fables in the third. Only the first two will be considered here. The third is explicit enough with its pervasive reliance on animal imagery. Like *The Injured Lady*, *A Tale of a Tub* draws on familiar folktale plots for its story of the three brothers Peter, Jack and Martin. The story begins characteristically with "Once upon a Time" (PW vol. i, p. 44). Swift avails himself of the nature of folktales, which is, according to Propp, to change and generate variants under the influence of new institutions, religions or simply circumstances,[20] and he combines three common plots or motifs: the mysterious will of a humble father; the rivalry between three brothers (or sisters); and a concern with clothes and their makers.[21]

The story of the old father who, feeling his end approaching, calls his sons to his bedside to inform them of his last will and testament is familiar in folktales. In Jacob and Wilhelm Grimm's "The Three Blessed Sons" the legacies are a cock, a saw and a cat. A variant version from the British Isles is entitled "Ass, Table and Stick".[22] Compared with such bequests, Swift's characters are better off with their magical coats, which

20 Vladimir Propp, "Fairy Tale Transformations," *Readings in Russian Poetics*, ed. L. Matejka and K. Pomorska, Cambridge Mass., MIT Press, 1971, pp. 94-114. In their edition of *A Tale* (Oxford, Clarendon, [1920] 1973, pp. xxxvi-xl) A.C. Guth-kelch and D. Nichol Smith mention, among Swift's possible sources, "The Three Rings", a tale also used by Boccaccio in the *Decameron*, a French adaptation of the former, "Les trois justaucorps" and Fontenelle's "Histoire de Mréo et de Eéne-gu." One or the other may have provided Swift with the general idea of the tale of the three brothers, but the similarities are slight. What follows does not want to re-open the debate concerning sources. It only purports to demonstrate that the satir-ist exploits a range of folktale associations.

21 E.W. Rosenheim (op. cit., pp. 119 - 135) discusses the clothes and the tailor, the episode of the Aeolists, what he calls "the narrative digressions", but not the tale of the three brothers.

22 Another version of the same story is, of course, the Biblical parable of the Talents but, in it, there is nothing magical or mysterious about the father's bequests to his sons, as there nearly always is in folktales.

possess unlimited wear. The father dies and the inexperienced sons are left to find their way in the world: to plunge into the tourbillion of the world and conquer it, as some versions of this tale put it. Indeed, they make an honourable start, in true folktale fashion: "they travelled thro' several Countries, encountred a reasonable Quantity of Gyants and slew certain Dragons." (ibid., pp. 44 - 45) Usually the youngest brother proves the most successful in turning his legacy to profitable account. In Section iv of *A Tale*, the second devoted to the brothers' story, the emphasis shifts from the use they make of their legacies to the rivalry that develops between them. In folktales, whether the protagonists are brothers or sisters, the elders frequently assume a dominant position and tyrannize over the youngest, until the latter, who is virtuous and courageous, is vindicated through a magical intervention or his own courage or virtue. In *A Tale* the initial situation is modified. The three brothers are the same age. However Peter soon behaves like the eldest. Therefore the ascendency he takes over his brothers is somewhat unnatural, although it follows the traditional folktale pattern. In different respects, the way he ill-treats his brothers, forcing them to take dry crusts for mutton and plain water for wine is reminiscent of such animal fables and tales as those of "The Fox and the Stork" and "The Bear and the Fox". As for the magical coats that can widen and lengthen as the brothers age and change, and will last them all the lives (ibid., p. 44), folktales are full of instances of garments with mysterious properties. "The Shoes that have danced" make their wearers invisible. Nor are tailors with their gooses, yards and needles uncommon (ibid., p. 46). They usually figure as creatures blessed above the ordinary. The Grimm brothers again have the story of a bold little tailor who impresses everyone with an inscription on his belt, and the British imp, Tom Tit Tot, is more magician than tailor.

The adaptation of folktale plots and motifs in *A Tale of a Tub* remains straightforward throughout. As they are supposed to form an ancient text, allegedly edited by a modern scholar, they are allowed to develop independently of the framing of editorial comment and, like it, they constitute a separate unit. Far more subtle is the use of folklore ingredients in *Gulliver's Travels*. The first thing to stress is that, in their case, the introduction of folklore motifs does not correspond to interruptions of the travel account, as already noted. The latter continues to ensure narrative continuity and can be said to hold the framing and the four-fold framed fiction together. As in the minor pieces mentioned above, the folklore ingredients represent a second level of fictional elaboration, woven into the first, which transforms what looked at first like an authentic travel report into a fanciful tale. The four long central segments of narrative in which the folktale motifs are operative – they usually comprehend most of the four books except a few pages at the beginning and at the end – are in each case delimited with precision, so that the transition between framing discourse and framed narrative is clearly indicated, even if it does not as a rule coincide with chapter endings. The moment Gulliver crosses a sea, or more exactly leaves his British merchantman, coincides with the beginning of the folktale deployment, and the moment he again sets foot on board a European vessel marks its end. The first effect achieved by the folklore element is to create four times a different fairy-tale atmosphere and world. As a result each voyage becomes an incursion into fairyland. It brings Gulliver into worlds different in scale or nature from the one he knows. Human nature four times undergoes a process of metamorphoses as typical of dreamland as of fairyland,[23] by comparison with which the merely simplified universe of folktales found in *A Tale* retains the same scale as ours. In the first two books, he meets pigmies and giants. In the third voyage, he discovers various sorts of magicians and potentates worthy of *The Thousand and one Nights*, which the public was to discover some years later. The lack of unity of the third voyage has often been deplored. The motif of legendary magic, however, can be seen as establishing a kind of link between its various episodes and as endowing the narrative of the third voyage with a common colouring, for want of any better unifying factor. Finally, with the discovery of the clever horses and unteachable human brutes in the fourth voyage, Gulliver enters a universe of animal tale and meta-morphoses more daring than Lucian's, but no less indebted to fairy tales with their birds and cats that help man, or humanized wolves that threaten him.

23 Kathleen M. Swaim (*A Reading of "Gulliver's Travels"*, The Hague, Mouton, 1972, pp. 35 - 36, 41), who also notes the fairytale character, prefers to refer to the universe of the *Travels* as one of metaphors, probably because she is more con-cerned with the allegorical dimension of the story. This fairytale quality makes a description of the voyages as a "rational journey" unsatisfactory (John M. Bullitt, op. cit., p. 9). Furthermore, to say as Real and Vienken do in "The Structure of *Gulliver's Travels*" (op. cit., p. 203) that Gulliver never leaves the real world when he crosses the seas may be correct on the satirical level and in so far as he feels he is a reporter and never leaves the surface of the earth. But the reader is not blind to the shift from circumstantial reality to fairyland as he is.

Although the transpositions of contemporary experience into fairytale settings becomes more a question of quality in the vision than of patterns, it is not impossible to recognize motifs specific to folktales woven into the travel plot. In the first voyage the Lilliputians are too small to be considered as the pigmies of "Herodotus, Aristotle, Pliny, Solinus, and other ancient authors".[24] They are as small as Tom Thumb, the Hazelnut Child, or the Danish Maia, who sleeps in a walnut shell. Every reader will remember the description of the troop of Lilliputian horse performing their mock skirmishes on Gulliver's handkerchief (PW vol.xi, pp. 40 - 41), which temporarily reduces the size of the Lilliputians, as though it intended to underscore the connection with these fairy tales. Gulliver performs the traditional gestures of taking up the tiny creatures and holding them on the palm of his hand or between his fingers. The Lilliputians are clever and mischievous like dwarfs and, with them, Gulliver adopts the attitude, recommended by fairy tales, of "pitting his good feelings against their bad feelings".[25] For the Lilliputians, on the other hand, Gulliver is an ogre-like giant, insatiable and potentially dangerous. They see him wade across the strait that separates their kingdom from the island of Blefuscu like the first ogre that Jack, the Giant Killer, kills on an island off the Cornish shore. In fact, a few Lilliputians take on the part of the legendary Jack when they decide to get rid of their embarrassing visitor, or at least to render him harmless by blinding him.

In the second voyage, Gulliver now finds himself in the position of Tom Thumb[26] or the Hazelnut Child. Living as he does among a race of giants, his small size is the occasion of many absurd adventures similar to those of the old nursery tale. Gulliver is not swallowed by a cow but comes very near being devoured by other animals. A spaniel catches him in its mouth and brings him to its master (ibid., p. 117). He is not killed by a spider but defends himself victoriously against two far more deadly rats (ibid., p. 93). He is not carried off by a raven, but by a monkey (ibid., pp. 121 - 123). He does not fall into a butter-pudding, but into a "Silver Bowl of Cream" (ibid., p. 108). The rôle of Giant Grumbo is

---

24 Walter Scott, see *Swift: The Critical Heritage*, p. 308.
25 Ruth Manning-Sanders, *A Book of Dwarfs*, London, Pan, 1963, p. 8.
26 Erich Rothstein, "In Brobdingnag: Captain Gulliver, Dr Denham and Master Tom Thumb," *Etudes Anglaises* 37: 129 - 141 (1984).

played by the farmer's baby, who nearly puts Gulliver into its mouth (ibid., p. 91).

"A Voyage to Laputa, Balnibarbi, Luggnagg, Glubbdubdrib, and Japan" has been seen to be mainly about magicians, would-be magicians and a Far East of absolute potentates in front of whose feet subjects kiss the ground. Islands fly like magical carpets, ghosts from the remote past are raised, queer experiments pursued by gnome-like scientists. Gulliver even meets immortal humans. What can be more natural, and aesthetically inevitable, but that this incursion into the universe of magicians should lead in turn to the most extraordinary adventure of all, the discovery of an island inhabited by intelligent and benevolent horses which, following the law of nature, have instinctively developed a comfortable way of life and organized themselves into a society that avoids tensions between groups and individuals? These horses prove ingenious and superior to men morally and intellectually, like the animals of certain fairy tales and fables. One is reminded of the celebrated "Bremer Stadtmusikanten", or "How Jack sought his fortune", its British equivalent, and "Puss in Boots". Numerous fables also describe societies of animals: colonies of frogs or kingdoms governed by a lion. The Houyhnhnms have also succeeded in reversing the relationship between man and beast and made themselves masters of a race of brutes, the Yahoos. At this point, *Gulliver's Travels* crosses the borderline between folklore invention and dreamland, the world beyond the looking-glass.

Swift uses folktale plots, folklore motifs and other fairytale ingredients in three different ways. *The Battle of the Books* transposes human activities into animal terms, and even, with the battle of the books itself, into the sphere of inanimate things. The transposition, typical of animal fables, is pushed one degree further to underline the ridicule of the debate between "Moderns" and "Ancients" and to dehumanize the "Moderns", who are responsible for the hostilities, by comparing their behaviour to that of unpleasant animals, mongrel dogs in particular (PW vol.i, pp. 141, 161). It explodes their claim to superiority as writers. *Meditation upon a Broomstick* offers another transposition of the same sort. The invidious comparison of man to a broomstick, which dehumanizes him, is both an attack on the lack of imagination of the clergyman, the alleged author, and a deflating symbol of the imperfect nature of man. With the chimney-sweeper in *A Hue and Cry* and the suggestion in *A Modest Proposal* that Irish landlords are ogres, Swift creates overtones that condemn the moral conduct of a man or class of people. In the former the metamorphosis of an earl named Dismal into a symbol of good luck also adds to the sense of humour characteristic of this piece of fake news. In the *Proposal* Swift trades on the innocent thrill of terror that the endings of folktales like "Hop o' my Thumb" or "Little Red Cap" inspire, to heighten both the horror of the situation and the fun of the joke that this proposal to end all proposals constitutes. In these cases Swift can be said to use the folklore ingredient to intensify the emotional impact of the satire, to lend it a touch of humour and to endow it with the vivid colours of popular imagination.[27]

By far the most frequent use of the folklore ingredients is, however, the third. The folktale is turned upside down. Where the reader was led to expect enchantment, he meets with disillusion. In this respect, the framed fictions have a second surprise in store for the reader. After discovering that what he believed to be an authentic taking of stand or valuable piece of information is just a fake, the reader receives a second shock. Folktales, fairy tales, fables and ballads are usually optimistic. They have been said to express whishfulfilment rather than an acceptance of the facts of life. In *The Story of the Injured Lady*, *The Last Words and Dying Speech*, *A Tale of a Tub* – where the reversal of the pattern is even underlined by the allusion to the brother's slaying of dragons at the beginning –, *The Mechanical Operation of the Spirit*, *A Tritical Essay* and *Gulliver's Travels*, things do not develop as the characters or readers expect and wish. Magic and wonder quickly evaporate. *The Story of the Injured Lady* reverses the pattern of "Cinderella": the scold wins the good party and the sweet young lady is left to weep over her fate. There is good reason to believe that this satire was composed with a view to ridiculing the Irish *aisling* or vision poem, a new fashionable form at the time. The *aisling* expresses a sense of loss. It represents the spirit of Ireland as a stately maiden, bright as an angel, weeping over her true mate, whom she has lost. The true mate is usually the Old or the Young Pretender.[28] Swift describes a situation between a woman and a man which is not unlike that described in the aisling, but he turns the radiant creature symbolizing Ireland into a homely folktale figure: a poor sempstress, prematurely worn by care and disappointment.

27 John M. Bullitt, op. cit., p. 86.
28 On the aisling, see Daniel Corkery, *The Hidden Ireland: A Study of Gaelic Munster in the Eighteenth Century*, Dublin, M.H. Gill, 1941, p. 128.

The reversal of the Cinderella pattern throws the blame for what happened to her on her own credulity and unpractical idealism. In a different way and more simply, *The Mechanical Operation* promises a delightful allegorical tale, but the story is not told: a laborious elucidation is given instead, so that the reader feels cheated. The story of Ebenezor Elliston turns out to be the very opposite of "The Rake and Rambling Boy", an anti-ballad about, not a jolly rogue, but a spiteful villain and unrepenting wretch.

A Tale pushes the device even further. Instead of discovering through trials and experience that their father's legacy is worth more than appears at first sight, more than the greatest wealth in the world, the three brothers, its satirical heroes, do everything to ruin the magical properties of their coats and transform them beyond recognition. Not one obeys his father's instructions and understands that virtue is preferable to worldly success. The youngest brother, or the brother who plays that rôle, does not come out the winner because he has proved the most courageous, virtuous and clever. Martin only gets off better than Peter and Jack because he is less daring than the others. This is not enough to marry a princess. His only claim to have overcome anything is to have retrieved his own coat from complete ruin in the nick of time. The world and its temptations prove too much for the brothers. As for the rivalry between them, it gives Peter, the most arrogant, the ascendency of an eldest brother over younger brothers once for all. The ending does not vindicate Martin in the eyes of the world and the readers, it only excuses him up to a point and shows him to be merely less unscrupulous than Peter and less easily carried away by his ideas than Jack. The magic of the coats has finally been an encumbrance rather than a benediction in disguise, because those who received them were not single-minded and ingenuous enough, like the heroes of folktales, to turn them to good account. Finally, the tailor, so often a beneficent and independent-minded character in folktales, is presented as a dangerous demi-god, worshipped by society and directly connected with its vices. In following him, rather than their father's will, the three brothers succumb to the temptations of materialism, vanity and worldliness: "Being now arrived at the proper Age for producing themselves," they fall in love with the "Dutchess d'Argent, *Madame de Grands Titres*, and the Countess *d'Orgueil*." (PW vol. i, p. 45).

In *A Tale* and *The Story of the Injured Lady*, it is the folktale plot that is inverted. The framed narratives open with an unstable situation: the death of a father, and a triangular relationship between two women and one man. The dénouement unexpectedly brings the opposite solution to that which is traditional in the tales indirectly alluded to. *Gulliver's Travels* proceeds differently, because it does not use fairytale plots, but only a colouring inspired from folktales and a number of folklore motifs. Each discovery of a new alternative world begins in wonder, but is followed by disillusion and turns into a trying experience. At first sight, the Lilliputians are delicate and wonderfully ingenious small creatures, quite clever in the way they deal with their monstrous visitor. They are like Tom Tit Tot, Rumpelstiltzkin, or the mannikin in "The Field of Ray-worth", with the added advantage that they look more men than goblins. Their miniature world looks like a paradise from Gulliver's height and with his short-sighted eyes:

The Country round appeared like a continued Garden; and the enclosed Fields, which were generally Forty Foot square, resembled so many Beds of Flowers. These Fields were intermingled with Woods of half a Stang, and the tallest Trees, as I could judge, appeared to be seven Foot high. I viewed the Town on my left Hand, which looked like the painted Scene of a City in a Theatre. (PW vol. xi, p. 29)

The Brobdingnagians are so tall that they look frightening. Everything around Gulliver is enormous beyond belief, from the blades of grass to the size of a bed or street. Certain events in the narrative are quite capable of communicating a thrill of horror to innocent readers: the first giant whom Gulliver comes across brings him "within three Yards of his Eyes" (ibid., p. 87), and the farmer's baby seizes him and gets his "Head into his Mouth" (ibid., p. 91). The inhabitants of Laputa are first described as incredibly absent-minded but harmless magicians. They are foolishly dressed, but travel on a flying island. Gulliver also begins by finding the experiments pursued at the Academy of Lagado fascinating. In the country of the Houyhnhnms he is so struck by the exceptional qualities of the horses that he at first pays little attention to the disgusting Yahoos, who had assailed him on his arrival. At the beginning of Book iv, the wonder is in fact reciprocal, as the horses are as surprised with Gulliver's readiness to learn from them as he is with their rational, or at least commonsense, attitude.

However, in each case, a more direct contact with the life of the country dispels the initial wonder created by the folktale colouring. The worlds which Gulliver discovers remain fairytale ones, but they progressively or abruptly lose their magical aura. The Lilliputians, who had appeared less deceitful than goblins, soon prove envious, conceited, cruel, and more dangerous than Tom Tit Tot or Rumpelstiltzkin, whereas the gigantic Gulliver plays the good fairy to them. On the other hand, the frightening Brobdingnagians turn out to be benevolent giants, or at least no worse than the common run of men. They are less dangerous to Gulliver than their animals or dwarfs, and it is finally Gulliver himself, the delicate and weak mannikin, who nearly endangers the peace of their country with his offer to give their king a recipe to make gun-powder (ibid., p. 134). With the juxtaposition of Books i and ii, there is the added irony that the smaller creatures are described as the nasty ones, whereas giants are comparatively kind and safe. The harlequin-like Laputans, who at first sight seem only eccentric and absent-minded, are soon found to be tyrants for the inhabitants of Balnibarbi. As for the scientists of the Academy of Lagado, they are no ingenious gnomes but silly wizards performing extravagant experiments like extracting sunbeams out of cucumbers or trying to read conspirators' secrets in their excrements (ibid., pp. 179, 190). The immortal Struldbruggs do not fulfil man's dream of immortality as accumulated wisdom. The older they grow, the more they degenerate physically and morally, without ever being able to die (ibid., pp. 212 - 213). Finally, in the country of the clever horses, Gulliver makes the painful discovery that he resembles the brutish hominids, the Yahoos, more than the reasonable horses, and this resemblance leads to his expulsion from their island. In each book, as the fairytale atmosphere is dispelled or turns sour, Gulliver is bound to recognize that, in whatever size or disguise, human nature remains basically what it is in England: sadly imperfect. In *Gulliver's Travels* the world of fairy tales is repeatedly made to belie its traditional nature and optimism. Men are more spiteful than goblins, giants more benevolent than men. Harlequins, wizards and immortal human beings betray their reputations for harmlessness, ingeniosity and wisdom. A commonwealth of beasts, so often shown in fables to be a replica of human society, is described as capable of teaching man a lesson.

The pattern of disenchantment is twice relentlessly developed, in Books i and iii, and twice with variations. In Brobdingnag Gulliver's situation becomes physically and morally more and more unbearable because of the difference in size between him and the giants, and in Houyhnhnmland, although he is delighted with the clever horses and desirous to spend the rest of his life among them, his imperfect nature ends up excluding him from their society, which comes as a terrible blow to him. Each time the fairytale character promises a contrast with Gulliver's Europe, and each time its charm evaporates, a process of comparisons set in, which shows that, in the world, "plus ça change, plus c'est la même chose". Under picturesque surface differences, Gulliver's new continents turn out to be not unlike his own.[29]

One ingredient that Swift uses to pervert the tale into an anti-tale, and to reverse its tendency to express a flight from reality into a process of awakening to circumstantial reality, is to load the account with a great wealth of concrete details about every aspect of the characters' gestures and adventures, to convince the reader that they are truly human. Folktales and fairy tales give a simplified picture of life and the outline of an experience. The reader is left to fill in this outline according to his own wishes. He is left to shape and dress the characters according to his dreams of a good or evil world. In *A Tale of a Tub*, on the contrary, he is spared no detail about the way the brothers transform their plain but magical coats to suit them to the predominant fashions of the day, or about the vexations that Peter inflicts on his two brothers. Concerning their dress, they are reported to add shoulder-knots one day and to go in for gold lace from Paris another day (PW vol. i, pp. 49, 51). In the same way, the concrete descriptions of Gulliver's experiences on his voyages, from the manner in which the Lilliputians feed him to the scene, in the last book, in which a young female Yahoo sees him bathing naked in a river and assaults him sexually, serve the same purpose (PW vol. xi, pp. 23 - 24; 266 - 267). This purpose is different from that of the Hogarthian vignettes in the framing fictions. In the tales of the framed fictions, the "realistic" touches are transposed to the scale and nature of the alternative worlds portrayed. At the same time the details of everyday activities are usually found to provoke the same passions in the characters, as we know in our world, so that the fairytale quality is only a fugitive first impression, nearly an illusion, that lasts only as long as the traveller's eyes have not adjusted to the scale of things in the country he is discovering. It must be added that this use of details is most consistent in the *Travels*,

29 In "Gulliver III, or, The Progress of Clio" (*First Münster Symposium*, pp. 228 - 229), Erich Rothstein detects a similar process of inversion in Swift's treatment of history. Swift, he argues, turns reported history into his own fiction, so as to prove the fictionality of what purports to be history. He shows that there too Swift submits interpretative patterns to the test of events, by which must be understood the test of a narrative logic in keeping with everyday experience.

because it fuses with a requirement of the genre. In a travel book the more unusual the experiences described, the more the narrator must vouch for their truth, and the story's authenticity to a large extent depends on such details.[30]

Swift's use of folktale plots and, more generally, of a folklore colouring calls for the following comments. As a device to create surprise and kill the pretence of authenticity of the framing fiction it is brilliant. So is Swift's invention. He does not only borrow from folklore sources, but imagines people, situations, whole ways of life in the spirit of tales and fables. He does not work in the spirit of a modern folklorist, however. His transpositions reflect the aesthetics of the classical age. On this point, his folklore fantasies, which are his most daring "fantastications", have frequently been misunderstood: a typical case of misreading due to changing literary conventions and the emergence of a new climate of sensitivity. It must be remembered that the classical conception of verisimilitude was mainly rhetorical. When Swift allows his imagination free scope in the framed fictions, he in fact follows the same principle of decorum that leads his parodic instinct to give precise renderings of current discourses in the framing of his satires. The latter have to be endowed with the proper degree of seriousness, but the "charm" of the former lies in their "extravagance" and irrepressible freedom of range. In its use of folklore colouring or plots, Swift's imagination, like that of his contemporaries, whether they are the imitators of the "Ancients" or the "Moderns", is unfettered by a conception of poetic truth subservient to the imperatives of philosophical science and psychology. Born of an age when mythological beliefs, superstitious legends, alchemy and magic had died for good and had not yet been claimed either as fields of investigation for new sciences nor as the expression of psychological processes, his fantasy ignores the categories "probable" / "improbable", realistic truth / extravagant lie, psychologically founded / gratuitous. It is the more fanciful for being unclaimed by any system of belief. Here again, Swift is seen to avail himself of the flexibility of existing conventions, and of the incompatibilities between different genres to heighten the satirical effect of practical joke.[31]

30 Everett Zimmerman, op. cit., p. 115.
31 On this problem, see my article "Misreading Contexts: Sir Walter Scott on *Gulliver's Travels*", *Reading Contexts* (SPELL 4), Tübingen, Gunter Narr Verlag, 1988, pp. 147 - 157. The words quoted in this paragraph are those used by Scott in his discussion of the *Travels*. In *The Origins of the Novel*, Michael McKeon

With the folklore element, Swift's art of satire is akin to that of the fabulists. For him as for La Fontaine, there is something, if not childish, at least childlike in a folktale or fable, and fantasy undermines the claim to excessive seriousness. The more serious and pompous the mimicry of the parody in the framing fictions, the greater the effect of deflation achieved by the framed fictions. *A Tale* widens the discrepancy to breaking point. Not only is the author of the prefaces and digressions simply the editor of the tale and a mere compilator, but he claims to make of the folktale, a childlike sort of writing, one of "the most finished and refined Systems of all Sciences and Arts" of its time (PW vol. i, p. 40). The blending of travel report and fairy tale in the *Travels* is more subtle but, however strongly they come to resemble at times the men and women of our world, Swift's Lilliputians, Brobdingnagians, Laputans, Houyhnhnms and Yahoos retain something of the nature of creatures like Puss in Boots, Tom Thumb or the fabulist's foxes and frogs. To the extent that they look more like characters out of fables than out of the satirist's experience, they are a source of irresponsible enjoyment and strongly contribute to making the purported author's claims as a serious contributor to the knowledge of his time a pose to take with a grain of salt.

Yet there is also something disturbing in the folklore colouring itself, which seems to be underlined by the way in which it is manipulated and made to evaporate. Folktales and fairy tales come too close to our most intimate dreams of good and evil for the deliberate and calculated suppression of their magic to leave us indifferent. The effect is complex. In

demonstrates how the modern notion of verisimilitude as a pretence of verifiable factuality or historicism developed (op. cit., pp. 53 - 54, 70, passim). His demonstration, which enlists the support of Gulliver, seems to me to be misleading on a point of some importance: it does not take into consideration the fact that the notion of verisimilitude which obtained at the time was not factual but rhetorical: it simply required that the means of expression be adapted to the subject. Now, as noted above, Swift precisely exploits to satirical ends his reader's familiarity with the older rhetorical conception of verisimilitude, when he intermingles the modes of realism and fantasy. To ignore this leads Michael McKeon to give a novelistic reading of the *Travels* which discounts the predominance of fantasy in the four voyages and its satirical function, to view Gulliver's story as a linear narrative of social mobility (ibid., pp. 339 - 347) similar to Defoe's *Robinson Crusoe*, and to limit the import of the satire to the social and economic struggle of its narrator. No one will dispute the fact that the social and economic problem is mentioned in the *Travels*, but it is evident that it does not have this central structural function.

so far as folktales are the expression of some of our deepest yearning, hopes and fears, Swift's inverted patterns can also be said to constitute that ultimate reference by which the world is judged in his satires. Many critics have said that they missed such a reference to an ideal in Swift. The folklore reference to the all's-well-that-ends-well of whishfulfilment is an absolute by which to assess man's failure to live up to his dream of perfection. The gap gives the measure of Swift's disillusion rather than of his pessimism. Finally, the inversions of patterns, with the proliferation of down-to-earth descriptive details in the development of the folktale motifs, create a movement forward which calls the attention unerringly back to a picture of the unpleasant realities of life. The more attractive, fugitive or amusing the illusion is at first, the more painful the process which brings the reader's mind back to the world of the framing fictions.

There is another aspect, too, and here *A Tale* and its critical history is informative. It is not just that the tale of the three brothers has been much neglected, whereas there has been no dearth of commentaries on the dedications, prefaces and digressions. When the tale has been discussed, it has been so in the terms proposed by the footnotes, some of them supposedly by Wotton, a scholar ridiculed by Swift. When this semi-fictitious Wotton encourages the reader to read the story of the three brothers as an allegory, in which Peter represents the Catholic Church, Jack Presbyterian sects and Martin the Anglican compromise, is he to be followed blindly, as the only acceptable guide? Certainly not. Swift even warns the reader not to with his general title and in a remark made by the purported author. First of all, he calls the story and the whole book "a tale of a tub", and then he suggests that reading the tale in the way Wotton recommends amounts to reading *Reynard the Fox* and *Tom Thumb* as dark Pythagorean treatises in need of elucidation (ibid., p. 41). Of course, it cannot be denied that the allegorical reading proposed by Wotton is not only possible but illuminating. The main objection is not that folktales do not lend themselves to allegorical interpretations, but rather that allegorical readings are too restrictive, if not downright distorting. Swift's own footnotes, added to the 1710 edition, raise further doubts about this sort of reductive interpretation imposed on the text. Whereas Wotton's comments quoted by Swift in other footnotes interpret the fiction with complete confidence (ibid., pp. 44, 45, 49, 50, 51), his own frankly admit that he cannot make sense of certain details (ibid., pp. 51, 100, 122, 123). These reservations on the part of the satirist himself suggest that folktales or fairy tales elude final descriptions or reductions to keys, though keys may be thrown to critics, as tubs are thrown by sailors to whales "by way of Amusement, to divert [them] from laying violent Hands upon the Ship" (ibid., p. 24). This is precisely what his inverted tales propose to do. But, simultaneously, Swift makes a plea for the ingenuous reader capable of enjoying good tales for themselves, and what do tales deal with but the important events of an individual's life: birth, love and death; man's passions; basic human relationships between members of a same family, neighbours, visitor and visited, or people in different social and economic positions; man's relationship to his natural surroundings, which provide him with what he needs to survive; and, more generally, man's innermost hopes and fears, as well as some of the very practical aspects of everyday life.

Such are the facts that the framed fictions focus on in the first place when they adapt folklore motifs and plots. These at the same time serve to universalize the portraits of the characters, and hence the import of the whole satire. *A Tale* shows the incidence of basic human relationships and social and economic pressures on the practice of religion. *The Story of the Injured Lady*, which presents the relations between closely connected countries as similar to those between neighbours and lovers, argues that they follow the same rules. As for *Gulliver's Travels*, its indebtedness to folktales would require a whole chapter to itself. Without going into details, the folklore ingredients can be said to stress the instability of the human character driven by passions, social and economic ambition, or mere restlessness, the individual's dependence on the people closest to him, his need for protection, approval or just interest on the part of others, as well as his fear of not being accepted by those he considers his likes and equals: all themes which are found in stories like "Tom Tit Tot" or "Tom Thumb". Fairytale motifs also allow Swift to show, as do the tales of giants, ogres, dwarfs and animals, that individual differences in look or habits raise suspicions and even hostility in the members of a community; that the unknown, the odd, the foreign, or whatever is out of the ordinary, can bring about reactions of mistrust and even defence; that size, greatness, or just peculiarity, are often felt as a threat by the common run of men; and, finally, that social hierarchy and solidarity are necessary to contain and discipline the disruptive effects of egoism, and to protect the individual against the forces of untamed nature. On all these points, it is worth noting that folktale themes are akin to those of travel accounts. Swift's framed folklore tales in his satirical fictions retain the folktale's way of looking at life as a private experience and adventure. Furthermore, tales have a way of looking at life *sub specie aeternitatis*. The products of human fantasy are timeless. Aesop's crows and foxes and Horace's Vulterius Mena and Philippus (Epistle I, 7) are contemporary with La Fontaine's storks and cobblers, and none has aged since. Now, it is evident that the presence of folklore plots and motifs in a satire do not make it any less topical. For readers, Gulliver will always remain a contemporary of Crusoe and Dampier. Peter, Martin and Jack are forever fixed in their memories as characters dressed for a Restoration comedy. Yet, by lending his representations of circumstantial reality the flavour of folktales – even if only temporarily – the satirist makes them look a little more like satirical fables. In *A Tale* the folktale resists the historical interpretation which Wotton's footnotes would impose upon it. It even contradicts it to the extent that three absolutely contemporary lives form the time scale of the narrative. It finally endows the three recognizably eighteenth-century characters with some degree of timelessness, not much perhaps, compared with Gulliver's fabulous hosts, but sufficient to detach them a little from their time and give them an ageless typicality. Through their association with a timeless folklore pattern, the contemporary details which help to invert this pattern, and the historical events, lose some of their historical specificity to become exemplary. Gulliver is no longer just an eighteenth-century traveller, a precursor of James Cook and the new type of colonialist trader, but the eternal incorrigible traveller, who contradicts Bacon and proves that travels have little formative influence and that men unlearn more quickly than they learn. This way of handling tales was to reveal itself particularly seminal for future writers, judging from its proud descendance: Voltaire's philosophical tales, and Dr Johnson's *Rasselas*, or, closer to us, George Orwell's *Animal Farm*.

III

The folklore element dresses up the facts of private, social, political and economic experience in its delightful colours. The discrepancy between the fanciful disguise or transposition of the framed fiction and the pretence that the document enclosing it is an authentic piece of journalistic or polemical writing is so patent that it gives away the show of seriousness of the latter at once, whether or not the demarcation between framing and framed fictions is structurally obvious. However the discrepancy is not always so marked. Swift uses other types of fictional narrative or dramatic patterns, whose nature cannot be so clearly distinguished from that of the letters, petitions, newsreports or pamphlets containing them, especially when they do not form a separate unit, as the dialogues of *Polite Conversation* do, but only a second level of fictional elaboration woven into the framing discourse. Sometimes the framing device seems to enclose no more than a faithful description of contemporary events: only an enlargement of one of those Hogarthian vignettes with which the alleged authors substantiate their claims to concrete existence. Such is the story of the end of Partridge, the astrologer, in *The Bickerstaff Papers*, or the account of the secret negociations between Versailles and London in *A New Journey to Paris*. Yet, these framed fictions have a different quality about them, which cannot be accounted for simply by a shift from discursive to narrative or dramatic modes of expressions. They also evidence a degree of literary elaboration that individual vignettes do not possess. They are to the vignettes of the framing fictions what a Hogarthian sequence or one of Hogarth's paintings are to his rough individual sketches. In each can be recognized the pattern of a literary genre or mode, which marks them off as fabricated rather than authentic, much in the same way as the folklore component does. Although the character of the framed fictions is, in this case, akin to that of the framing structures, one tending towards descriptive or dramatic "isomorphic" realism, and the other aiming at faithful imitation or "mimesis", enough divergence of aims, and enough fantasy in the framed constituent, show through to reveal a lack of coherence between the two and betray the fake, as in the cases analyzed above. However the satirical effect no longer results from their incompatibility being blatant and the whole looking preposterous, but from the maintaining of a deliberate ambiguity.

Needless to say, as with the folklore ingredient, the integration of the literary artefact within the satirical fiction, and the nature of its development, vary from work to work. On the other hand, whatever the extent of the development, it lends the satirical fiction dramatic interest and thrill, whereas the folklore atmosphere supplies a sense of innocent wonder and the shock of surprise. As dramatic interest and wonder, or childlike enjoyment, do not exclude each other, Swift sometimes combines folklore colouring with one of these narrative or dramatic patterns. He does so in *A Tale of a Tub* and *Gulliver's Travels*, of course, but also in minor pieces like *A Hue and Cry* and *The Story of the Injured Lady*. Besides being endowed with a folktale quality or pattern, these four works relate stories of intrigues and betrayals. Gulliver's account is that of his voyages into fairylands, but each of his four incursions into fairyland also turns into a story of betrayal.

These narrative and dramatic plots, or hints of plots, which supply the satires with dramatic interest, can be said to fall into two categories: on the one hand, what could be called the stories of conspiracies, grouping accounts of betrayals, personal spite, collusions against an innocent person or group, court intrigues, cabals of ministers or political plotting, and, on the other hand, scenes and stories of comedies of manners. Deceitfulness and underhand dealings give their stamp to the former. These include, apart from the four works listed above, where the folklore colouring and the conspiracy plot combine, "Mrs Harris's Petition", *A New Journey to Paris, A Letter from the Pretender to a Whig Lord, The Humble Petition of the Footmen of Dublin* and *An Examination of Certain Abuses*. The plots and themes inspired by the comedy of manners inform, or its atmosphere pervades, the framed fictions in *The Bickerstaff Papers*, "A Description of the Morning", "A Description of a City Shower", "A Satirical Elegy on the Death of a late Famous General", *Directions to Servants*, and, to quote its full title at least once, *A Complete Collection of Genteel and Ingenious Conversation, According to the Most Polite Mode used at Court and in the Best Companies of England: in Three Dialogues*. Their general concerns are the obvious great and little failings of individuals and society, the great comedy of man's benign vices.

Frauds, betrayals, underhand dealings and conspiracies have been indispensable ingredients in the writing of one type or another of stories or dramas, in the same way as love affairs or adventures, ever since literature has existed. They belong to these standard plots or patterns of experience that literature has always exploited. Conspiracies had been the staple of Elizabethan and Jacobean drama, as they are today of the spy story or thriller. In Swift's lifetime, the genre that drew on this vein of inspiration was the scandalous contemporary memoirs or the secret history.[32] They sometimes took the form of unauthorized publications of

32 When they were pieces of pure fiction, memoirs and secret histories were particularly apt to be introduced by the kind of editorial framing encountered in Defoe or Swift. McKeon calls it "the parody of the discovered manuscript topos" (op. cit., p. 56), which is not quite appropriate to account for its structural function.

private papers. Pat Rogers adds: "More particularly, secret history had come to mean scandalous accounts of private caballing, hole-and-corner intrigue, backstairs diplomacy."[33] In England such works mostly came from the pens of those hacks that Swift and his friends made a point of ridiculing in their satires. Their continental counterparts were also frequently translated into English, like Marie D'Aulnoy's famous *Mémoires de M. d'Artagnan*, which later inspired Alexandre Dumas' *Three Musketeers*. There is a flavour reminiscent of Dumas, if in a lighter humorous key, in Swift's *A Hue and Cry, A New Journey to Paris* and *A Letter from the Pretender*. The second is allegedly a report on the secret negociations that the Queen of England and her ministers were conducting with Versailles, under the nose of England's allies, to bring Marlborough's protracted wars to an end. The highlight of the story is a typical meeting, which the English poet and plenipotentiary Matthew Prior is supposed to have with Madame de Maintenon and another enigmatic figure in a vineyard adjoining the garden of Louis XIV's mistress. Swift's pieces of fake news may equally be said to have been inspired by his own work as an historian. While he was spreading false news to amuse himself in his spare time, he was also working at the project of a secret history of the very same negociations, the *History of the Four Last Years of the Queen* (1711 - 1713), which, he hoped, would correct the misrepresentation of facts by enemies of the government.

A Tale of a Tub contains both a folktale about three brothers and the story of Jack and Martin's private cabal to overthrow their brother's tyranny. *Gulliver's Travels* makes considerable use of conspiracies and betrayals. In Lilliput the eminent services that Gulliver renders the crown make several ministers envious of his prestige. They form a cabal against him, which nearly costs him his life. When Gulliver accidentally lands in Brobdingnag, the giants' country enjoys peace and stability thanks to the sound government of an enlightened monarch (PW vol. xi, p. 138). This time Gulliver himself comes near playing the trouble-maker, when he privately proposes to give the king the recipe for gun-powder with the intention, he says, to enable him to "destroy the whole Metropolis, if ever it should pretend to dispute his absolute Commands" (ibid., p. 134). On Laputa and Balnibarbi conspiracies are an endemic evil. With their flying island the Laputans try to crush the opposition of the other island

33 *Grub Street*, p. 193.

in much the same way as Gulliver suggested that the king of Brobdingnag should use gun-powder against those who might resist his command. Furthermore, on board the flying island, there are frequent cabals of ministers. In Book iii, Gulliver does not get involved personally, but one of the victims of these cabals is his friend and host Lord Munodi (ibid., p. 175). Conspiracies are such a widespread evil on the two islands that their academy has made a specialty of research on the problem of their detection. Finally, "A Voyage to the Houyhnhnms" begins with one type of conspiracy, the mutiny of Gulliver's sailors to dispossess him of his ship (ibid., p. 222), and ends with what is for him another kind of betrayal when, yielding to pressure from the other horses of the community, his master decides to part company with him (ibid., p. 279). Deprived of the noble creature's friendship, Gulliver considers his forced departure as a new exile. The sequence and patterning of the main conspiracies and betrayals in the *Travels* is evidence of their dramatic importance. They can be said to shape Gulliver's adventures and life. In this respect, the conspiracy pattern is more important than the travelling one, which simply transports the hero from his world into various dream-lands and holds the four parts together.

Altogether different is the turn that frauds and conspiracies take in the two petitions and *An Examination of Certain Abuses*. All three are instances of heavy framing, with the result that no continuous narrative pattern is allowed to emerge, only a second level of fictional elaboration. The underhand dealings are not told as a story. They are the purported authors' expression of their conviction that a vast conspiracy is afoot, which they have to expose to protect themselves or their friends. What distinguishes the framed element from the rest of the discourse in these cases is that the enunciator's argument turns into a lucubration, which can even border on fantasy. "Mrs Harris's Petition", the most factual, is based on the fact that a servant has been defrauded of her savings, and she accuses other servants of this petty larceny. The footmen's petition and *Certain Abuses* draw sombre pictures of mysterious manoeuvres on the part of a no less enigmatic and elusive enemy, Dublin bucks in one case and Tory Jacobites in the other. In the first place these pieces are their authors' complaints and, to that extent, their form falls within the province of the study of the framing fictions. A look back is inevitable here. To take *Certain Abuses* as an illustration, its purported author, the citizen of Dublin responsible for the framing fiction of public protest, is one of those decipherers of plots described in the *Travels* as typical of

Laputa and another island, Tribnia – an anagram for Britain –, of whom Gulliver writes that they are Artists

very dextrous in finding out the mysterious Meanings of Words, Syllables and Letters. For Instance, they can decypher a Close-stool to signify a Privy Council; a Flock of Geese, a Senate; a lame Dog, an Invader; the Plague, a standing Army; a Buzard, a Minister . . .   (ibid., p. 191)

Certain Abuses shows in action what the *Travels* describe. The author opens his "examination" with a request to the authorities of the city of Dublin to introduce certain regulations to force cheesemongers, fishmongers, costermongers and other hawkers, who go about town advertizing their products and services, to change their unintelligible cries into intelligible ones. As he puts it, to shout *"Herrings alive, alive here"* when you sell dead fish is a stupid lie (PW vol. xii, p. 218). But his mind quickly shifts from this banal observation of street life to suspicions (ibid., p. 223) and from suspicions slips into mere assumptions, none the less presented as certainties (ibid., pp. 224 - 225), until it becomes obvious that, in each hawker's cry, and then in each punch house sign, the citizen smells treachery to the Whig government. The alleged author ends up proposing a picture of universal conspiracy, where everyone is plotting against everyone else. It is this vision of universal conspiracy that forms the framed fiction in the sense defined above. It is woven into the texture of the alleged author's framing discourse, but, once again, it has nothing to do with the original purpose of the "examination", which is a plea for reform and order. From an accumulation of hints a frightening vision develops. There is not a step that the author takes around the city that does not bring him further proofs of villaneous plotting. On a punch house sign, an irrelevant animal, eagle, lion, raven or crow, holding a ladle plunging in a bowl of punch, becomes a rallying sign for Catholic malcontents, or Tories favourable to the Stuart and Catholic Pretender. The fishmonger's cry of "by my sole, buy my sole" is deciphered as meaning *"buy my Soul, buy my Soul"* and explained as a way used by those opposing the Settlement of 1689 to discourage the population from taking the oath of fidelity to the protestant king (ibid., p. 226). Even dogs have been contaminated by this universal disease:

The Dog, who perfectly understands the Term of Art, and consequently the Danger he is in, immediately flies. The People, and even his own *Brother Animals* pursue: The Pursuit and Cry attend him perhaps half a Mile; he is well worried in his Flight;

104

and sometimes hardly escapes. This, our Ill-wishers of the *Jacobite* Kind, are pleased to call a *Persecution*; and affirm, that it always falls upon *Dogs* of the *Tory* Principle.

(Ibid., p. 221)

Though the conspiracy remains the product of a heated partisan brain, and though the accumulation of hints and suspicions is never allowed to take a narrative form, and thus become something separate from the alleged author's obsession, the impression of general conspiracy that *Certain Abuses* contains is exciting. It calls up a forceful vision of explosive situation, which satisfies the reader's craving for action, as the hints of folktales do his sense of wonder and fantasy.

The conspiracy motif or plot is a recurrent one in the work. It is even present in the polemical writings. *The Conduct of the Allies* accuses those who were believed to make money out of the war with France of wanting to prolong it, of working against England's interests and of deceiving the Queen and the nation as to the real situation. *The Drapier's Letters* try to turn the story of a licence obtained through bribery into a history of general conspiracy to ruin Ireland. The figure of the conspiracy is usually deliberately hyperbolic in its applications. But the reader comes so often across this concern that it is difficult not to see a personal obsession in it. On the other hand, it must be granted that the two political parties were so constantly levelling charges of obscure plotting at each other through the journalists in their pay that conspiracies may also be said to have been in the air. Swift himself once wrote that he had the impression of living "in a plot-discovering age" in which an innocent man of the wrong political persuasion could be "seized and imprisoned, and forced to lie several months in chains, while the Ministers were not at leisure to hear his petition, until they had prosecuted and hanged the number proposed."[34] Whatever its source, there is no doubt that the conspiracy is always a fiction, whether in the satires or in the polemical discourses,[35] and that Swift is particularly fond of it, because it affords inexhaustible possibilities for suspense, because it contains in germ all "the exciting qualities of evil" that can stimulate a satirist's imagination.[36]

---

34 PW vol. ix, "A Letter from Dr Swift to Mr Pope" (dated Jan. 10, 1721), p. 33.

35 J.A. Downie, *Jonathan Swift: Political Writer*, London, Routledge and Kegan Paul, 1984, p. 158.

36 Nigel Dennis, *Jonathan Swift: A Short Character*, London, Weidenfeld and Nicolson, 1965, p. 48.

The other fictional plots that Swift uses to shape and colour the framed fictions, so as to make them look irrelevant in the kind of writing the satires purport to be, are in a different key. Their source of inspiration is the then popular comedy of manners. The rather loose canvas of *Directions to Servants* or "Verses on the Death of Dr Swift" allows the satirist to string together scenes which feature butlers, cooks, footmen or Swift's own acquaintances as comic characters. In the former, the descriptions of servants' misdemeanour to illustrate the rules of conduct of the profession read like so many stage directions in a farce. The following are two of the recommendations made to chamber-maids:

> When you sweep your Lady's Room, never stay to pick up foul Smocks, Handkerchiefs, Pinners, Pin-cushions, Tea-spoons, Ribbons, Slippers, or whatever lieth in your Way; but sweep all into a Corner, and then you may take them up in a Lump, and save Time.

> When you spread Bread and Butter for Tea, be sure that all the Holes in the Loaf be left full of Butter, to keep the Bread moist against Dinner; and let the Mark of your Thumb be seen only upon one End of every Slice, to shew your Cleanliness.
>
> (PW vol. xiii, pp. 55, 56)

More elaborate, though less extensive, is the use of a comic framed narrative in *The Bickerstaff Papers*. The whole polemic engendered by the first piece of the series, Bickerstaff's counter-almanac, has already been seen to follow the pattern of a comedy in three acts. The staging effect would have remained purposeless, however, had the central piece of the hoax been missing. This takes again the shape of a separate fiction: the account of Partridge's defeat ending in his alleged death. The first part of his story is then presented dramatically through the polemical exchange, but the second is directly reported. For once this narrative piece is well integrated, so that it does not look like a foreign body within its context. Yet it is surprising both dramatically and formally in so far as the report of this death is the unexpected fulfilment of an almanac prediction and a sudden new development of the action, as well as a readily identifiable literary set-piece in a context of random current polemics: an exemplary death-bed scene. The description of the solemn leave-taking of the dying soul had the status of a minor genre. It was generally associated with church oratory rather than the comedy of manners, and, of the funeral oration, Swift's narrative has the solemn character and pathos. However, the death-bed scene was not unknown in comedy, as the widely different cases of Ben Jonson's *Volpone* and Molière's *Le médecin malgré lui* testify. What usually justified its presence in a comedy was that the comic character was either faking dead or recovered unexpectedly. The case of Partridge is similar: he is said to die though he does not do so actually. Swift may also be said to use the dying man's last words to remind his readers of another popular genre: the rogue's dying speech, which he turned into another hoax: *The Last Speech and Dying Words of Ebenezor Elliston*. Rogues are notorious heroes of popular comedies, and the implication makes the death-bed scene highly ambiguous by suggesting a connection between the astrologer's activities and those of the criminal underworld. The comic use of the death-bed scene turns Partridge into a stock comic character: a typical blocking figure.

Another interesting case is *Polite Conversation*, which contains a genuine play. Wagstaff's pompous introduction announces a "treatise" (PW vol. iv, p. 99) and a complete art of conversation in three dialogues. What the reader gets, however, is only a thin handbook, which is, in fact, not a handbook at all, but another comedy in three acts, prefaced with a list of characters and a brief argument giving the outline of an action. The names of the characters are reminiscent of those of Restoration comedy or of Sheridan's in *School for Scandal*. They have names Lord Smart, Mr Neverout, Colonel Atwit and Lady Answerall. The three dialogues obey the classical rules for the unities of place and time. Though the action begins on the Mall, most of it plays at Lady Smart's, over breakfast, dinner and a game of quadrille. The time the action takes to unfold is less than the prescribed twenty-four hours. The third unity is not forgotten either. The action itself consists in the relationships that form, or do not form, through the conversation of the characters. There is less scandal than in Sheridan's comedy, but more complimenting and teazing:

Ne[erout]. Well, Miss, if I must be hanged, I won't go far to chuse my Gallows: It shall be about your fair Neck.
Miss [Notable]. I'll see your Nose Cheese first, and the Dogs eating it.
(Ibid., p. 170)

The picture of society is recognizably that of the eighteenth-century comedy of manners, but the relationship between action and gestures is reversed and, consequently, the nature of the dialogues is perverted. Regarding the relation of words to action in comedy, it is usually the development of the action and of the behaviour of the characters that lead these to display their wit. In Swift's dialogues it is the impulse to use such and such an already stale phrase that prompts the gesture and the action. Handkerchiefs are dropped, snuffboxes offered, tea poured or spilt, dishes passed around and footmen sent on errands for the sole sake of making conversation and of allowing a character to use a clever phrase or pun. The colonel seems to cut his thumb on purpose to allow the ladies to put in their remarks:

> *Lady Answ[erall]*. Ay, that was your Mother's Fault; because she only warned you not to cut your Fingers.
> *Lady Sm[art]*. No, no; 'tis only Fools cut their Fingers, but wise Folks cut their Thumbs. (Ibid., p. 138)

The whole action is orchestrated to allow the characters to use well-worn phrases, poor puns, weak rhymes, sometimes with even little a-propos:

Col[onel]. Madam, I must needs go home for half an Hour.
Miss [Notable]. Why, Colonel, they say the Devil's at home. (Ibid., p. 133)

This perversion of the function of witty dialogues renders the comedy non-comic, or comic at a secondary level: that of the parody of a genre. It turns the characters into automata, and their repartees into a grating imitation of wit, and the plot into an enactment of hollow activities.

The analysis of the folklore colouring given to several framed fictions has demonstrated that Swift often reverses folktale patterns or creates a fairytale atmosphere only to dispel it. In this respect, the folklore ingredient frequently constitutes an interpretative factor, more than a dramatic plot. It underlines the opposition between the ideal and the real. This is particularly evident where the folklore component combines with what has been called, for simplification's sake, the conspiracy story. When the charm of folktales fails and the magic evaporates, what remains is the dark reality of the conspiracy. The concrete details with which the life of the characters is portrayed were said above to jeopardize the fairytale atmosphere, and the conspiracy story deals it the final deathblow. It also gives the change a dramatic turn. In *A Tale of a Tub* the story of the three brothers takes a turn for the worse when Peter tries to defraud Martin and Jack of what is their inheritance by right, their fundamental equality before their father – underlined by the fact that they are the same age –, and again when Martin and Jack conspire to take their revenge on Peter. In *Gulliver's Travels*, when conspiracies, betrayals or other underhand dealings begin to threaten, the wonder of the fairy tale vanishes, and the reader's attention is brought back to the sad reality of man's frailty. Conspiracies kill the magic. In "A Voyage to Lilliput" this moment comes rather late, with the ministers' cabal against Gulliver, shortly before his departure. As often noted, it is symbolic that the Lilliputians should decide to deprive the cumbersome giant of those very short-sighted eyes that have deceived him into thinking these treacherous mannikins much nicer than they really were. In the third voyage the enchantment disappears almost at once, as the sad reality of the Laputans' shortcomings – more numerous than their achievements – intrudes after a few pages already. After that, the rest of the voyage leads Gulliver from one disappointment with magic to another. "A Voyage to the Houyhnhnms" is a little different in that it contains two conspiracies, as seen above. The first, the sailors' mutiny, opens the gate of fairyland for Gulliver. It makes his admiration for the horses, who are in full control of their passions, inevitable, and his growing misanthropy explicable at the end. The second, which results in his being expelled from the horses' fairyland touches him the more deeply as coming from the very creatures he most reveres. It leaves him bitter, as people are, who have been let down and betrayed by those they loved and trusted. In fact, before entering each fantastic country Gulliver is reported to fall asleep or described as ready to drop from exhaustion, and at the end of each voyage he appears like a man who has been bewitched and awakens from a dream: it is as though, on landing in each new *terra incognita*, he had fallen into a drowsy state and imagined all that happened to him there,[37] so that each geographical discovery in the *Travels* is also an incursion into dreamland. Three times the dream turns to nightmare and Gulliver is happy to wake up. The fourth time the dream is pleasant and he feels depressed at being awoken. He finds it difficult to adjust back to reality.

---

37 PW vol. xi, Book i, pp. 21 and 78; Book ii, pp. 85 and 144; Book iii, pp. 154 and 156, but there is no mention of sleep or weariness at the end of the voyage, only of direct contacts with magic and magicians in the course of the narrative; Book iv, pp. 223 and 284.

When the folklore colouring is not there to superimpose the interpretative pattern of an awakening to reality on the dramatic or narrative pattern of another literary artefact, the latter, which has already been said to lend dramatic interest to the framed fiction, sometimes behaves like the folktale pattern and becomes itself interpretative, though perhaps not so conspicuously. It does so either by acquiring a suspicious literary polish, which is no longer in keeping with the promise for blunt information or naked argument of the framing and betrays the lying fiction, as seen in *The Bickerstaff Papers*, or by distorting the conspiracy story or comedy-of-manner plot in a way that recalls the reversals of the folktale and fairytale patterns, as in *Polite Conversation*. "The Fable of Midas" belongs to the first category: printed as a half-sheet of purely topical comment on a political event, it has the appearance of a literary fable on a semi-legendary figure. More frequent are the pieces belonging to the second category. The verse descriptions of city life at dawn or under a shower turn out to be parodies of pastorals, and sad inversions of their ideal picture of life.[38] As for *A Hue and Cry* and *A New Journey to Paris*, they have the flavour of pages from mock histories rather than true pieces of news.

With their framed fictions in form of fable, burlesque secret history, burlesque death-bed scene, mock pastoral, mock elegy or mock comedy, Swift's satirical fictions look, when the folklore colouring is absent and when the narrative or dramatic pattern is both a dynamic ingredient and an interpretative factor, like parodies of actual polemical or journalistic pieces, verisimilar fakes, containing other parodies, fanciful mock pieces. On one point, at least, the satirical use of the narrative and dramatic plots as interpretative patterns is similar to that of the folklore element: it also defeats the reader's expectations by reversing or burlesquing the usual developments. But the effect is not exactly the same. Like the mock epic, the burlesqued literary plot or simply the polished lying pattern does not so much aim at shocking the reader into a new awareness of how sad reality is, as at presenting it as falling far short of the image of life usually proposed by literature.

38 Nora Crow Jaffe also notes the use of the device in the poetry in connection with her discussion of raillery (*The Poet Swift*, Hanover, University Press of New England, 1977, p. 23). Roger Savage, "Swift's Fallen City: 'A Description of the Morning'", *The World of Jonathan Swift*, ed. Brian Vickers, Oxford, Blackwell, 1968, pp. 176 - 179. P. O'Hethir, "The Meaning of Swift's 'Description of a City Shower'", *ELH: A Journal of English Literary History* 27: 204 - 205 (1960).

The conspiracy stories or comedy-of-manner situations have a different relation to circumstantial reality from the folklore colouring. The latter trades on its association with the literature of the marvellous and of innocent enjoyment. It toys with the notion of a distancing from everyday life and flight into the world of dreams. In the handling of dramatic patterns that conspiracies and comedy-of-manner situations constitute, Swift, on the contrary, takes pains to underline the close parallel between what the framed fiction reports and what exists outside the text, in circumstantial reality. In the *Travels*, which play with both distancing effects and the use of parallels with everyday experience, Gulliver's conversations with his hosts have no other purpose but to remind the reader that, in fact, he is not discovering new worlds but his own. This drawing of parallels is constant. The narrator's comparison between Tribnia - Britain and Balnibarbi on the score of discoverers of plots is a good illustration of the procedure. Where no such discussion enlightens the reader, the turn of events is such that the parallel with what happens in our world, or between one world and another in the *Travels*, is easy to draw. In a different way, the imbroglio of conspiracies described in *An Examination of Certain Abuses*, the secret negociations in *A New Journey to Paris*, and the ridiculous dialogues of *Polite Conversation* are specifically reported as referring to events taking place outside the text. By turning literary patterns into mock patterns and by maintaining some doubt as to whether the narrative or dramatic content is pure fantastication or report of facts, they seem to say: this is what really happens in the world, and the world is worse than literature or history ever represent it. Literature idealizes, even when it seems critical. Through the dramatic patterns of the conspiracy and comedy of manners, fiction and reality become to some extent interchangeable. However subjective and distorted the alleged writer's views may appear, the satirical fiction postulates some sort of rough equivalence between the world he lives in and what he tells the reader. In so far as they refer to the world outside the text Swift's great comedies of vice and the little tragedies of virtue narrated in the framed fictions overlap with the trope of the gratuitous game, to which the journalistic and intellectual debate of the period is compared. They consequently lend the game pleasant or unpleasant, comic or semi-tragic, overtones.

There remains to say something about what is achieved by presenting circumstantial reality as a world of conspiracies and low comedy. The first thing to stress is that, even where they do not develop into full fictional plots but remain in an embryonic state, the elements of conspiracy and comedy nevertheless exhibit the usual universalizing force of dramatic patterns.[39] Cabals, collusions and underhand dealings, what has been called conspiracies, create the explosive and slippery situations that the framed fictions present. But they are also great evils in the world. The conspiracy story is used to articulate the narrative pattern and the moral reflexion of the satire. It is not just, like ambition, poor education or wars, a feature of life that comes in for criticism. Fictional though they may be, conspiracies are an epitome of the creeping evil of a treacherous world. And what a terrible picture Swift draws of its consequences. The conspiracy story shows in action how faith, trust, devotion, frankness and generosity can be undermined in society. Men or parties have recourse to underhand dealings to satisfy their thirst for power and wealth, their egoism or ambition. Plotting is a way of getting rid of one's opponents, while avoiding open confrontation. On this head, it ranks with unfair trials, assassinations and wars as a criminal means towards an unjustifiable end. As for its effects, conspiracy is first of all cruel. Conspirators stop at no baseness. They display boundless energy and ingenuity in the pursuit of their goal and to cover up their meanness. Gulliver's impeachment at the end of his stay in Lilliput is a shameful story of ingratitude. The enviousness of a few disappointed ministers succeeds in obliterating all memory of his great services to the whole nation. From the point of view of society, conspiracies favour not freedom but tyranny, as can be seen with the policy led by the king of Laputa to crush oppositions. The greater the intellectual refinement of a country, the worse are the disruptive effects of underhand dealings. They engender universal suspicion and fear and provoke counter-measures that result in a general psychosis, of which *An Examination of Certain Abuses* gives a vivid impression.[40] Conspiracies are also a psychological evil. They do not only exist as facts in the world, but in the minds of men and women. In the episode of the horses' expulsion of Gulliver, in "Mrs Harris's Petition" or that of the footmen of Dublin, but particularly in *Certain Abuses* there is more than a hint that fear of betrayal often becomes self-deception and a dangerous blindness leading to madness in the most extreme cases. Conspiracies, cabals and underhand dealings

---

39 Paul Ricoeur, op. cit. pp. 69 - 70.
40 C.J. Rawson has also observed "the chaotic vitality" of evil (op. cit., p. 51), but he sees anarchy as the worst type of evil for Swift (ibid., pp. 82 - 83).

show creeping evil exultant and victorious, undermining social life and individual psychology: this is the vision of evil that Swift opposes to his friend Pope's duncehood. Pope describes duncehood as a disease suffocating and paralyzing life in *The Dunciad*. For Swift, evil is a much more sinister force because both dynamic and destructive, and because its agent is always man driven to violent action by his passions, vices and weaknesses.

By comparison, the comedy-of-manner ingredient looks pale. It deals with what is obvious, and it lacks the sense of deep treacherousness and evil that conspiracies suggest. The dirt of "A Description of a City Shower", the moral depravation of "A Description of the Morning", the numberless blunders listed in *Directions to Servant*, and the casual way in which the news of Marlborough's death is received in "A Satirical Elegy on a Late Famous General" are at best the sad, if also laughable, expression of much human mediocrity. The repenting astrologer who, on his deathbed, admits that his almanacs contained only lies, the ladies of "Verses on the Death of Dr Swift" and the characters in *Polite Conversation*, are harmless, disingenuous, and uninventive. No great passion or faith animate the characters of the comic fictions. They symbolize the mediocrity of their society, and their conversations the poverty of their interests, spiritual life and occupations. Such minor failings are minor evils. They do not endanger society and draw either Swift's amused scorn or his impatient rebuke. They are more reminiscent of Pope's portrayal of duncehood in so far as they are engendered by people's dullness, indifference and inexcusable complacency. Life is not threatened in these cases: it is made stale. Dirt and rottenness call for no more than the energetic action of a good cleaning.

IV

The reasons why the framed fictions have been referred to as the truly satirical constituents of the complex satires ought to be fully clear by now. Whereas the framing components are merely deceptive wrappings, it is the framed fictions that expose the sophistries of the current discourses parodied. They are the source of the two types of disjunctions that produce the satirical effect. On the one hand, their unexpected nature in their immediate context creates a rupture with the framing, so that both appear to pull in incompatible directions, one towards fanciful or literary artificiality and the other towards a pretence of authenticity. On the other hand, there are the reversals or inversions of traditional patterns within the framed fictions. These disjunctions serve two closely related satirical ends: one is strategic and concerns the reading process, and the second is structural and connected with the characterization, and consequently the reliability, of the purported authors of the pretendedly authentic documents.

Concerning the strategic function and its influence on the reading process, the previous chapter has indicated that the framing device serves to delineate the space of an exclusion, which is equivalent to a condemnation. It is possible to see now how this is achieved. The fictitiousness of the framed component undermines on the rebound the claim to factuality of the framing discourse. Because in one way or another the framed component never fully fits in with the framing discourse, the text does not answer the reader's expectation. Worse, it proves unreliable. It is not what its external form, its peritext, announced. When Gulliver's account of his travels turns out to be a fairy tale, or Wagstaff's "full and compleat . . . Body of Refined Sayings" (PW vol. iv, p. 115) a poor comedy, the truth value of the framing document or preface is denied. That the reader was at first taken in by the pretence of objectivity changes little about the emptiness of the purported author's claim to be taken literally. Concerning the second type of disjunction, even if reversing or perverting the traditional patterns of tales, secret histories or comedies of manners, or simply utilizing them as irrelevant examples of too well-polished fictions, means no more than creating new lying folktales, scandalous chronicles or low comedies, these are at least presented in such a way as to challenge the universe of beliefs for which their original models have become a routine vehicle.

The first sort of disjunctions calls into question the seriousness of a large number of contemporary publications, as well as the inexplicit, often wrong, assumptions about their reliability. The second entertains, at the same time as it shocks the reader into a new awareness of the unpleasant facts of life. Both breed mistrust, since they expose various writing practices and types of fictions as dishonest, half-honest or merely impulsive fabrications. With his satirical denunciations, Swift neither denies the desirability of plain reports and sound discussions, nor asserts the impossibility of producing them, as some modern writers would today when they are confronted with the same uneven balancing of "blindness and insight" in the world. He only deplores the fact that much printed trash falls far short of the standards of a decent honesty and plain commonsense that he struggled to promote in his more didactic writings, like his sermons.

As for the structural function of these disjunctions, it is equally crucial, because it highlights the connection between the unreliability of the text and the characterization of its purported author. It shows this unreliability to be rooted in human fallibility. Indeed, the disjunctions are not just flaws in the text which put the reader on his guard. They are also flaws in the minds of the fictitious authors through whom Swift voices his criticism of man and society. Nothing better confirms the fact that their characterization is more functional than psychological, and strictly subordinated to the parody of genres, than the rôle played by the text's flaws in creating their personality. The characterization of the authors can be slight or distinctively drawn. But there is no doubt that the personality emerges most vividly where the flaws, the disjunctions, are most marked. Whether the alleged writer is alone responsible for the framed fiction or only its editor, the discrepancies in his publication lend him a feature that distinguishes him from any novelistic character and narrator, and more generally from anyone else in life, the reader in particular.[41] Swift's best-known personae are victims of various kinds of blindness. The disjunctions in their texts, which represent the flaws in their minds, make them prone to error. They are unaware of the discrepancies in their writings. But their errors of judgment do not escape the reader. So it is their blindness that makes them appear different from those who read them. When, in *A Tale of a Tub*, a hack edits a folktale as though the story were a work of recondite philosophy or history in need of annotations (PW vol.i, pp. 40 - 41), or when Gulliver reports his travels to fairylands – or is it his dreams ? – as though he had discovered real continents and islands like Christopher Columbus or James Scott, when Wagstaff proclaims himself arbiter of good manners and saviour of

41 In the ongoing debate about the scope and nature of Swift's impersonations as fictional devices, there has been an unfortunate tendency to consider the alleged authors in the satirical fictions as full characters, in whose suffering and alienation the reader can feel involved, as with the characters of a novel. It is necessary to indicate why this is hardly possible. But to point out the difference is not the same as saying that the portrayal of an alleged author need show no consistency or that his character cannot be presented as having suffered or suffering, hoping, fearing or rejoicing. To be credible he must have some feelings and ideas, apart from experiences.

the art of conversation as Beau Brummel and Beau Nash were to do soon after, they do something that is not only foolish, but inadmissible. In these extreme cases, the gap between the avowed intentions of the framing discourse and their non-fulfilment in the framed fictions is such, and the alleged author's refusal to see his mistake so final, that there is something schizophrenic about his work. *A Modest Proposal* is a mad one, not because it is inhuman – that makes it simply cruel –, but because it presents the Irish landlords as legendary ogres and the poor people of the country as so many Hop O' My Thumbs, though its author does not realize this. With the flaws in the texts, Swift can be said to give a structural expression to the eighteenth-century notion of the flawed nature of man.[42]

The transition, or lack of it, from polemics or journalistic report in the fake documents to the popular tale, story of conspiracy or social comedy in the framed fiction, always illustrates, not only a flight into wild fancies, but also, and more importantly, the triumph of an impulse to fictionalize. For Swift, fiction-making seems to be inescapable, and it always bears the stamp of subjectivity. One invents a story and sees oneself cast in a particular rôle as a result. According to the circumstances, the fiction-making can be more or less outrageous. It varies with the degree of the individual's self-centredness or blindness. After the discrepancies in the text, the fictionality of the framed component functions then as a second evidence of the fictitious author's blindness, error or unreliability, which the satire sets out to expose. In the worst cases, when the mind succumbs to the temptation of fictionalizing, and subjectivity is left to its own devices, Swift believes, like Hobbes, that "a great fancy is one kind of madness", and that people prone to such fancies, "entering into any discourse, are snatched from their purpose by everything that comes in their thought, into so many and so long digressions and parentheses that they utterly lose themselves".[43] Hobbes's expla-

42 Paul Fussell, *The Rhetorical World of Augustan Humanism*, Oxford, Clarendon, 1965, pp. 84 - 85.

43 *Leviathan*, London, Routledge, 1924, p. 41. John M. Bullitt (op. cit., p. 144) adds that a sort of "mechanical rigidity" usually accompanies an excess of subjectivity. Many of Swift's polemical pieces are in fact critical appraisals of such deceptive fictionalizing and rôle playing. Ronald Paulson has analyzed the stylistic features of such outbursts of fancy in *Theme and Structure in Swift's "Tale of a Tub"* (pp. 1 - 86), whereas Carole Fabricant has drawn attention to the fact that Swift became increasingly "less indulgent to the vagaries of the imagination" in the course of his life (op. cit., p. 58).

nation is a fitting description of what happens to the alleged authors' minds in *A Tale* and *Mechanical Operation*.[44] It applies to *An Examination of Certain Abuses*, and a case can also be made for the fairytale colouring in *Gulliver's Travels* and the comedy of manner in *Polite Conversation*. They too present what can be labelled a bolting or running away of the imagination on the part of their respective authors. In all these instances, the hiatus between the framing discourse and the framed tale or comedy, which is one between intention and performance, shows that the rôle into which the alleged author or editor has cast himself is one he cannot fill to satisfaction because he is unsuited for it. The satirical fictions show that, as an aspect of subjectivity, fictionalizing is a daunting obstacle in the pursuit of truth seen as the result of observation, which was the truth valued by the period. The medium of expression may look scholarly, objective and trustworthy, but subjectivity defeats such aims.

Even where the discrepancy between framing and framed fictions is minimal and the gap discreet, so that it contributes nothing to the characterization of the purported author or editor of the piece, enough fictionality appears to betray a suspicious confusion between historical facts and fiction and to reveal, on the part of the implicit writer or editor, a congenital incapacity to know and represent reality as it is. As already mentioned, in the two poems about London or *A New Journey to Paris*, the alleged editor or author proposes a picture of life in one case reshaped by the conventions of the pastoral and in the other case by those of the scandalous chronicle, although all three pieces are offered to readers as straightforward reportage. Fixed thinking patterns and writing habits can be discerned among the causes of a sort of fictionalizing that weakens their apparent truthfulness. No discourse is ever completely objective. Here the distortion may be slight, because the purported editor or author is not carried away by passion or imagination, and consequently has a reasonable control of his medium of expression, but it is there nevertheless. Furthermore, in so far as authorship is presented as a collective undertaking, often intended to reflect the views of prospective readers, the deficiencies revealed by the discourse, the gaps in the text, reflect a general human infirmity, at the same time as they function as the

44 Robert H. Hopkins, "The Personation of Hobbism in Swift's *A Tale of a Tub* and *Mechanical Operation of the Spirit*", *Philological Quarterly* 45: 372 - 378 (1966).

satirist's shock tactics to bring this infirmity to man's consciousness. On this point the study of the framed fictions confirms that of the framing discourses. The human mind is enclined to cherish fictions rather than facts.

With their incoherences, the satirical fictions seem to suggest that any apprehension of reality is more or less chaotic. In this sense, the framing discourses are no longer the only representations of the way the mind sees things and facts and the only parodic spreading out of the observable to be the better able to dissect it. The whole satirical fiction, with its disjunctions and fanciful fabrications becomes a caricature and an embodiment of the dangers of subjectivity. In presenting the disjunctions in the text as an effect of the flaws of the minds that write them, Swift even relates the incoherences of his fictions to the other manifestations of disorder in man's life: cabals, conspiracies, betrayals, and other underhand dealings, wars, or the harmless inconsequences and little failings of the comedy of manners, which he portrays in his framed fictions.[45] He hints that bad writing and bad policy are two facets of a same evil, which has its roots in the imperfection of human nature. Behind the perception of man's difficulty to know the world and himself can be once again recognized the Lockean conception of human understanding. With his framed tales Swift, however, contributes an original insight to the theory: his intuition that the mind is all too often content to live off self-spun fictions.

As important for his satires as this conception of human understanding is the conception of language that evolves from it. Swift does not believe, like Aphra Behn and Defoe, that words represent facts and things in any simple way. In their realistic romances they assume that language opens a transparent window on to the life of other people. Their fictions are shaped by the conviction that reality is *out there* and that language is designed to represent it. This atomistic conception of language postulates a direct correlation between language and reality: between each object or action in the universe and the word that corresponds to it. In his *History of the Royal Society of London* Thomas Sprat speaks of a "return back to the primitive purity, and shortness [of style], when men deliver'd so many *things*, almost in an equal number of

---

45 For Ricardo Quintana (op. cit., p. 69), irrationality is, besides egoism, one of the great evils in the world for Swift.

words."[46] Such language, Sprat argued, was the ideal tool that science needed. That Swift rejects the view as unfounded is well known from the *Travels*, which contain a discussion of the nature of language. Its criticism of what could be called the Royal Society position deserves special attention. The reader is quickly made aware that Gulliver's ideas concerning language do not coincide with his performance. He is presented as a down-to-earth and practical ship surgeon, who wholeheartedly subscribes to the recommendations of the Royal Society to travellers. His aim is to give a faithful report of his discoveries:

> Thus, gentle Reader, I have given thee a faithful History of my Travels for Sixteen Years, and above Seven Months; wherein I have not been so studious of Ornament as of Truth. I could perhaps like others have astonished thee with strange improbable Tales; but I rather chose to relate plain Matter of Fact in the simplest Manner and Style; because my principle Design was to inform, and not to amuse thee.
>
> (PW vol. xi, p. 291)

Coming as it does at the end of "A Voyage to the Houyhnhnms" such a statement sounds odd and downright ironical. Gulliver is even ready to go further than Sprat: he reports with undisguised interest a project from the Academy of Lagado tending to dispense with words altogether and to replace them by the objects themselves that they refer to:

> since Words are only Names for *Things*, it would be more convenient for all Men to carry about them, such *Things* as were necessary to express the particular Business they are to discourse on.   (Ibid., p. 185)

On the other hand, it is clear that Gulliver is not as detached and objective as he claims. When he tries to do better than the real or fictitious travellers of his time, William Dampier, Robinson Crusoe or Montesquieu's Usbek, and to avoid airing the prejudices of his race, he falls into the opposite error. His open-mindedness leads him to adopt the views of the countries he visits, and his inside glimpses of their customs are more than once as biased as those of other travellers, though for opposite reasons. When he comes back from Brobdingnag, he sees everything in England with the eyes of the giants. His account also shows him to be repeatedly carried away by his subjective impressions or the intoxication

---

46 Op. cit., p. 113. On Swift and the contemporary conceptions of language, see Ann Cline Kelly, "After Eden: Gulliver's (Linguistic) Travels", *ELH: Journal of English Literary History* 45: 35 - 54 (1978).

of language, especially when he describes his country. In the middle of his description of his stay among the Houyhnhnms, whom he admires as much as he learns to despise England and Europe, the reader overhears him speaking to his master of human wars in terms bordering on enthusiasm, the very tone in which he had recommended the use of gunpowder to the king of Brobdingnag, and which he should have found out of place in the situation:

I could not forbear shaking my Head and smiling a little at his Ignorance. And, being no Stranger to the Art of War, I gave him a Description of Cannons, Culverins, Muskets, Carabines, Pistols, Bullets, Powder, Swords, Bayonets, Sieges, Retreats, Attacks, Undermines, Countermines, Bombardments, Sea-fights; Ships sunk with a Thousand Men; twenty Thousand killed on each Side; dying Groans, Limbs flying in the Air: Smoak, Noise, Confusion, trampling to Death under Horses Feet: Flight, Pursuit, Victory; Fields strewed with Carcases left for Food to Dogs, and Wolves, and Birds of Prey; Plundering, Stripping, Ravishing, Burning and Destroying.

(Ibid., p. 247)

In this sense, Gulliver's voyages into what looks at first sight like fairylands are also indirectly an apt tale about the delusion of language and its fabrications. The dream of "plain style" which avoids subjectivity and relies on the weight of facts can only be an illusion.[47]

In fact, Gulliver is an inconsistent narrator not merely because of the structural ruptures in the text. He is always so engrossed with the task in hand, whether he is recording his own observations or the discourses that he held to different interlocutors, that he is usually content to put side by side discoveries, fragments of conversations or facts. One thing or impression drives out another. The more detailed the report, the more incapable Gulliver is to compare his experiences and to find a pattern in them. Because he limits his effort to observing and reporting, he suffers from a kind moral and critical anaesthesia, which makes him accept whatever is before him or focus his attention on whatever he is recording. Because he takes his uncomplicated view of language from the Royal Society, language deceives him and makes him as unreliable a narrator as Wagstaff's vanity makes him an unreliable guide in the matter

47 Martin Price considers the "plain style" as Swift's ideal in the matter (op. cit., p. 31). Whether the satirist believed in the capacity of such a style to escape the pitfalls of subjectivity remains doubtful. Even his didactic writings tend to oppose one kind of subjectivity to another, in the hope of reaching a consensus acceptable to all parties.

of "polite conversation". Language is unreliable, Swift repeats in all his great satires, however it is used.[48] Objective reportage is an illusion. Borrowing the words of a modern historian, the satirist can be said to reject the seventeenth-century notion of an "isomorphic relationship between language and nature" in favour of the eighteenth-century linguistic assumption that language "reflects the structure of the mind."[49]

This imprisonment of the self in its own representations and in the web of language is not the whole lesson of Swift's satirical fictions. However important it is to stress the share that the folklore, conspiracy and comedy-of-manner ingredients have in establishing the subjectivity of the purported authors' or editors' outlooks, the propensity of the blind and ignorant self to fictionalize, and the way the mind of man can remain trapped in the subjective fictions he spins for himself owing to the limitations of language, it is equally capital to stress the fact that man is not irremediably locked up in subjectivity, blindness and error, as any reader of *Gulliver's Travels* knows. A real possibility of overcoming these limitations exists, and it resides in the nature of fictions again.[50] Continually Swift's satires remind the reader that it is possible to break free from the prison of self. They express his belief that the mind of man can reach beyond subjectivity and fictionality and is not condemned to pursue wild chimeras, like Don Quixote. The escape is made practicable by a critical approach to the problem, or by satire with its disturbing disjunctions precisely, which are equivalent to shifts of perspective. The same devices that serve to betray the subjectivity and incoherence of the alleged authors' or editors' visions also serve to transcend their limitations in so far as they are perceived as expressive incoherences. In a world of language where every utterance tends to become a fiction, Swift plays one fiction against another, doing and undoing patterns. He seems also to have understood something fundamental about narrative and dramatic fictions that theoreticians often forget: their freedom to shape their own courses, independently of their author's will. Sometimes they do so regardless of the laws of practical experience, which they contradict. When this happens they lie and in the detection of the lie resides the

48 Angus Ross, op. cit., pp. 34 - 35.
49 Murray Cohen, op. cit., p. xxiv. Paul Fussell (op. cit., p. 8) has also insisted on Swift's indebtedness to Locke.
50 A fact recognized by Everett Zimmerman (op. cit., p. 87), who writes: "Swift's conception of self includes a recognition that the world existing beyond is at least to some degree available as a counter-balance to individual assertion."

truth. Sometimes actual facts or events shape their plausible course. Satire makes use of both possibilities. Either the lie is exposed by reversing the pattern, or the weight of the facts reported belies the views of the purported author. *He* may not be aware that what he reports gives the lie to his initial intention or to his comments, – or he must not notice it, because his function requires him not to –, but the reader cannot help realizing it. The unexpected turn taken by the plot of a framed fiction, and the hard facts, in the form of other people expressing differing views or of events contradicting expectations and opinions, bring, if not the alleged author, at least the reader back to circumstantial reality, or at least a more accurate perception of it, like the blows struck by the flapper, which prevent the Laputan lord from "bouncing his Head against every Post". They give him the corrective jolt which makes social life possible, a social life in which the alleged author, by his incapacity to extricate himself from his subjective outlook, fails to take a constructive part. In so far as the framed tales mislead the reader they contribute to give an image of human error,[51] but, when they betray their own fictionality, they show the triumph of life over fiction, of truth over error, and of communication over solipsism.

Nothing is simple in Swift's satires. When the alleged authors are shown to be carried away by their subjectivity and imagination, or misled by the hold that certain conventions of genre have on their imagination, a superior critical imagination, and a set of other literary conventions, narrative and dramatic, or at least a nimbleness of mind in toying with contradictory fables, enable the satirist to rise above the deceptions. In this sense his folktale, conspiracy and comedy-of-manner plots are first of all the sugar-coating on the lies, as the concrete details of everyday life are their unsavoury substance. But it is not sufficient to say that, with the sugar-coating, Swift simply meets the classical and Augustan requirements for literature to please as well as teach. The plots or overtones of his framed fictions are also the expression of that secondary imagination that releases the intellect from the prison of its subjectivity and from the shackles of fixed, because habitual, thinking patterns. The

---

51 It seems more accurate to say that Swift offers an image of human error than of the relativism of all views, as Françoise Lapraz-Severino argues in *Relativité et communication dans les "Voyages de Gulliver" de Jonathan Swift* (Paris, Didier, 1988). In his *Travels* Swift's imagination repeatedly moves beyond the traveller's experience of changing customs and values to the inescapable fact of human imperfection, which is absolute and not relative.

realistic trappings of the fake contributions to the literary and journalistic debate of the period are forgotten. The new-style traveller and disciple of the Royal Academy, the projector of *A Modest Proposal*, or the anonymous author of "A Description of a City Shower" are no longer credible writers offering their serious observations or reflexions on the contemporary scene. They fully appear as fictional mouthpieces and, even more important, as producers of lying fictions. Lilliput, Laputa, the Ireland of ogres and London are no longer real places on a map: they become symbolic. A ship surgeon's travels, the breeding of children to provide the rich with a new kind of delicate meat, and the cleansing of London by a sudden summer shower, assume their true character as fables about human life. In the process, the literary motifs of the framed fictions play a central rôle as both a source of fictionality and a means of detecting this fictionality.

By giving full play to combinations of folklore, conspiracy and comedy-of-manner ingredients, to inversions of familiar narrative and dramatic patterns, the satirist juggles with his fictions in a way which is not so much meant to impress the reader as to make the fictions attractive before they become acceptable to the intellect. The popular fictions of the framed narratives and dramas force the reader's imaginative consent and his acceptance of their visionary and corrective message. As they are not discursive, they only require him to acquiece in their humorous or grim way of looking at life, and this imaginative consent short-circuits the arguments of the framing discourses, which are those of the fallible alleged authors. In the process, subjective reasoning and biased imagination are defeated by the secondary critical, or satirical, imagination, which is also the voice of commonsense and practical experience, capable of transcending the limitations of subjectivity and habit. Many of Swift's contemporaries felt a positive attraction to fictions which, for them, were able to convey as much, if not more truth than factual reports. They explored the ways in which language could shape a man's views of himself with respect to society and its predominant ideologies. Novelists in particular were soon to conclude that it was possible to construct an alternative reality out of lies and to create a new type of fiction that would be true without being slavishly factual. For his part Swift preferred to think that it was only possible to invent corrective lies out of a world of language. His attitude was more ambivalent than theirs. On the one hand, he loved fictions because he delighted in little deceits of all kinds. They appealed to his sense of humour and to his imagination as means of tricking readers into playing a game for which he set all the rules. On the other hand, and on the contrary of what has been put forward,[52] he was impatient with the idea that language could only express subjectivity and that there was no way out of its fictions. This, as a satirist he could not accept, as his ultimate aim was to ridicule the errors of man and society as they existed and not as they were perceived by those who committed them. Not only were deceits to be exposed, not only was the obstacle of subjectivity to be overcome: satire must also reach back to circumstantial reality, and his objective in combining framing devices and framed fictions was to make this possible. As will be seen below, this satirical device paves the way for a special type of images which focus on various types of social, economic, political or religious behaviour. The choice of these images is emblematic, and in keeping with the nature of the framed fictions. They also distort reality because they belong to the distorting fictions but, as they are presented in contexts which give full play to undeceiving strategies of all sorts, the distortions are not a source of illusion: on the contrary, they complete the satirical denunciations by giving it a direction.

The view presented here of the way language and, above all, fictions work perhaps leaves the impression that very few uses of the former are fully suited to raise discourse above the status of mere personal or collective opinion, and to steer the reader clear of the mysterious, but ambiguous, ways of uncontrolled sympathy or rejection. Such seems nevertherless to have been Swift's deep conviction, judging from the fact that, besides the type of satire that he favoured, he had recourse to only two other forms of expression, both of which betray the same distrust of equivocal thinking: namely, dialectic with its conflicting arguments and counter-arguments which keep a check upon each other;[53] and didactic writing, which guides the reader firmly out of the maze of deception and self-deception. He seldom entrusted, not his thoughts, which were meant to remain private, but his messages to the reading public to other modes of expression than these three.

52 See above note 67, p. 61.
53 James A.W. Rembert, op. cit., p. 103.

Chapter 3

The Metamorphoses of the Body

At the core of Swift's satires and, in general, of their framed tales, stories or comic fragments, there are then images of a particular type. They form certain loose motifs, which constitute the third level of Swift's fictionalizing of reality. Their common denominator is the human body, what it wears and how it behaves: in other words, the body and its metamorphoses. They contain the satires' main explosive charge, in the sense that they refer explicitly to life and society and are easily identified as critical of them. Not all the fictitious journalistic or polemical pieces exhibit folklore, conspiracy and comedy-of-manner constituents; not all popular tales, fables, pages of fictitious history and fragments of comedies of manners are framed; and, clearly, the fictions of the human body do not figure in all the satires. They are, however, another essential feature of the best-known satires, which combine all three structural devices. On the other hand, few texts deal exclusively with the body. The reason is easy to see. In order to develop, the fictions of the body need a narrative or dramatic support: otherwise they remain tropes. This is precisely what happens when the body is mentioned in polemical writings, or in the framing discourses of satirical fictions.

In fact, throughout the work, the body is the source of numerous tropes, as are folktales, fables, figurative proverbs and anecdotes. It is even possible to say that the two types of tropes are typical of Swift's general style, as metaphors from trade, shopkeeping and agriculture are of Defoe's. Here again, it is these very tropes which, developed on a larger scale, provide the fictions of the body discussed in the present chapter.

The same volume of *Irish Tracts: 1728 - 1733* (PW vol. xii) that has served to illustrate Swift's recourse, in his polemical writings, to imagery from fables and folktales, also contains countless examples of references to the body. In *A Short View of the State of Ireland*, the political situation in an Ireland governed from England is compared to "the Condition of Patients, who have Physick sent them by Doctors at a Distance, Strangers to their Constitution, and the Nature of their Disease" (ibid., p. 8). Writing about the treatment that an intelligent man may expect from other people when he ventures into politics, Swift describes him as "mounting the Ladder, and every Hand ready to turn him off, when he is at the Top" (*The Intelligencer*, Numbers v and vii, ibid., p. 39). Using another image reminiscent of his early work and toying with two meanings of the word body, he continues:

And in this Point, Fortune generally acts directly contrary to Nature; for in Nature we find, that Bodies full of Life and Spirit mount easily, and are hard to fall; whereas heavy Bodies are hard to rise, and come down with greater Velocity, in Proportion to their Weight; But we find Fortune every Day acting just the Reverse of this.   (Ibid.)

Dealing with the lack of currency that prompted *The Drapier's Letters*, another *Intelligencer*, Number xix, contains no less than four comparisons between Ireland and the health of the human body. Here is one of them:

this Complaint for the Want of *Silver*, may appear as ridiculous, as for a Man to be impatient about a *Cut-Finger*, when he is struck with the *Plague*: And yet a poor Fellow going to the *Gallows*, may be allowed to feel the Smart of Wasps while he is upon *Tyburn-Road*.   (Ibid., p. 55)[1]

A Vindication of his Excellency John, Lord Carteret offers two allusions to dissection. One is about a real surgeon who, apparently, had been offended by the Earl of Galway and had put aside a hundred guineas to purchase the earl's corpse at his death "to make a Skeleton of the Bones, stuff the Hide, and shew them for three Pence; and thus get Vengeance for the Injuries he had suffered by its Owner" (ibid., p. 157).[2] Swift recommends an improved version of the same treatment on whosoever professes great friendship to someone and then runs him down unjustly behind his back. Such a vile person, he suggests in an outburst again reminiscent of *A Tale of a Tub*, ought to be flayed and dissected alive by his victim. The victim should

to the View of Mankind, lay open all the disordered Cells of his Brain, the Venom of his Tongue, the Corruption of his Heart, and Spots and Flatuses of his Spleen – And all this for *Three-Pence*.   (Ibid., p. 158)

1   Similarly, other significant allusions to health and the body in the same volume on pp. 71, 79, 263, 291.
2   As will be seen below, items such as skeletons were often exhibited to the public as a popular entertainment.

126

One more example will suffice to provide the reader with an inkling of the diversity of such tropes and images inspired by the human body. This is to be found at the beginning of *Maxims Controlled in Ireland*, where Swift asks the reader to "conceive a nation where each of the inhabitants had but one eye, one leg, and one hand" (ibid., p. 131). Such sampling of body imagery from Swift's later work echoes his early work and highlights a quasi medical interest in the human anatomy and the way the human animal functions. This same interest is to be observed in his satirical fictions.

The human body and clothes are a source of perennial concern and fascination.[3] The two terms are frequently opposed to each other. They belong to a set of similar oppositions that go back to the origins of culture and on which man's very distinction between culture and nature is founded.[4] It is true that the way in which people dress may vary considerably between one civilization and another. Certain ages favour gorgeous or stiff clothes, while others prefer light and comfortable ones. The difference cannot always be accounted for by the climate. Other factors, mostly human and economic ones, intervene. Of late years, our Western world has laid the stress on the body, and even nudity. But today's "nudity is only a garment, or worse a uniform, among others", as a philosopher reminds us.[5] In spite of changing fashions, the antithetical relationship between the body and what it wears has nevertheless remained the same throughout the history of mankind, and so has the language of clothes, however differently people may have dressed in each civilization and age.[6] For this reason, Swift's fictions of the body are one of the aspects of his satires most likely to interest the readers of any age.

Swift seems to have understood better than anyone else how he could turn man's interest in clothes to creative account. He was well aware that they did not only afford protection against the inclemencies of the weather. They serve social and psychological functions, as he knew.

3 The body and its representations have been the subject of several studies from psychoanalysts, semeioticians, literary scholars and many other specialists over the past decade. For a brief introduction to the subject, see *Etudes de Lettres* 2 (1983).

4 Claude Lévi-Strauss, *L'homme nu*, Paris, Plon, 1971.

5 Jean Brun, *La nudité humaine*, Paris, Fayard, 1973, p. 51.

6 For Jean Brun, the history of man is that of his desire to escape from his nakedness and the history of fashions is history itself (op. cit., p. 18).

People wear them to project an image of themselves, which in turn helps to define their relations to others and even to their whole environment, animal as well as material. This is why the satirist made the body and its clothes one of the central features of his satirical art. As might be expected from what precedes, his interest principally focused on clothes as signs of rank, status and wealth, but he did not ignore their deeper psychological and sexual functions for all that.

This being said, one could hardly imagine a more radical contrast between seventeenth- and eighteenth-century fashions in dress and those of the twentieth century. Whereas clothes today fit the human anatomy and aim at being comfortable, Swift's time was one of great artificiality and refinement.[7] The daringness of the previous period was severely repressed. Sumptuous and voluminous garments enveloped the body in such a way as to render it unrecognizable.[8] The body was pushed into the background and, when a reaction set in, the attacks were directed, not against the general cut and shape of clothes, but only against the excesses of refinements. The Puritans, who were responsible for this reaction, never questioned the principle itself that clothes should conceal the anatomy as much as possible, because the repressing tendencies of clothing agreed with their religious convictions. It was left to satire to make the most of the fact that the better concealed a thing is, the more one wishes to see through the disguise. As will be seen below, dressing and undressing the human anatomy are at one and the same time two aspects of Swift's fictional use of the metamorphoses of the body and, repeatedly, an image of the satirical process itself. It must be added that he was not the only one to make use of the possibilities offered by clothes and the body as images and sources of comedy. His Scriblerian friends have all been noted to capitalize on the body in their writings,[9]

---

7 Paul Fussell, op. cit., pp. 216 - 218. These pages discuss the rôle of clothes at the time with reference to *A Tale*.

8 John Carl Flügel, *The Psychology of Clothes*, London, The Hogarth Press,[1930] 1950, pp. 111, 149, 156. One of Flügel's theses is that there always exists, in any period, a correspondence between the form of clothes, architecture and current ideas.

9 The Scriblerian Club, formed about 1713, was an association of friends, of which Pope, Swift, Arburthnot, Gay, Parnell, Congreve, Lord Oxford (Harley) and Atterbury were members. Pat Rogers writes: "One of the main principles of Scriblerian humour, in fact, is an awareness of the satiric power of physical misadventure." (*Literature and Popular Culture*, Brighton, Harvester Press, 1985, p. 78).

though none of them seems to have done so as systematically as he has from the beginning of his career, not even Pope. Furthermore, Swift is the most audacious of them all in his treatment.

The eighteenth century's display of extravagant fashions was not the only reason that Swift and his contemporaries had to show a special interest in man's physical appearance. The progress in the study of anatomy and the anthropological discoveries of travellers certainly played an equally important rôle. To begin with the latter aspect, the Western world was becoming better acquainted with other populations, other races and other ways of life. Not only did travel literature offer accounts of cannibals, but the nakedness of the savages was much stressed and discussed, along with other strange customs. Here were people who lived according to the law of nature and felt no shame going around unclad. They did not behave more indecently for being naked. Were they not closer to a state of innocence? Were not clothes signs that civilization had destroyed some of Western man's natural virtues? If everyone more or less agreed that the "Divine Law" had been an improvement on the law of nature, the encountering of such radically different customs clearly caused embarrassment. This embarrassment finds frequent expression in the writings of contemporaries. Every reader remembers Crusoe's bizarre appearance on his desert island: the goatskins clumsily sewn together which he wears as he goes about his daily toil and the cumbersome umbrella that he carries with him on every occasion; and yet he lives in a tropical climate, where nakedness would not only be possible, but more comfortable. After rescuing Friday, a naked savage, from the cannibals of a rival tribe, one of the first things Crusoe does is to give him clothes in which to conceal his nakedness. To the modern reader, not only is Crusoe's reaction amusing, but the eagerness with which Friday complies is odd too. Crusoe's strange getup does not so much illustrate the narrow utilitarian notion of dress as protection as the Puritan one of a simple but complete covering of the human animal. It is in this context that the nakedness of the Houyhnhnms and Yahoos must be appraised, and also, more generally, the recurrent opposition between dress and nakedness in Swift's satires.

As for the other historical factor, the progress in the medical science, it had an even more direct influence on this eighteenth-century fascination with the body, as a result of the recent developments in the study of anatomy. Religious barriers no longer prevented dissections from being performed openly, and the new spirit of experimentation was particularly pronounced in the field of medicine.[10] The study of anatomy and surgery had been, or was being, introduced in universities, and medical schools were opened. Quite apart from that, one consequence of wearing heavy clothing was a lack of personal hygiene, which undoubtedly was the cause of numerous minor ailments. As Flügel puts it: "Beneath the scent, the powder, and the gorgeous trappings, the body was often dirty and ill-kempt – a condition well in keeping with the almost total lack of washing or sanitary equipment that distinguished even the palaces of that time."[11] As the rapid increase in periodical publications of advertisements for beauty products as well as for soaps, powders, creams and other similar items testify, the body hidden from view by the heavy clothing had its revenge.[12]

Philosophically, anthropologically and medically, the human body had in consequence become an object of very general, and not always very healthy and innocent, interest for the public at large. The development of extravagant fashions to conceal a large part of the human anatomy combined with this more intellectual or personal interest to make the body a central concern of the period. Few studies of Swift escape the necessity of discussing, or at least mentioning, his views on the subject, which means that they usually touch upon some aspect or other of his imagery of the human body. Whether the subject is the three brothers' coats, the religion of the Aeolists or the dissecting of a "beau" in *A Tale of a Tub*, the eating of infant flesh in *A Modest Proposal*, or the human size and shape in *Gulliver's Travels*, the focus on man's body and clothes is only too obvious. They are a source of literary invention constantly put to satirical use in the fiction, yet the development of the motif has not been

---

10 Descriptions of dissections and other experiments were regularly published in the *Philosophical Transactions of the Royal Society*, London: see Nos 157: 14, 538 - 539; 165 : 813; 174: 15, 1121. Concerning Swift's reading of the *Transactions*, see Robert C. Olson, "Swift's Use of the *Philosophical Transactions* in sec. v of *A Tale of a Tub*", *Studies in Philology* 49: 459 - 467 (1952).

11 Op. cit., p. 223.

12 To my knowledge, there exists only one brief survey of such advertisements. Most of its illustrations are drawn from the middle years or the second half of the century, and it only touches upon the case of the beginning of the eighteenth century. However it is a valuable one: Jean-Michel Lacroix, "La Publicité des produits pharmaceutiques dans la presse anglaise du XVIIIe siècle", *Le Corps et l'âme en Grande-Bretagne au XVIIIe siècle*, eds Paul-Gabriel Boucé and Suzy Halimi, Paris, Publications de la Sorbonne, 1986, pp. 37 - 47.

investigated on a global scale and what he writes on clothes has received less attention than what he says of the body. Comments have usually been limited to a registering of the reader's disgust at what seems to be "Swift's *physical* repulsion from humanity",[13] and his audacious portrayal of "how loathesome human beings are".[14] Another line of analysis has been to consider Swift's "excremental vision" from a psychoanalytic angle.[15] Central to the psychoanalytical approach is a study of his scatological poems, those few pieces of writing more or less exclusively devoted to the fictions of the body: "Strephon and Chloe", "Cassinus and Peter" and, more particularly, "The Lady's Dressing Room" and "A Beautiful Young Nymph Going to Bed".[16] The purpose of what follows is not to investigate further the meaning of the scatological element, but to examine it in the wider perspective of the fictions of the human body.[17]

It goes without saying that, as a structuring device, these fictions are different in nature from the folktale, conspiracy and comedy-of-manner patterns analyzed in the previous chapter. It has already been said that they are unable to function independently of these other patterns, whose support they need for their development. The folklore tales, conspiracy stories and snatches of comedy provide a continuous thread and the dynamic impetus that the metamorphoses of the body lack by themselves. Even when it ceases to be a trope and becomes an actor, the body can only be represented as what it looks like at different points in its various activities and in varying postures: tiny David threatened by a colossal Goliath, a scrawny Don Quixote rushing at full tilt at windmills.

13 George Orwell, "Politics v. Literature: An Examination of *Gulliver's Travels*", quoted from *Jonathan Swift*, Penguin Critical Anthologies, p. 345.

14 T.S. Eliot, "Cyril Tourneur", *Selected Essays*, London, Faber, 1972, p. 190. See also John M. Bullitt, op. cit., p. 170.

15 This line of argument, initiated by G. Wilson Knight, has led to Norman O. Brown's brilliant study: "The Excremental Vision", *Life against Death: The Psychoanalytical Meaning of History*, London, Routledge and Kegan Paul, 1959, pp. 179 - 201. Carole Fabricant (op. cit., p. 24) has recently questioned the validity of this psychoanalytical explanation and convincingly argued that "the excremental vision" was more likely to be a feature of the Dublin landscape in the middle of which Swift lived as a Dean of St Patrick's.

16 SPW, pp. 519 - 527, 528 - 531, 476 - 480, 517 - 519.

17 On the body motif in the poems and a review of recent views on the subject, see Everett Zimmerman, "Swift's Scatological Poetry: A Praise of Folly", *Modern Language Quarterly* 48: 124 - 144 (1989).

Although not exactly static, such gestures must be grafted onto an existing dramatic or narrative pattern, like the postures of a mime onto the framework of a show, in order to form continuous narrative patterns. On the other hand, the body creates images. Incapable of producing vast patterns by themselves, these images of the body nevertheless have a quality that even folktales do not possess. They offer unlimited possibilities for descriptive elaboration, so that they are what readers tend to remember with or without the help of illustrators. In other words, the human body becomes a central feature in another type of vignettes. A first type was said above to give readers isolated glimpses of everyday life, which were used by the satirist to anchor his fake framing discourses in the circumstantial reality of the period. This second type of vignettes differs from it in two ways: on the one hand it transposes man's everyday life into the fanciful worlds of the framed fictions, and on the other it tends to develop into clusters of images.

With the fictions of the body, Swift comes closest to the powerful visionary spirit of Hogarth and Daumier. Like them, he may have been blind to landscapes but, as soon as there is a human figure to hold the centre of the stage, a scene takes shape. At the same time, the fictions of the body develop something that folk literature, conspiracy stories and comedy of manners contain in germ with their interest in clothes, disguises, metamorphoses, bodies eating and eaten, posing or acting.[18] Finally, the body is also one of the oldest and most popular sources of comedy, a comedy that Swift relished in the popular shows of the time: harlequinades, feats of contortionists or exhibitions of waxworks, skeletons and other curios. At times, when the folklore or comedy-of-manner colouring seems to get lost or fails to appear clearly, the fictions of the body can be said to keep their spirit alive in the meantime, so intimately are they related.

In so far as the fictions of the body form memorable vignettes, they are individually not very different from the tropes and images of the polemical writings. Yet, apart from the fact that they make up chains, they also relate to the text that contains them in another way. They become central to the plot, enlivening it, and acting as the focus of attention and

18 In "Un Corps devenu récit" (*Etudes de Lettres* 2: 7 - 18 (1983)), IVàn Almeida suggests that fictions of the body are not only a frequent motif in popular tales, but that popular tales can also be construed as discussing the very problem of the representation of the body in their own narrative terms.

the central theme, whereas they tend to be peripheral when they appear in the discursive framing discourses, which are modelled on the polemical writings – although it must be granted that no critic on *A Tale* failed to notice the importance of the description of the three oratorical machines from "The Introduction" (PW vol. i, pp. 34 - 38) or of the dissecting of a "beau" in "A Digression concerning Madness" (ibid., pp. 109 - 110). Such passages are rightly felt to be a key to the spirit of the satire, and any discussion of *A Tale* is considered to be incomplete if it does not include some comment on them, but they are not central to the mimetic framing fiction, only to its argument.

Swift proves most inventive when speaking about the body. He is said to have been the first writer to create a bespectacled hero in English literature.[19] Yet he has done far better. There are many ways of drawing attention to the body in art and life, and Swift describes most of them. Firstly, there are certain ways of dressing and behaving that achieve that goal: from the shoulder-knots and gold lace added to the plain coat inherited by Peter from his father, to the Earl of Nottingham's disguise of a chimney-sweeper, to the harlequin Laputans, the reader of Swift's satires is invited to watch an extravagant masquerade of characters in various attires. From the regular occupants of pulpits, "stage-itinerants" or mountebanks' stages, and gallows to the rope-dancing of the Lilliputians, he is treated to a complete review of acrobatic shows and exhibitions of feats of agility. The body can be denuded, rather than dressed, in order to attract attention, and Swift occasionally presents cases of a partial or complete literary strip-tease. Sometimes the strip-tease does not stop at mere nudity: it goes even further to dissection. Death can also draw attention to the physical aspects of the body, as sculptors and painters know. There again Swift makes no bones about pushing the device to the point of cruelty: he has the body taken to pieces, or even eaten.[20] His most original and celebrated device, however, is his use of the two ends of the telescope to enlarge or reduce the size of the body in the first two books of *Gulliver's Travels*. Far from being an easy trick, as Dr Johnson suggested,[21] it was truly modern and innovative, and remains so today.

19 Pat Rogers, "Gulliver's Glasses", *The Art of Jonathan Swift*, ed. Clive T. Probyn, London, Vision, 1978, p. 179.
20 A procedure John M. Bullitt seems to object to: he accuses Swift of "depriving the objects of his satire of all natural humanity" (op. cit., p. 170).
21 James Boswell, *The Life of Samuel Johnson*. See *Swift: The Critical Heritage*, p. 205.

To have the three Brobdingnagian scientists study the tiny Gulliver through a magnifying glass, whilst all the time Gulliver sees the Brobdingnagians as human beings enlarged twelve times, was nothing less than a literary invention of genius.[22]

II

First in importance among the fictions of the body, by dint of the sheer frequency with which they recur in Swift's satires, are the images of clothes, and of the body dressed and overdressed. Swift never ceased to return to the subject and, in spite of the considerable changes in fashion that have taken place between the high-heeled shoes, silk stockings, embroidered breeches and coats, shoulder-knots and periwigs of Louis XIV's time and our own blue jeans, Mao shirt-collars and mini-skirts, these images of the body dressed and overdressed continue to fascinate men and women.

Clothes figure prominently in the arts between the English Restoration and the French Revolution, as they also did in the everyday life of the upper classes. The refinements of fashion found artistic expression through portrait paintings, and in the vogue of the Italian opera, as well as in the form of more popular entertainments like masques and masquerades. Literature inevitably responded to this ubiquitous social importance of the way people dressed. From Molière to Beaumarchais and Sheridan, comedies made use of clothes by having their characters follow, and sometimes even discuss on the stage, the fashions of the day. From using dress as a comic prop on the stage to making it the target of satire was just one step.

To a large extent Swift's interest in clothes is that of a man of his time. He was never rich, but moved in fashionable circles. In London he was often seen in the company of ministers and even at court. In Dublin he knew whoever was worth knowing at the Castle and in the Church. A good coat and periwig were indispensable to him, and his correspondence sometimes gives the impression that they were his most precious possessions, such was the care he took over them. His satires certainly reflect these everyday worries and the great importance that dress had for anyone who led a similar lifestyle. To these personal reasons was later

22 Compare PW vol. xi, pp. 103 - 104 and pp. 112 - 113.

added a political one, in that after his forced retirement to Ireland he also showed increasing concern for one of the country's few economic assets: the manufacture of cloth from Irish wool. He wrote tracts to defend it against the encroachment of foreign imports: *A Proposal for the Universal Use of* Irish *Manufacture* (1720) and *Proposal that All the Ladies Should Appear Constantly in Irish Manufactures* (1729).[23] These tracts once more make direct allusions to the unwise expenditures arising from following the tyranny of fashion, and Swift can be counted upon to find an unusual comparison to underscore the point he is making: "The lavishing of all which money is just as prudent and necessary, as to see a man in an embroidered coat begging out of Newgate in an old shoe" (PW vol. xii, p. 127). But they are also evidence that, by that time, dress was no longer merely a source of individual worry, but rather a matter of national economic concern. Whatever the motivation behind their use may have been, the fictions of the body dressed and overdressed provided Swift with an inexhaustible fund of satirical imagery.

In order to proceed from the straightforward to the complex cases, mention must first be made of the mock comedy, *A Complete Collection of Genteel and Ingenious Conversation.* The characters of its framed fiction, the Sparkishes, Smarts and Nobles of the dialogues, can only be imagined clothed in the full attire of Swift's contemporaries, complete with wigs, embroidered coats, shoulder-knots, lace, silver fringes, high-heeled shoes, and silk stockings. The men also sport embroidered handkerchiefs, snuffboxes and swords,[24] which were necessary adjuncts when it came to displaying one's good manners, and a certain style of leisurely life consisting of walks on the Mall, morning calls upon the ladies, conversations over tea and dinner, and "Quadrill until Three in the Morning" (PW vol. iv, p. 130). From powdered hair to embroidered coat, every item is intended to beautify the human animal and to increase man's feeling of self-importance. Swift's use of clothes in this case is similar to that of the comedies of the period with their "beaux" and toasts.

Clothes put in a discreet appearance, albeit of a different kind, in *The Story of the Injured Lady.* The contrast between the injured lady, once a pretty woman but now a faded mistress, and her rival, the ill-favoured shrew who marries the paramour, is mainly physical. However, as the

23 PW vol. ix, pp. 11 - 22 and PW vol. xii, pp. 119 - 127.
24 PW vol. iv, pp. 153 - 154, 147, 131.

moral tale also has economic and political overtones which relate it to the tracts mentioned above, the author underlines the connection between his folktale figures on the one hand and the sad plight of Irish weavers and the general situation of the country on the other by once again employing two images of clothing. The first describes the offended lady, Ireland, going about "always mobbed and in an Undress, as well out of Neglect, as indeed for want of Cloaths to appear in" (PW vol. ix, p. 4). The second, a concealed protest, describes the way in which the discarded mistress is repaid for her "Love, Constancy, and Generosity": she is given the office of seamstress, not even to her former paramour and his shrewish wife – which would have been vexing enough –, but rather to their "Grooms and Footmen" (ibid., pp. 7 - 8), which makes the slur additionally painful and her financial situation more desperate still. This image is an allusion to the fact that Irish cloth was considered both unfashionable and below the notice of gentlemen and ladies. On the other hand, the implications are here again that garments are visible marks of social and economic distinction.

Far more interesting from a satirical point of view is the use of clothes as disguises. As already noted, it is usually to be found in connection with the conspiracy motif. Not all stories of plotting and underhand dealings mention disguises and, even when they do, not all grant them the same importance. However, for the satirist, disguises are there to be pierced and their wearers are there to be unmasked. In this respect, the use of the motif is intrinsically related to a basic strategy. It should also be noted on this point that Swift's satires actually utilize very old material. Myths, legends and tales offer numerous similar instances of characters who put on the garments of a rival or enemy whose identity they want momentarily to adopt.

Three satires feature disguises in their fictions and use them as a metaphor for the unmasking of the villain: *A Hue and Cry after Dismal*, *The Humble Petition of the Footmen of Dublin*, and *An Examination of Certain Abuses*. To these can be added a fourth, *The Battle of the Books*, where the development of the motif probes deeper and becomes a criticism of the nature of man, not unlike that contained in *A Tale of a Tub* and *Gulliver's Travels*. *A Hue and Cry* is a simple story of literal unmasking. As seen in the previous chapter, the Earl of Nottingham and his man Squash have adopted the undignified habit of chimney-sweepers, in order to spy on the activities of English troops in Dunkirk and, if possible, to thwart the efforts of the Tory ministry to come to a peaceful settlement with France. They have even blackened their faces to be sure of passing incognito. A punning on "black" is evident here, and the double-entendre is particularly successful. Swift blackens his victims' faces to blacken their character, because they have tried to blacken the reputations of their political enemies. The climax of this amusing piece of deception follows their arrest. When the soldiers splash them with pails of water to reveal the true colour of their skins, Squash does not change colour because, under the soot, he retains the complexion of the true "Black-a-more" that he is (PW vol. vi, p. 140). As for the earl, nick-named Dismal, after much scrubbing he does not become pink, but merely shows "some dawning of a dark sallow Brown" (ibid.), which leaves no doubt about his identity, whilst serving to reveal his true nature. The breaching of the disguise suggests the baseness of the earl's political manoeuvres, and the meanness of his character which, the satire adds, cannot be washed clean, in other words reformed. The overall satirical effect is the result of a perfect convergence between the folklore ingredient, which provides the disguise, the conspiracy pattern, which provides the impetus for the action, and the fiction of the body, first disguised and then stripped bare, through which the satirical unmasking is effected. Simple as it is, the choice of the disguise and the action of tearing it away are a splendid example of Swiftian satirical wit.

Not altogether different, though more indirect and subtle, is the way *An Examination of Certain Abuses* and *The Humble Petition* use the motif of clothes as disguises. The case of the petition is particularly characteristic. In it the footmen call upon the Dublin authorities to punish counterfeit footmen who, they claim, wear in public the same "*Green Coats*, and sometimes *laced*, with long *Oaken Cudgels* in their Hands, and without Swords" (PW vol. xii, p. 235). They insist that such counterfeits are a danger to their profession and represent a threat to public order. They will be satisfied with nothing less than the punishment of the offenders. They recommend setting them in the stock or whipping them (ibid., p. 236). The target of this satire seems at first to be the high opinion that footmen have of their profession, but soon, by one of those ironical twists of which Swift is so fond, the satirist makes it clear that some Dublin bucks have fallen so low as to imitate footmen.[25] As for the dress motif itself, it is handled in such a way as to convey the impression that the footmen in question wear their livery as a distinctive social

25 See Herbert Davis's introduction to PW vol. xii, pp. xxxiii - xxxiv.

mark, a sign of privilege and an emblem of their virility. The livery also becomes a kind of uniform for them. It gives them a sense of belonging to a corporate body, whose interests must be taken into consideration and which can, if need be, exert pressures on the authorities. In other words, the clothes motif becomes the pivot of a socio-economic argument in the satire.

In the last three cases mentioned, conspiracy and disguise through clothes are inseparable. The clothes motif becomes the visual embodiment of the conspiracy, of the underhand dealings, or simply of a vague fear of such things. Because of the nature of clothes, the satire, whether it is personal or general, whether it is political or social, takes on an extra dimension as a comment on the manners and organization of a society. Although the clothes of the disguise are the images by means of which the satirical unmasking is achieved, their significance as clothes, as emblems of a class or way of life, is not altogether forgotten. This remains the same as in the comedy of manners of *Polite Conversation*.

With *The Battle of the Books* Swift uses clothes to draw a far more critical portrait of a category of men, the "Moderns", in their dispute with the admirers of the Ancient authors. In this satire the characters do not wear the sumptuous garments of contemporaries, but mediaeval suits of armour, necessary to venture into battle. Suits of armour have a long history not just as heavy protective clothes, but as disguises as well. They are also designed to strike terror into the hearts of enemies. They are symbols of virility and valour and, in legends, they are a type of clothes particularly appreciated by those who want to usurp somebody else's identity, as no one can recognize a man encased in a heavy suit of armour with the visor of his helmet lowered. The satirist remembers all these significations in *The Battle*. No reader can forget the vision of the encounter between Virgil, "in shining Armor, compleatly fitted to his Body", and Dryden, whose armour is so much bigger than his body that, when he lifts up his visor, his "Face hardly appeared from within" (PW vol. i, p. 157). Swift adds that Dryden's "Helmet was nine times too large for the Head, which appeared Situate far in the hinder Part, even like the Lady in a Lobster, or like a Mouse under a Canopy of State, or like a shrivled Beau from within the Pent-house of a modern Perewig" (ibid.). This image of ill-fitted garments is central to the portrayal of the "Moderns". *The Battle* says that their clothing is of their own fashioning and that they are the worst clad for that reason (ibid., p. 147). Bentley, another member of the fraternity, turns up on the battlefield in a suit of armour "patch'd up of a thousand incoherent Pieces" (ibid., p. 160). The image throws up numerous suggestions. The "Moderns" talk big and would like to impress the public. They claim to be original, but they are dependent on borrowings in a way not commensurate with their pretentions. Their borrowings do not constitute wholes. Any reputation they may enjoy is usurped, because it has been acquired fraudulently. More fundamentally, their disguise is meant to help them to be taken for somebody else and to escape the limitations of their own selves.[26] At least it gives them this illusion. The image also leads to another train of thought. Twice *The Battle* stresses the equivalence of books and bodies. The books in the Royal Library where the hostilities begin are the authors' bodies. The text mentions "two mighty Armies of *Antient* and *Modern* Creatures, call'd *Books*" (ibid., p. 153). Translated into the language of books, the image of ill-fitting clothes suggests impressive volumes with impressive bindings concealing thin contents, hotch-potches of useless trash, such as the hack purports to offer in *A Tale of a Tub*.

What is at stake in *The Battle* is the discrepancy between pretensions and performance, between appearances and reality, between seeming and being, which finds its most complete expression in *A Tale* and *Gulliver's Travels*. Concerning the latter, it is sufficient to note here that few characters in literature are so constantly concerned with clothes as the natural covering of their bodies as Gulliver is. From the tale of the secret pocket in which he conceals his glasses to his vain attempt to prevent the Houyhnhnms from finding out that his clothes are not his natural covering, Gulliver shows clothing to be as crucial a preoccupation of man in any situation as either food and shelter, a point on which he is in full agreement with his contemporary Robinson Crusoe. He also attaches great importance to the attire of the populations he discovers. This becomes particularly evident in the cases where the fashions differ from those of Europe, as in the case of the Laputans. Their clothes, mathematically designed and geometrically cut, are as ill-fitted as the suits of armour worn by the "Moderns" in *The Battle*. They betray an exacerbated intellectuality, a spirit of abstraction which ignores the more subtle and rounded forms of life. The cut of their clothes shows their unbalanced personalities. There will be ample opportunity to return to the problem of clothes in the *Travels* in the discussion of the next group of

26 Jean Brun, op. cit., pp. 45, 47.

fictions of the body but, having made allowances for the different folklore patterns onto which the dress imagery is grafted, it is already possible to say that what refers to *A Tale* below applies to the *Travels* as well.

Some works "are rich in local virtues but have only a loose or tenuous overall form", R.S. Crane once remarked, whereas others are unified but relatively barren of pleasure or significance.[27] His observation applies to the offhand way in which Swift handles the folktale pattern in the framed fiction of *A Tale of a Tub*. The folktale pattern is a tenuous unifying factor. On the other hand clothes, which are technically a mere motif in the story, are given a prominence that they are never endowed with in folktales. Most of the adventures that befall the three brothers relate to their inherited coats. These coats are a source of endless imaginative elaboration on the part of the satirist, and they, more than anything else, are responsible for making the tale more meaningful than the mere sum of its parts. It can even be said that the satirist's strategies examined so far have no other purpose but to invite a reading of *A Tale* as the story of what happens to clothes and the bodies wearing them.

The previous chapter has already given to understand that the tale of the three brothers is not so much a history of the three Christian denominations confronting each other in the British Isles, as an account of the relationships of these at the end of the seventeenth century, as well as, more generally, of the real state of people's religious convictions. It is true that the story-teller uses expressions like "in an Age so remote" or "in those Days" (ibid., pp. 48, 51); but, by nature of their very vagueness, they are as typical of what is to be found in any folktale as the "Once upon a Time" with which it begins, and so they cannot be interpreted as referring to any specific events of the past. On the other hand, the actors in the story wear modern dress and lead modern lives, like those in *Polite Conversation*. When the three brothers, the main actors, first appear in good society, the narrator emphasizes the fact that they meet "with a very bad Reception" (ibid., p. 45), because they are not dressed like other people. The secondary actors, their contemporaries, "fill up Parliament–, Coffee–, Play–, Bawdy-Houses" (ibid., p. 47). Fashions originate in Paris (ibid., p. 51), whilst the setting is, in the main, upper-class London. Another preliminary remark to make is that, in the tale

27 *The Language of Criticism and the Structure of Poetry*, Toronto, Toronto University Press, 1953, pp. 182 - 183.

itself, Swift seems to have avoided mentioning religion, God and religious belief in direct connection with the story of the three coats.[28] The two mentions of religion occur, as will be seen below, in connection with society's deification of fashionable clothes and Jack's reaction against Peter's shameless and extravagant endorsement of this deification. A religious reading of the text is possible only at a secondary level of interpretation, but hardly in connection with the plot itself and its development, where clothes worship and Aeolism are mere social creeds, or ideologies which dictate social rituals. On the level of events, the antagonism between the two extremist brothers is social: an opposition between two ways of living. Finally, the narrator explicitly states at the beginning of the story that Peter, Martin and Jack tamper with their plain coats with the express purpose of courting "the Dutchess *d'Argent*, *Madame de Grands Titres*, and the Countess *d'Orgueil*" (ibid., p. 45). The choice of these allegorical names clearly conveys the idea that, in their society, "one of the purposes of decorative dress was . . . to emphasise distinctions of rank and wealth", for the benefit, not only of the aristocracy, but of their imitators as well.[29] What follows furthermore demonstrates that Swift is directly concerned with the dynamics of fashions as an expression of social and sexual rivalries, which result either from envy or admiration and lead to imitation.[30]

To write about the potential of these variations played on the motif of clothes is not easy. As soon as one ventures out of the safe ground of allegorical interpretations in terms of Catholicism, Anglicanism and Presbyterianism – safe because these are accompanied by footnotes and seem to have received Swift's approbation – the images acquire a sort of indeterminacy, whilst at the same time speaking more universally. But the loss of a strict equation between image and idea is the price one has to pay to understand this third constituent of Swift's first great satire. *A*

---

28 On this point the fictions of the body confirm Ronald Paulson's impression that the coat imagery should be considered in terms of man's "conduct and morality", rather than in terms of faith and motives (*Theme and Structure in Swift's "Tale of a Tub"*, p. 150). Summing up the traditional interpretation of what he calls the allegory of the coats, he adds: "It has been noticed by critics that the allegory of the coats is strikingly unreligious, almost secular in tone. Speaking of religion in terms of clothes has seemed impious, and certainly nothing that can be called religious sentiment is to be found in Peter, Martin, or Jack." (p. 149).

29 J.C. Flügel, op. cit., p. 111.

30 Ibid., p. 138.

Tale extends the use of what ought to be called here clothes symbolism further even than in *The Battle*, and only the *Travels* offer a development on the same scale.[31]

The story of the three coats encompasses the sections numbered ii, iv, vi, viii, and xi. In the father's will, the coats are the only legacy and, consequently, the only objects susceptible of being a source of visual imagery. The fact that, in contrast to what often happens in folktales, all three brothers receive the same bequest, does, however, make the latter's importance more conspicuous. The rest of the will contains recommendations: the brothers are urged to live in good harmony, "together in one House like Brethren and Friends, for then you will be sure to thrive, and not otherwise" (PW vol.i, p. 44). It soon appears that women, money, titles and pride make them forget these precepts. The story of the coats itself can be divided into two parts: in the first (sections ii and iv), under the leadership of Peter, but as one, the brothers disobey their father's instructions and add to the magical plain coats which they have inherited anything that the fashion of the day requires. In the second part (sections vi, viii, xi), Martin and Jack are shown to be trying to undo this damage. They would like to restore their coats to their original state, in keeping with their father's last wishes.

Of the coats that the three brothers inherit from their father, the tale says little, except that they are plain and will grow or adapt to the bodies of the brothers, who are enjoined to "wear them clean, and brush them often" (ibid., p. 44). The relationship of the coat to the body is not as a disguise, this time, but as a useful and welcome covering, which will last them "sound and fresh" as long as they live (ibid.). The development of the story makes it clear that it wraps up a mere "sensless unsavory Carcass" (ibid., p. 48), an "inward Mass" (ibid., p. 97) which can suffer from worms , spleen or cholic (ibid., p. 66). This "mass" needs preserving from various diseases, and it is prone to "Turbulence and Convulsions within" (ibid., p. 97), which often result in the emitting of belches, the breaking of wind or in other still more unsavoury manifestations. The coats serve to protect man against warm and cold (ibid., p. 125) and as a

31 When he develops the pictorial side of his fictions of the body in *A Tale* and elsewhere, Swift seems to be well aware that, to use the words of a semeiotician, "what you can see is even more polysemic than what you recount", but that, on the other hand, the body as a reality only becomes intelligible in a narrative (Ivàn Almeida, op. cit., p. 13).

covering to a not very appetizing mass of bones, muscles and entrails. Because of their plainness, they are a guarantee of modesty – two characteristics that Jack and the Aeolists, like Peter earlier, though for opposite reasons, lose sight of at the end of the tale. The same characteristics come in for further discussion at the end of *Gulliver's Travels*, when the Houyhnhnms find out that their human visitor's clothes are an artificial covering which can be removed. They approve of its use: to their eyes, the Yahoo anatomy – and consequently the human one, which so closely resembles it – is ugly. The Yahoo himself being naturally immodest, the horses conclude that it is wise of man to do what he does. Practical but unobtrusive clothes, both tales propose, are a sign of elementary decency, a requisite for man, and at the same time a symbol of his humanity. With the contrast they provide between the naked Yahoos and Gulliver, the *Travels* further underline the fact that the wearing of clothes by humans, unique amongst animals, also distinguishes civilized man from the savage. This was, as already said, a highly topical subject at the time.

Little developed as it is, the image of the plain coat is explicit. It shows first of all that Swift shares with his contemporaries the general conception of clothes as useful and distinctly civilized, on condition, he adds, that they be practical. As for the opposition between this simple garment and the body, which it conceals, it is in the pure Christian tradition. According to this tradition, "attention devoted to the body [is] prejudicial to the salvation of the soul", and clothes help to direct man's thoughts away from his anatomy.[32] Swift goes further. As he is sensitive to ugliness and deformities, he feels that clothes exist not so much to beautify the body as to erase physical inequalities. When he writes that the coat must grow with its wearer, he seems to imply that the best kind of wrapping is that which is adapted to the human anatomy, accepted for what it is, and which similarly avoids either embarrassing or imposing on others. Were it not that it is described as "plain", the coat would undoubtedly be recognized as the mystical dress which transcends the opposition between the body and its covering, abolishes the distinction between being and seeming, and proclaims the spiritual perfection of its wearer.[33]

32 J.C. Flügel, op. cit., p. 57.
33 Jean Brun, op. cit., pp. 11 - 12. The philosopher finds this metaphysical conception of dress expressed in Matth., 28,3; Mark, 9,3; 16,5; Luke, 9,29; 24,4; John, 20,12; Revelation, 16,15; and Swedenborg, *The Sky*, 177 - 181.

The significance of what happens to the three coats in the course of the story is revealed in its full complexity via the two seemingly irrelevant descriptions of the worship of tailors, and of the Aeolists, which interrupt the course of the narrative. Both are in fact eccentric elaborations on the motif of clothes. What other explanation could there be for Swift making his reader lose the thread of the tale, for the first time barely two pages after the start, but to stress the importance of clothes? In this sense, the three pages (ibid., pp. 46 - 48) about clothes worship could even be regarded as completing the exposition. As for the passage on the Aeolists, it represents an even longer interruption of the narrative (ibid., pp. 95 - 101), coming immediately after the crisis which leads to the open rebellion of Martin and Jack against Peter. With the help of the main digressions, it works to delay the dénouement, yet it also reasserts the thematic importance of clothes after a stretch of narrative which has a little lost track of them, by giving a new instance of the false understanding that people have of the social significance of their artificial covering. The twin descriptions of the two sectarian worships and their related philosophies set off a whole train of highly suggestive associations of ideas which enrich considerably the range of connotations of the story of the coats.

The description of the cult people make of clothes begins with that of their worship of tailors. In their society tailors have become lares or household divinities. Without the due propitiation of these hungry and pitiless demi-gods, there is no hope of succeeding in the great world in which it is the brothers' ambition to live. They soon learn to their own cost what it means not to worship at the shrine of such lares, in other words, not to sacrifice to the tyranny of fashion and luxurious living. The central idea put forward by this elaboration of the clothes religion is, of course, that tailor worshippers deliberately distort the original purpose of dress which, according to a certain Christian tradition referred to above, was simply to draw man's attention away from his physical nature. From a means to an end, clothes become for them an end in itself. They are no longer a necessary covering, and a mark of modesty or humanity, as the dying father had taught his sons to believe. Clothes worshippers value appearance above everything else. They have solved once for all the perennial problem of appearance and reality, or, more precisely in this case, seeming and being, by privileging the former at the expense of the latter: for them the essence of man's being as a civilized creature lies in the way he dresses. This way of looking at man has become so deeply engrained amongst clothes worshippers that, in the imagery of *A Tale*, it colours their religious practices and their vision of the world as well as of themselves. They have made the basis of their philosophy the worn – and, around 1690, already outdated – metaphor of the firmament as an ample cloak which envelops the world. They see man himself as "a *Micro-Coat*, or rather a compleat Suit of Cloaths with all its Trimmings" (ibid., p. 47). The clothes are the man, or the man is his clothes. Some worshippers extend the refinement of their implicit ideology further still, and conceive of man's nature as formed by a carcass enveloped by "two *Dresses*, the *Natural* and the *Celestial Suit* (ibid., p. 48). The former dress shows that what all too often passes for man's moral stature in society only consists of the way he wears his clothes. Swift sarcastically underlines the point by having his ingenuous hack ask: "Is not Religion a *Cloak*, Honesty a *Pair of Shoes*, worn out in the Dirt, Self-love a *Surtout*, Vanity a *Shirt*, and Conscience a *Pair of Breeches*, which, tho' a Cover for Lewdness as well as Nastiness, is easily slipt down for the Service of both" (ibid., p. 47)? The *"Celestial Suit"* is neither celestial nor a suit: all the spirituality of which it is capable is another display of refinement according to the tastes of the time:

the Faculties of the Mind were deduced by the Learned among them in this manner: *Embroidery*, was *Sheer wit*; *Gold Fringe* was agreeable *Conversation*, *Gold Lace* was *Repartee*, a huge long *Periwig* was *Humor*, and a *Coat full of Powder* was very good *Raillery*: All which required abundance of *Finesse* and *Delicatesse* to manage with Advantage, as well as a strict Observance after Times and Fashions.

(Ibid., p. 48)

Fashionable ornaments serve as moral sense, intellectual achievement and good manners. As for the carcass, it is just a tailor's dummy to hang clothes on.[34] Gorgeous clothes make man look different from what he is and tend to breed contempt of the body. As it is described, the ideology of the tailor worshippers gives a vivid illustration of that constant illusion in the history of man that fashion can help one to escape from the cage of one's ego, and to create a new, a better, identity for oneself, at the same time as it dissolves all the pluralities within the social body or one of its classes into the identical.[35]

34 J.C. Flügel reminds us that Carlyle used another image, that of the clothes-horse (op. cit., p. 157).
35 Jean Brun, op. cit., pp. 16, 19.

At the beginning of *A Tale*, the three brothers are presented as making this ideology their own. As men in search of social status, a social status founded, as seen above, on titles, wealth and pride, they become imitators of their social betters. Swift seems to have described them in the same terms as the contemporary new rich. Their ambition leads them to follow the frantic succession of fashions, by which one class of people try to keep ahead of their imitators to retain their distinct rank.[36]

Peter himself is both like his brothers and different. As the first half of the tale already demonstrates, he is the only one whom the clothes ideology suits perfectly, because he is a natural lover of clothes. To satisfy his taste, his plain "micro-coat" *must* become a double, or even treble, coat. He is the one who, ignoring his father's injunctions, urges his brothers to beautify their coats with whatever successive fashions require: shoulder-knots, gold lace, flame-coloured satin for lining, silver fringes, embroidery with Indian figures, points tagged with silver (ibid., pp. 49, 51, 52, 53, 54, 55). It is he who recommends the ornaments which, accumulating inside and outside, transform the original coats beyond recognition. Because only finery will pass muster in good society, he goes even further than his brothers and ends up wearing, apart from the triple coat, "three old *high-crown'd Hats* . . . on his Head, three Story high, with a huge Bunch of *Keys* at his Girdle, and an *Angling Rod* in his Hand" as a sign of his superiority (ibid., p. 71). Whether hat, keys and rod are interpreted as the Catholic Pope's three distinctive attibutes is of secondary importance in the dress context. What is significant is that these extra details present him as a man who enjoys sartorial exhibitionism and whose way of dressing corresponds to "an extensive sublimation of the Narcissistic elements from body to clothes."[37] These additions to his costume are an expression of his sense of his superiority. They also show him to be quite conscious of what he is about: they are intended to make him look more impressive than his brothers and give him authority. Sorcerers used to do the same. That they also make him look like a cross between a clown, a housekeeper and a gentleman farmer going fishing is only due to the effect of satirical distortion.

There is no better confirmation that Swift uses Peter's sartorial exhibitionism to expose the illusions created by the wearing of sumptuous clothes than the fact that the satirist also presents him as a clever charla-

---

36 J.C. Flügel, op. cit., p. 130.
37 Ibid., p. 100.

tan, who understands the world better than his father's will. Peter does not forget that, for all their submission to fashion, people are none the less as much concerned with their carcasses as with their smart coats and, like other quacks in the eighteenth century, who advertised their products in almanacs and periodicals, he makes a living out of various medicines he sells to preserve and cure these carcasses, whose very existence clothes worshippers try to ignore as much as possible. In other words, he cleverly exploits the situation created by extravagant fashions that he loves. The story of Peter's coat is that of his absorption into the world.[38] This absorption makes him blind to higher spiritual values, and even to the more elementary existential problems, such as happiness, health, or the notion of social solidarity, which are present so constantly in Gulliver's mind. He belongs to the same category of characters as those of *Polite Conversation*. He makes use of his external appearance to shine in society and succeed in life.

After their quarrel with Peter, Martin and Jack rediscover their father's will and set about putting their coats to rights. Each proceeds according to his temperament, and consequently they achieve very different results. Martin quickly realizes that some of the harm cannot be undone. He slowly and carefully strips away as much gold lace, as many fringes, Indian figures and points tagged with silver as he can. But he is above all anxious not to tear the magical cloth of the original coat to pieces:

> where he observed the Embroidery to be workt so close, as not to be got away without damaging the Cloth, or where it served to hide or strengthen any Flaw in the Body of the Coat, contracted by the perpetual tampering of Workmen upon it; he concluded the wisest Course was to let it remain, resolving in no Case whatsoever, that the Substance of the Stuff should suffer Injury. . .   (ibid., p. 85)

In the above quotation, the expression "Subtance of the Stuff" is interesting, as is that of "the Body of the Coat". They remind the reader that the story is not simply about any sort of coat, but rather about man as a "micro-coat", or about man more concerned with his appearance than his being. Martin's attitude is described in simple narrative terms, but it is difficult to assess. One reason may be that, whereas Peter is what psychologists would call a case study, Martin is proposed as an example to follow. Nevertheless, to the extent that his attitude is contrasted to Peter's sartorial exhibitionism, it would seem to represent "the duty

38 Martin Price, op. cit., pp. 78 - 79.

type", who reacts against the excesses of refinement.[39] What Martin is trying to save in repairing his coat is the modesty and decency of the human character: the nature of a being neither overbearingly proud, nor disgustingly immodest. On the other hand, he has no special compunction about continuing to wear those ornaments which he has been unable to unstitch. This does not suggest resignation on his part, only that no one can claim to wear the mystical dress in this world. Unquestionably, he is the only brother who understands the ambiguous psychological and social functions of dress. He neither finds it wise to scorn clothes nor advisable to flaunt them. He advocates a compromise. By accepting to wear the coat with some remnant of ornaments, he shows that he is neither ashamed of his physical nature nor careless of his appearance. He neither wants to yield to the frivolities of a predominant class nor to embarrass everybody by adopting the extreme opposite attitude. By contrast, Jack is so impatient that he destroys his coat.

The first thing to say about Jack is that he is another case study, like Peter. He exhibits all the traits of the man who rebels against dress.[40] He has not resigned himself to wearing clothes and, given the chance, he more or less unconsciously destroys what he feels to be a straightjacket. Jack despises the very ends for which coats were invented. In winter he goes about "always loose and unbuttoned, and clad as thin as possible, to let *in* the ambient Heat" and in summer he wraps himself up "close and thick to keep it *out*" (ibid., p. 125). It is his skin and muscular eroticism which makes him reject clothes as he does. In addition, he is totally indifferent to his appearance, has no sense of decency and only a weak desire to protect his body.

The story of how Jack gets rid of the ornaments on his coat serves to show two things. On the one hand, it demonstrates that Jack's action is destructive to more than just his coat and, on the other, it highlights the kind of metaphysical justification, or ideology, upon which his destructive work relies, in order to make his gesture of defiance towards Peter and his rejection of clothes worship acceptable. With regard to Jack's rough handling of his magical coat, the reader follows the process of its degradation with increasing astonishment: Jack "strips", "tears", "pulls", "rends", and "flays off all", until he finds himself in "a ragged, bobtail'd

39 J.C. Flügel, op. cit., pp. 97 - 98.
40 Ibid., pp. 91 - 94.

Condition" (ibid., pp. 87, 88). But all this apparently thorough destructive work completely fails to change the character of the decorative dress. Whereas Martin's coat recovers "the State of Innocence",

his own was either wholly rent to his Shirt; or those Places which had scaped his cruel Clutches, were still in *Peter's Livery*. So that he looked like a drunken *Beau*, half rifled by *Bullies*; Or like a fresh Tenant of *Newgate*, when he has refused the Payment of *Garnish*; Or like a discovered *Shoplifter*, left to the Mercy of *Exchange-Women*; Or like a *Bawd* in her old Velvet-Petticoat, resign'd into the secular Hands of the *Mobile*. Like any, or like all of these, a Meddley of *Rags*, and *Lace*, and *Rents*, and *Fringes*, unfortunate *Jack* did now appear. (Ibid., p. 88)

He continues rubbing his coat every day against rough walls, in order to eliminate the last remnants of lace and embroidery. In his fury, he even sullies the coat (ibid., p. 122), with the result that the rags no longer serve their rôle of modest covering and protection. To this must be added that, in so far as he adopts an attitude which is directly the opposite of Peter's, he acts as his brother's rival. Like him, although in a different manner, he seeks after status and power, and he wants to impose his ideas and attract disciples.

According to the clothes philosophy, the human anatomy, and likewise the inward man, has no value in itself and, as clothes have become all that is noble, human and alive in man, "carcass" is a suitable word with which to describe the more humble side of his humanity. But, when all belief in the value of coats is dismissed as ill-judged, there remains nothing to believe in but the "sensless, unsavory" mass of flesh and the "carcass", and there is no barrier left to prevent a total loss of self-respect and moral and physical depravity. This is what happens to Jack.

Nakedness, the revelation of the carcass, is the link between the ragged condition of the coat, whose substance has been damaged, and the anti-religion of the Aeolists. In this fiction, Swift describes Jack's and his disciples' conception of human nature. To the clothes worshippers' overvaluation of dress, they oppose their total disregard of it, with the result that their attire draws attention back to the body's physicality and eroticism. This attitude betrays an even greater ignorance of the original purpose of clothes. For the Aeolists, Swift says, the "sensless, unsavory Carcass", not the coat, is the whole man, and this carcass is animated by a "*Spirit*, or *Breath*, or *Wind*" (ibid., p. 95).[41] What counts is no longer breeches and shoes and snuffboxes, but belches, wind and gripes, the mechanisms of the digestive system, and sex – and not even the circulation of the blood, Swift seems to be implying, which had been one of the great medical discoveries of the previous century. Man's humanity is reduced to its lowest animal denominator: that of a hyperactive physical organism. The protuberances of the body, namely the ears, the nose, the genitals and the buttocks, are mistaken for the seat of spirituality and called "spiritual Excrescencies" (ibid., p. 129). No wonder, then, that Jack and the Aeolists behave with such little modesty and in such grotesque manner:

> At other times were to be seen several Hundreds link'd together in a circular Chain, with every Man a Pair of Bellows applied to his Neighbour's Breech, by which they blew up each other to the Shape and Size of a *Tun*; and for that Reason, with great Propriety of Speech, did usually call their Bodies, their *Vessels*. When, by these and the like Performances, they were grown sufficiently replete, they would immediately depart, and disembogue for the Publick Good, a plentiful Share of their Acquirements into their Disciples Chaps. (Ibid., p. 96)

Long before our century, Swift had realized that sex and excretion organs are closely related and that, as Yeats's Crazy Jane tells the Bishop, "Love has pitched his mansion in / The place of excrement". At the same time, he stresses the fact that the importance which the Aeolists grant to man's animal nature by scorning appearances has stifled true spirituality or, at least, distorted its nature as effectively as the opposite attitude of the tailor worshippers. Jack has convinced himself and his followers that the human body is self-sufficient as well as divine. Is it going too far to suggest that he is here as much an embodiment of the contemporary philosophical sensualism as of Nonconformism?

What is particularly puzzling is why Swift associates Jack and the Aeolists' attitude to clothes with Puritanism. The virulence of his attack is all the more surprising as his conception of dress bears much resemblance to that of the contemporary Nonconformists. Perhaps it is this similarity that accounts for a greater degree of satirical distortion in this

---

41 For Ronald Paulson (op. cit., pp. 114, 103 - 122), this metaphor of the body in *A Tale* is of Gnostic origin and an image of the dissenters' view of man as self-sufficient. This may be the case, but it is at least as important to stress the relevance of his fictions to current manners.

case. Anyway, there results from it a difficulty of interpretation. It must be first of all remembered that, in his fiction, Jack's fury is directed against the excess of ornaments added to clothes, but not against Peter's "artificial sartorial body" itself.[42] That Jack continues to resemble his brother in spite of his efforts to restore his coat to its original simplicity proves first that he has no understanding of the true use of clothes and second that, in spite of his temperament, he is powerless against the predominant tastes of society. Martin was well aware of the limits that his action could have. Jack's behaviour implies an equal ignorance of the nature of his coat and of that of his body. Moreover, the radical elimination of ornaments does not solve the problem of the fundamental ambiguity of clothes. To Peter's "sublimation of the Narcissistic elements from body to clothes", he substitutes a type of dress which redirects attention to the body. Instead of becoming a safeguard against immorality, the absence of ornament even endows the natural and artificial curves of the anatomy, Swift's "protuberances", with sexual connotations. Such a usually harmless organ as the nose is then capable of arousing undesirable emotions. The ultimate result is that to disregard the ornamental function of dress is the surest way of awakening prurience and giving the body more central importance than it should have.

Swift's criticism is social and political as well as psychological and moral. Jack and the Aeolists are not simply reacting against the tailor worshippers and those who court "the Dutchess *d'Argent, Madame de Grands Titres*, and the Countess *d'Orgueil*." What they challenge is a type of social distinction which appears mainly based on such superficial criteria as the wearing of fashionable garments, and they can rightly be suspected of wanting to overthrow their opponents, much as the "Moderns" want to overthrow the "Ancients" in *The Battle of the Books*. Their attitude represents a threat to the social order, in the same way as Peter's policy leads to corruption. What the Aeolists propose is in fact a sort of prefiguration of libertinage as an instrument of subversion. Their revolt against civilization considered as a source of restraint, and their cult of a physical spontaneity, are shown to lead them to manifest a "strange Disposition to Nastiness and Dirt" (PW vol. ix, p. 263), not unlike that of the Yahoos.

---

42 J.C. Flügel, op. cit., p. 222.

For all their difference, both the clothes symbolism of the tailor worshippers and the anatomical symbolism of the Aeolists represent inversions of values.[43] A Tale describes not one, but two such inversions. The tailor worshippers are guilty of overvaluing appearances, and of living by them. Jack and the Aeolists, by rejecting this overvaluation of appearances and without really wanting to do so, fall into the opposite trap of reducing human nature to a mass of guts. Both attitudes express the same wish to transform reality in an attempt to change man. Both ideologies are equally dangerous for man to follow and give an oversimplified picture of his double nature.

The coat imagery in A Tale tells an altogether different story from that reconstructed with the help of the footnotes. With the fate of the magical coats, the story of the three brothers can be once again observed to move beyond the customary allegorical reading of the satire as a new apocryphal version of the Christian myth of man's disobedience and of the divisions between Christians. The two cults mentioned in it are both non-religions: the former, as a deification of worldliness, comes close to a cult of wealth, and the latter, as a reaction against worldliness, represents another kind of materialism. The exfoliation of the coat imagery shows that the very choice of dress and fashions to satirize the attitude of churchmen and believers alike place the tale of the three brothers at least as much in the literary category of the criticism of social manners as of religious criticism. The two fantasies of the tailor worship and of the Aeolists have no other purpose but to make the underlying principles of each attitude imaginatively more explicit by presenting them as the world views of two anti-religions. To assert this is not to deny that Peter can embody a certain Catholic attitude, Martin an Anglican one, and Jack a Presbyterian one; rather, it shows that the central range of associations is slightly different, much richer and much wider. The satirist deplores both excesses, of extreme worldliness and of a type of unworldliness, which he detects among his contemporaries. When he shows Martin steering a safe middle course, he seems to be recommending the third brother's attitude as the right one and offering the image of the plain coat worn with care and simplicity as an example of ideal, rather than practical, conduct. It is not Anglicanism, but a proper attitude to our own spiritual and animal nature, that the imagery proposes as the

43 Martin Price, op. cit., pp. 78 - 79.

good attitude to adopt. Several years later he takes up the same image in the *Travels*, in order to make much the same point.

The social symbolism of the coats and the religious allegory do not coincide, unless it is assumed that the three main characters of the tale are taken to represent the social attitudes of three types of clergymen: Peter, the Jesuit or High Church prelate who dreams of social assimilation in the higher spheres of the aristocracy like the new rich or ambitious upper merchant class – the fact that Peter is a successful salesman reinforces the parallel; Jack, the Low Church or Presbyterian minister who rejects worldliness as irreligious and implicitly battles to have his honest intentions, his merit and his work judged at their own value, as did craftsmen and smaller traders; and Martin, the clergyman who adopts a supple and pragmatic attitude which avoids offending anybody, at least as far as is consistent with his religious mission. This being said, there can be no doubt that the clothes motif is an aspect of the satire likely to continue to interest readers because of its rich suggestiveness, whereas the allegorical element has come to sound outdated and nearly everything has been said about it that needs saying.

This account of the fictions of the body dressed would be incomplete without a few remarks on the body dressed in rags described in other works. In Ireland Swift was at least as accustomed to seeing the body poorly dressed around him, as he had been to seeing it overdressed in London. In his work, dire poverty has its dress, like wealth. This dress borders on nakedness, yet it is still a dress of a sort. Besides the already mentioned lady of *The Story of the Injured Lady*, who goes about "always mobbed and in an Undress . . . for want of Cloaths to appear in", but who is still comparatively well off, there are the much more terrible portraits of beggars. They are not just slovenly dressed like Jack in *A Tale*. In Book ii of *Gulliver's Travels*, they are described as wearing rags covered with lice, and the rags leave the sores, tumors and infirmities of the body in full view of anyone approaching them:

There was a Woman with a Cancer in her Breast, swelled to a monstrous Size, full of Holes . . . a Fellow with a Wen in his Neck, larger than five Woolpacks; and another with a couple of wooden Legs, each about twenty Foot high.

(PW vol xi, pp. 112 - 113)

As for the lice crawling on the beggars' clothes, they are what Gulliver finds most disgusting. He could see, he explains, distinctly the Limbs of these Vermin with [his] naked Eye, much better than those of an *European* Louse through a Microscope; and their Snouts with which they rooted like Swine. (Ibid., p. 113)

There is an intriguing parallel between this description of the beggars' rags and that of the three brothers' coats in *A Tale*. Like the latter, the beggars' clothes are themselves not a single dress: the lice cover the rags, so that they seem to wear their rags and a layer of lice; but instead of adding pride of appearance to the main dress like the shoulder-knots, gold lace and embroidery with Indian figures, or of at least concealing human frailty, the lice make the rags look totally inadequate as covering. This message is underscored in the above quotation by the use of the word "naked", which is transferred from the body, the object depicted, to the eye of the viewer in the expression "naked Eye", and by the comparison of the lice to pigs rooting in the earth. The wearing of such rags is actually represented as worse than mere nakedness. Not only do the rags not conceal the mass of flesh and bones and its sores as it should but, far from protecting the body, they add to its physical discomfort and the ills of life.

This same vision of rags as unprotective and unconcealing undress recurs in *A Modest Proposal*. The proposal even opens with it. This time the beggars' outfit is not examined under the microscope, but multiplied by the hundreds and even thousands, which is as shocking:

It is a melancholly Object to those, who walk through this great Town, or travel in the Country; when they see the *Streets*, the *Roads*, and *Cabbin-doors* crowded with *Beggars* of the Female Sex, followed by three, four, or six Children, *all in Rags*, and importuning every Passenger for an Alms. (PW vol xii, p. 109)

It goes without saying that rags do not inspire any ideology, or "religion" to use the imagery of *A Tale*. Ideologies assert the privileged status of an influential group or attempt to justify it. Rags are simply connected with squalor, the sad circumstances in which the unprivileged live. They are the badge of deprivation, loss of self-respect and reversion to the near animality portrayed in the Yahoos. If finery is an arrogant assertion of rank and wealth which tends to make the wearer forget his frail human condition, rags convey the impression that a significant proportion of men and women in the world are denied the possibility of developing a true sense of self-respect and of feeling truly human. Swift's various kinds of "undress", especially the rags covered with lice, are reminiscent of similar instances of anti-dress or anti-decoration found in myths or legends: pictures of bodies covered with excrements or dust or other unpleasant covering symbolizing the state of nature as opposed to that of culture.[44] The body dressed in rags is not exasperating in the way the sloven attire of Jack and of the Aeolists is: their self-display is indecent. What poor clothes fail to cover properly is the saddening and pathetic spectacle of human misery.

Between the straightforward use of clothes in *Polite Conversation*, the motif of disguise in the conspiracy stories and the sophisticated treatment of the clothes motif in *A Tale*, the *Travels* and *A Modest Proposal*, there does not seem to be much in common. Clothes are put to widely different uses. They serve to develop an economic argument, to symbolize hypocrisy or villainy, and to caricature mistaken attitudes and beliefs. Yet above and beyond these differences can be detected one similarity, for clothes are also connected consistently with the idea of the true worth of man, of his honesty towards himself and others, and of his self-respect, a self-respect of which he is all too often deprived by others or which he is all too ready to sacrifice in the pursuit of wordly gain. Above all, it is clear that dress is not so much for him a kind of protection and decoration as a means by which he tries to hide and to transform himself. Man, Swift's metamorphoses of the body dressed remind us, changes clothes to substitute the costumes of rank and social position for that of his native condition, which he is all too enclined to forget. In this the rich are inevitably more successful than the poor. But man's excessive concern with his appearance or a complete state of destitution are equally sure ways of emptying him of his very being.

III

The respective fates of Peter and Jack and that of the beggars have suggested just how closely related clothes and nakedness are. The body overdressed is a body that begs to be undressed, or, rather, stripped naked. The fashions of his time made Swift realize the possibilities opened up by this paradox for his satires, long before the champions of libertinage, Choderlos de Laclos, Sade or John Cleland exploited it in their novels. The body stripped naked, dissected or put to death – these

44 Claude Lévi-Strauss, op. cit., p. 348.

last two being other ways of stripping it naked – forms the second group of his fictions of the body. Clearly, the satirist is not concerned with their erotic appeal: for him, strip-tease means moral dissection.

Here again Swift draws from the same sources as myths, legends and tales, in which losing one's clothes is frequently equivalent to regressing to a state of nature, to losing one's strength, growing thin and weak, and to being exposed to death.[45] To a generation of people who either invested much of themselves in their clothes or who felt reassured by what they wore, all these connotations of the idea of nakedness must have sounded alarming. Coming across a naked man was an unsettling experience, and a man deprived of his clothes was a man stripped of the marks of his rank, education, wealth, religion, as well as of protection and social support and the sense of being a creature apart. Nakedness appeared as great a leveller as death – which was also why they were closely connected.

To many readers, the motif will principally bring to mind two of his poems, as already said before: "The Lady's Dressing Room" (1730) and "A Beautiful Young Nymph Going to Bed" (1731), both daring descriptions of undressing. But other instances, similar and different, abound in the other satirical fictions. Sometimes these incorporate veiled glimpses and partial exhibitions of parts of the body that are shameful to a greater or lesser extent. Sometimes the motif of stripping is elaborated just enough to overstep the limits of propriety, and sometimes it is not. Jack, with his ruined coat, certainly reveals more of his anatomy than is consistent with good manners, which puts him outside the pale of acceptable society. On the other hand, when Gulliver undresses before his Houyhnhnm master, who is simply curious to know what he looks like without his artificial covering, he does so as far as modesty allows. Finally, the unmasking of satire – for which the undressing is a central metaphor, as already noted with reference to the disguise motif – can at times be ruthless, as the body stripped naked becomes the image of a body spewing and excreting. In these instances, the reader is no longer witness to the breaching of a pretence, of a false appearance, but rather to the revelation of essential human frailty.

Swift's often deplored coprophilia and his "excremental vision" are, in fact, one aspect of this more comprehensive dominant image of the body stripped naked, dissected and put to death. What has been called their

45 Ibid., pp. 26 - 27, 307.

obscenity should be regarded as an extreme degree of satirical unmasking, and as occasional "retorts to degeneracy"[46] – moreover it is not so much obscene as uncompromising. The vision of Caelia excreting, on which "Cassinus and Peter" ends (SPW, p. 531), is of the same order as, and in itself no more shocking than, those discussed above of the beggars' bodies covered with lice or of the Aeolists' immodest behaviour.

Swift makes the most of people's fascination with the human anatomy. He even has a predilection for the cases which offend the canon of classical statuary: bodies aging or decayed through lack of care and disease. His satires also give expression to an embarrassment that seems to have been a new feeling at the end of the seventeenth century: a phenomenon of fairly recent date. At the same time, he probably reckons that people will always be like his Lilliputian soldiers, when they are ordered to parade between Gulliver's legs:

His Majesty gave Orders, upon Pain of Death, that every Soldier in his March should observe the strictest Decency, with regard to my Person; which, however, could not prevent some of the younger Officers from turning up their Eyes as they passed under me. And, to confess the Truth, my Breeches were at that Time in so ill a Condition, that they afforded some Opportunities for Laughter and Admiration.

(PW vol. xi, p. 42)

Swift's nearly obsessive awareness of man's physical nature is, of course, not limited to this fascination and embarrassment.

Except in the poems already mentioned, the fictions of the body stripped naked never play the same extensive part that the story of the body dressed does in *A Tale* or *A Hue and Cry*. The reason for this is not far to seek. The possibilities of metamorphosing the body with changes of clothes are endless, whereas undressing can only be a final act. When it is part of the motif of the avatars of the body dressed, however, the fiction of the body stripped naked always represents a crucial moment in its development. In "The Fable of Midas" it characteristically coincides with the climax of the satirical portrait. The verses conclude with the image of the modern Midas, the Duke of Marlborough, divested of his *"Golden Spoils"* (SPW, p. 102). Otherwise undressing is the subject of limited passages or flashes of the imagination. At any rate, what it does not possess in extension, it compensates for by its memorable vividness.

46 Nigel Dennis, op. cit., p. 57.

More than any of Swift's satirical fictions, *Gulliver's Travels* is full of the cumbersome presence of the human body. For the Lilliputians, the "Great Man-Mountain" (PW vol. xi, p. 34) is not only a danger, but an enormous organism to feed. Every day it needs for its sustenance no less than six cows or oxen and forty sheep in meat, "together with a proportionable Quantity of Bread and Wine, and other Liquors" (ibid., p. 33). But "A Voyage to Lilliput" is not just the story of an enormous body, which the inhabitants of an island admire, feed and use to their own advantage before they decide to get rid of it: it is also that of a swarm of tiny, nimble and dexterous bodies, endowed with cleverness and cunning, which surround that huge body. When Gulliver wakes up on the shore after his shipwreck, he feels no less than forty of them climbing around on his body like big ants (ibid., pp. 21 - 22). In Brobdingnag Gulliver finds that his physique is totally inadequate to cope with the situation. Not only are the giants a threat to his security, but even small animals and birds represent a danger. Furthermore, the huge bodies of the Brobdingnagians, which at close quarters look like ours would under the microscope or through the telescope, are a nightmare to him. Even the young maids of honour at court, who probably comprise a bevy of some of the best-looking girls in the country – the equivalent of today's film starlets – appear frightening and disgusting to him:

Their Skins appeared so coarse and uneven, so variously coloured when I saw them near, with a Mole here and there as broad as a Trencher, and Hairs hanging from it thicker than Pack-threads . . . (ibid., p. 119)

In the third voyage, far from having achieved the ideal of the life of pure intellects, devoted to the pursuit of knowledge and wisdom, the Laputans, the academicians of Lagado and the Struldbruggs offer three illustrations of how man's physical nature gains revenge when its claims are ignored. Finally, amongst the Houyhnhnms and Yahoos, Gulliver is made increasingly aware of his sad resemblance to the latter, as compared to the unpretentious and comely anatomy of the horses. From being physically cumbersome in the first two books of the *Travels*, the body becomes mentally and morally so in the last two. Man's physical nature is of central concern in the satire. Dress, food and shelter, which have been seen to be Gulliver's recurrent preoccupations as a traveller, as well as significant motifs, are merely aspects of this more central motif, which is tightly woven into the texture of the hero's adventures and is inseparable from the narrative. It would hardly be going too far to say that Gulliver's adventures are those of his body, more often than those of his mind.

The peripeteia of this cumbersome body, which is the focal point of Swift's satire, is not only that of an organism fed, dressed and sheltered, but also that of a body concealed at times for protection, or out of a sense of modesty, and sometimes unwillingly revealed. The passage quoted above referring to the Lilliputian officers who, marching under the arch of Gulliver's legs, cannot resist looking up, shows once again that the covering of the body is never complete, and that it often discloses more than it is supposed to. New or worn, clothes always reveal as much about the human anatomy as they conceal, a fact which is well known. In the first voyage, modesty prevails: when he wants to relieve himself, Gulliver does not denude the necessary part of his body in the open. He creeps into a secularized temple, the only building large enough to receive him, or he waits for the night to protect his privacy (ibid., p. 29). Young men and naughty ladies in Lilliput may imagine as much as they like: Gulliver's clothes cover his body. On only one occasion does he display a private part of his anatomy, and then he does so in all innocence. When he opens his fly to extinguish the fire that has broken out in the empress's apartments, his action can surely be judged as merely boyish. Moreover, it takes place at night. In the circumstances, only a warped mind could take offence.

In Book ii are to be found the first traces of an immodest undressing of the body. Certainly, the nine-year old Glumdalclitch, Gulliver's little nurse, who dresses and undresses him when she gets a chance is as girlishly innocent as Gulliver was in the above scene. For her the tiny man is effectively a living doll. Nevertheless the situation is awkward: after all, Gulliver is a fully-grown man, although twelve times smaller than a Brobdingnagian, and he understandably feels ill-at-ease:

This young Girl was so handy, that after I had once or twice pulled off my Cloaths before her, she was able to dress and undress me, although I never gave her that Trouble when she would let me do either my self.   (Ibid., p. 95)

Indecency becomes a more serious issue when, at court, the maids of honour – the word "honour" has an amusing resonance in the circumstances – use Gulliver as a sex object: Gulliver remembers that one of them "would sometimes set [him] astride upon one of her Nipples" (ibid.,

p. 119). More generally, it is in the land of the Brobdingnagians that all anatomies, owing to their sheer size, appear at their most vigorous. Whereas in Lilliput, propriety was assisted by the miniaturization of human nature, so that immodesty could only be cerebral, in Book ii physical vitality and the human anatomy become obtrusive because of the sheer size of the giants.

In the third voyage, in many respects so different from the other three, the motif is as clear to see as ever. Gulliver is the privileged observer of the revolt of the body against the intellect, or of their divorce. In contrast to Book ii, Book iii describes a loss, and even the disappearance, of physical vitality and activity. Instead, abstract, mechanical and unproductive activities take their place.[47] In some of these activities, the body even becomes the object of detached experiments, which lead to what used to be called the mental alienation of their authors. At the same time the reader is treated to another instance of the body being stripped naked. At first an appearance of propriety is maintained: the traveller is struck by the speculative attitude of the Laputans, and by their lack of concern for the way they dress. He is impressed by this show of unworldliness. There is even a delicacy in the Laputans' manners that he had not found amongst the Lilliputians and Brobdingnagians. While new clothes are prepared for him, Gulliver is asked to wait, for six days, in a sort of fitting room and private apartment (ibid., p. 162). However, an uneasy sense of indecency soon grows within the reader, when it becomes clear that this exaggerated delicacy is connected with their exacerbated intellectuality. The body is not literally undressed, as in Books ii and iv, yet the presence of matters of the flesh becomes more and more apparent. The geometrical cut of the Laputans' garments evidences two great failings in their wearers: they scorn and try to ignore their physical nature and, in doing so, their general attitude becomes hostile to life itself. Gulliver soon learns that their scorn of the flesh has led their wives to find consolation with lovers from the subject island of Balnibarbi, since their husbands are too wrapped up in their speculations to pay attention to their need for affection. Moreover, what he had first taken for unworldliness is in fact linked with a thirst for destruction: the inhabitants of the flying island want to exterminate all those who rebel against their domination, and the image of the flying island crushing

47 Kathleen Williams, *Jonathan Swift and the Age of Compromise*, Lawrence, Kansas University Press, 1959, p. 173.

rebels is an image of cerebral activity destroying physical life. Though the natural philosophers at Lagado have a different attitude, and are not guilty of the same extreme intellectuality as the Laputans, their researches are marred by what, to a twentieth-century reader, suspiciously looks like misguided use of the human intelligence and a Freudian compensation for a devious sexual development. They are dirty and unkempt creatures, who perform nauseous experiments and show an obsessive interest in the biological processes of food absorption and evacuation. As for the Struldbruggs, their bodies become so ravaged with decrepitude, as they grow older, that it is the death toll for their minds. The Laputans simply look odd, but the other two groups of characters cause the body to look dirty, ugly, devoid of vitality and sadly mortal. In Book iii, the avatars of the body, which this time do not concern Gulliver personally, become serious, and the change of emphasis paves the way for the last voyage.

In "A Voyage to the Houyhnhnms" Gulliver is literally, albeit privately, stripped naked. This provides a contrast to the strip-tease of the Brobdingnagian maids of honour, which had been voluntary and indecent, and to Glumdalclitch, who had been child enough not to see any harm in handling the tiny visitor like a doll. In Book iv, Gulliver conceals his nakedness as long as he can from the horses, since he is aware that it is the secret of his dress that distinguishes him "from that cursed Race of *Yahoos*" (ibid., p. 236). When his secret is found out, he owes his host an explanation and a demonstration:

I therefore told my Master, that in the Country from whence I came, those of my Kind always covered their Bodies with the Hairs of certain Animals prepared by Art, as well for Decency, as to avoid Inclemencies of Air both hot and cold; of which, as to my own Person I would give him immediate Conviction, if he pleased to command me; only desiring his Excuse, if I did not expose those Parts that Nature taught us to conceal. . . Whereupon I first unbuttoned my Coat, and pulled it off. I did the same with my Wastecoat; I drew off my Shoes, Stockings and Breeches. I let my Shirt down to my Waste, and drew up the Bottom, fastening it like a Girdle about my Middle to hide my Nakedness.

My Master observed the whole Performance with great Signs of Curiosity and Admiration. He took up all my Cloaths in his Pastern, one Piece after another, and examined them diligently; he then stroaked my Body very gently, and looked round me several Times; after which he said, it was plain I must be a perfect *Yahoo* . . .

(ibid., pp. 236 -237)

Though there is a certain delicacy in the proceeding, the strip-tease is as complete as in "The Beautiful Young Nymph Going to Bed", and the strict privacy in which the scene takes place does not make things any less painful for Gulliver. Imagine Robinson Crusoe deprived of his heavy costume of animal skins, appearing naked before Friday: his situation cannot compare with that in which Gulliver finds himself. When he removes his clothes before the astonished horse, the human body is doubly stripped naked. In the first place, Gulliver is forced to expose his anatomy of a poor forked creature to the view of an animal judge – which is, in itself, bad enough as he feels that his clothes give him his identity as a civilized European and as a human being. Secondly, his exposed nakedness leads to the verdict that, physically, he stands lower than the worst creatures he has ever encountered. The reasonable horse concludes that Gulliver's anatomy is not only similar to that of the Yahoo in its essentials, but also inferior "in point of Strength, Speed, and Activity, the Shortness of [its] Claws" and in several other aspects (ibid., p. 260). Worse still, the horse finds the human shape so odious that he has "therefore begun to think it not unwise in us to *cover* our Bodies, and by that Invention, conceal many of our Deformities from each other, which would else be hardly supportable" (ibid.). The horse's kindness does not make his judgment any less galling for Gulliver, and when, soon after, as if to confirm the cogency of its conclusions, Gulliver is sexually assaulted by a young female Yahoo, who finds him bathing naked, he can only feel that he has been stripped of all the insignia of his human superiority. Thus concludes the story of what happens to Gulliver's body.

A survey of the fictions of the body in Book iv would, however, be incomplete without an account of the Yahoos, and of what happens to their bodies. The Yahoos are mainly naked bodies, and the shape of these bodies contrasts with the attractive form of the horses. They combine ugliness, dirtiness, deformities, a total lack of modesty and weaknesses resulting from intemperance with an uncommon animal vitality. Above all, they belong to the same zoological species as Gulliver, they are hominids, as he realizes all too well. The more inescapable the resemblance – at his arrival on the island he had not noticed it –, the more callous his attitude towards them becomes. At the precise moment when the Houyhnhnm master discovers the secret of the clothes, Gulliver is thinking of making himself new clothes with the "hides of *Yahoos*" (ibid., p. 236), and it is soon after he comes to recognize his kinship with them that "the Skins of *Yahoos*, dried in the Sun" supply the leather of his shoes (ibid., p. 276). Finally, it is their skins again, and their fat, which provide the materials needed for the construction of the canoe in which Gulliver sails back to the world of men. His attitude to the Yahoos is in every respect similar to that of the projector who proposes the consumption of human flesh to Irish landlords in *A Modest Proposal*. The cruel irony of Gulliver's treatment of Yahoos has often been noted: the suggestion seems to be that you can always rely on man to treat his brethren inhumanly. But within the framework of the fictions of the body clad and stripped naked, it takes on a simpler meaning. Finding himself in a world so different from his, where the links in the chain of beings are inverted, Gulliver has come, like Crusoe to attach too much importance to his clothes as a distinctive feature of his humanity and as his ultimate tie to civilization and to his species. Deprived of his clothes, he loses his bearings. The contradictions in his attitude are symbolic. His walking in shoes made out of almost human skin – the word "hide" dehumanizes it without concealing the evidence – goes further: it amounts to trampling all over a condition which he vaguely sees as his own, although he refuses to accept it. This refusal is the source of his misanthropy: he hates himself for being a Yahoo. But the misanthropy is founded on an error of judgment, for the clothes imagery suggests that Gulliver is not a Yahoo. He fails to recognize what even the horses see clearly: namely, that what is important is not that he is physically a Yahoo, but that he wears clothes and is a teachable creature, ready to learn, to imitate and improve – at least when given sound models. The *Travels* point out that his "Teachableness, Civility and Cleanliness astonished [his master]; which were Qualities so opposite to [the Yahoos]" (ibid., p. 234). His mistake is to accept the horses' prejudiced views, when they run down the human anatomy by comparing it to that of the Yahoos. Deprived of what he considers the emblem of his humanity, his clothes, he all too readily comes to see himself as nothing more than an inadequate body.

At the same time the body provides a link between the "realism" of the traveller's account and the fairy tale's inverted patterns. Its fictions articulate the two other components of satire and, as a result, find themselves structurally at its centre, as the central subject around which all the others gravitate. *Gulliver's Travels*, like the tale of the brothers Peter, Martin and Jack, is a story of the body clad, but even more – and this is the significant difference – of the body stripped naked, as indeed a sense of the presence of the human anatomy underneath the clothes pervades the whole satire. Clothes and the naked anatomy are again central images which draw attention to the complexity of human nature. It is because of them, not because the hack or Gulliver discuss this or that general topic, that the two satires are satires on man. *A Tale* is concerned with appearances. In it, the fictions of the body serve to illustrate the aberrant implications of extreme social attitudes, which amount to a kind of philosophical folly, ignorance of the true nature of man and neglect of elementary moral sense. The *Travels* for their part deal with the inescapable truth that man is a being of flesh. In them, the fictions of the body bring out the moral and intellectual implications of ordinary prejudices or failings, those of man in civilized society or of a Robinson Crusoe confronted by a totally new reality.

What happens to Gulliver and what he sees others do brings out the fact that man's physical nature is the source of his energy and health as well as of his frailty and sickness, that all men are equal in their animality, that a large part of their life is spent in trying to meet the needs of the body and in obeying or disciplining its impulses, and that it must neither be made too much of nor too little, as both attitudes render man inhuman. The alternating of moments when clothes are the focus with views of, or allusions to, the naked body shows both man's reluctance to accept his physical nature for what it is, and the opposite mistake of his giving it too much importance, to the point of forgetting the greater importance of the life of the mind. The characters' attitude towards clothes and nakedness, ever ambiguous, a mixture of pride, curiosity, disgust, fascination and wilful neglect, conveys the impression that it is difficult to be totally and utterly human. Dressed or undressed, the body becomes a global symbol of the illusions man lives on, of the empty claims he makes for himself and others and, more particularly in the *Travels*, of his inability to reconcile the contrary needs of his nature and to meet the demands of moral, spiritual, social and animal life at the same time.

From the fictions of the body stripped naked to those of the body put to death and dissected, there is but one step, and even this is sometimes so minimal that the skin comes off with the clothes. These images are for Swift another way of stripping human nature naked and an extension of the same satirical strategy of moral dissection. They push the satirical device further, and their emotional impact is all the greater for it. In *Gulliver's Travels*, nudity is more often suggested than portrayed and, where it is depicted, the description stops at the external appearance of the human anatomy. With the strip-tease of the poems, the stripping naked transgresses the frontiers separating anatomy from the less aseptic science of physiology, or else it turns into a dismantling of the body that is meant to reveal that there is decrepitude lying in wait for it. The dissection which, like the undressing, need not be literal or complete each time, is presented as the stripping away of just one more layer of the ornament or protective covering with which man has attempted to forge a falsely secure sense of identity for himself, or has tried to conceal his true nature from himself and others. The naked body shows man denuded of the pride of rank, wealth and all the marks of his power and prestige. But a young and healthy body can still be a source of vanity and illusion. On the other hand, when it is described as a decaying anatomy, a mass of bones and organs and dead flesh, the body confronts man with the incontrovertible truth of his mortality, and of the equality of all, and it deprives him of the comfort of his last illusions. Two early satirical fictions have remained famous for their vivid physiological notations: *A Tale of a Tub*, and its outgrowth, the more specifically physiological *Discourse concerning the Mechanical Operation of the Spirit*.

Swift displays a specialized interest in anatomy and physiology. He is fond of describing the way organs function. He delights in utilizing the contemporary mechanistic jargon of medical studies and goes so far as to invent spurious physiological mechanisms to account for certain opinions and intellectual attitudes. He does so in his description of the sect of the Aeolists and of the fate of Jack in *A Tale*, as has already been noted. *The Mechanical Operation of the Spirit* puts forward a similar type of mock physiology:

Now, the Naturalists observe, that there is in human Noses, an *Idiosyncrasy*, by Virtue of which, the more the Passage is obstructed, the more our Speech delights to go through, as the Musick of a Flagelate is made by the *Stops*. By this Method, the Twang of the Nose, becomes perfectly to resemble the *Snuffle* of a Bag-pipe, and is found to be equally attractive of *British* Ears . . . (PW vol. i, pp. 184 - 185)

In a similar way, several aspects of Puritan preaching and its effect receive strictly physical explanations.

Quantitatively, physiology plays a much less important part in *A Tale* than in *The Mechanical Operation*. On the other hand, *A Tale* contains some the most ruthless images of dissection proper. They are found — and this is particularly interesting — in the hack's introductory pieces and digressions which, unlike the story of the three brothers, are not about dress and the body. They are not numerous, and yet they have struck readers for two reasons: some of them are so unexpected in their context as to stick out like sore thumbs, and they are usually the most shocking and unbearable images. On closer examination, however, they are not as isolated as they look. The framing discourse is scattered with references to the human anatomy used figuratively. These constitute an important motif. They are all of the same nature and serve three functions: the human anatomy is a metaphor for the written word and the literary work; it figures in the discussion of inspiration, or what could be called the physiology of composition; and it plays a rôle in certain Hogarthian vignettes referring to the life of the period in so far as this life is connected with the causes of inspiration. A link between the three categories is provided by words like "carcass" (PW vol. i, pp. 28, 77), "flaying" (ibid., pp. 20, 109), "devouring" and the action of consuming flesh (ibid., pp. 21, 36 - 37, 117). These images of the body are introduced in such a way as to follow a loose progression and form a structural contrast with the images of the body dressed in the tale itself, as they recur in further parallels. The more overdressed the brothers become, the more obsessed they are with their coats, the more insistent the images of dissection become, until the moment when Jack's tearing of his coat and the purported author's apology of madness draw the two threads of imagery together, in order to effect the satirical climax.

Regarding the use of the body as a metaphor for the literary work, little need be said apart from the fact that it is the least conspicuous and that its character is similar to that found in *The Battle of the Books*. Indexes are referred to as the posteriors of books (ibid., p. 91), whilst twice the writer describes the action of satire as a lashing of the body (ibid., pp. 29, 30).[48] As for the descriptive physiology of inspiration and writing, Swift might have called his mock scientific explanation "Physicological", a term he chooses to employ to define another phenomenon (ibid., p. 37). Though developed erratically and perfectly fanciful, his description constitutes a fairly consistent theory of how works are inspired and composed, and how they affect readers. Each process is presented as resulting from an organic function. He has his hack argue that the physical health of the writer is fundamental to inspiration, and that *A Tale* originated amongst the same disorders of the body as all other great schemes that imperil the stability of society: the

48 For other similar illustrations of the metaphorical use of the body, see pp. 20 - 21, 64, 117, 132.

grand designs of conquerors, philosophical systems, new religions, or sectarian beliefs like Jack's Aeolism. According to the purported author, a particular diet produces specific vapours in the head, which must find an outlet somehow. He sums up his theory thus:

Now, I would gladly be informed, how it is possible to account for such Imaginations as these in particular Men, without Recourse to my *Phoenomenon* of *Vapours*, ascending from the lower Faculties to over-shadow the Brain, and thence distilling into Conceptions, for which the Narrowness of our Mother-Tongue has not yet assigned any other Name, besides that of *Madness* or *Phrenzy*.   (Ibid., p. 105)

This is how fictions are produced, and men prefer them to reality because they are more impressive or beautiful. By postulating this direct relationship between the physical health of the writer and the quality of his productions, the satirist's physiology of literary activity makes it possible for him to utilize the life and character of the man as an image of what his work is worth.[49] He explains in the same manner how readers or an audience are affected.[50]

Swift does not clarify the link between the physiology of composition and the Hogarthian vignettes about dissection, or between that and the image of the body as a mass of guts. But when, at the beginning of "A Digression in the Modern Kind", he unexpectedly and without explanation has his hack writer mention his experience of holding lectures on a dissected carcass until it stank (ibid., p. 77), he does at least suggest that a rotting body can stir a writer's inspiration as surely as a woman's charms or "Pudenda" (ibid., p. 92), and that his alleged author is momentarily exchanging his identity as a traditional Grub Street hack living in a garret for that of a Warwick-Lane physician. It prepares the reader for the fascination and horror elicited by the allusions to the woman flayed alive, and to the "beau" stripped of his clothes and skin, whose persons, comments the hack in a splendid understatement are much "altered . . . for the worse" (ibid., p. 109). With these two images, the reader is treated to an experiment in open bowel surgery, a somewhat disgusting experience which, whatever the purported author may say about the blessed state of moral blindness, brings the imagination back

---

49 It is as though Swift had anticipated the development of eighteenth- and nineteenth- century biographical criticism, which was soon to be applied to his own work, and warned readers against its biases.

50 See also pp. 27, 37 in *A Tale*.

imperatively to the corporeal state of man. Here again, Swift seems to be suggesting that the loftiest planes of man's imagination, spirituality and intelligence are still affected by his physical and mortal nature. He impresses upon the reader his vision of man incapable of rising much above the imperfection of his flesh. Needless to say, he does not believe every word of his physiological theory. His reducing of the life of the mind to a purely physical dimension is a fictional move similar to his having Gulliver or his tailor worshippers believe that the essence of humanity lies in their clothes. Nowhere else, neither in his poems nor in *The Mechanical Operation* did he go so far as in *A Tale* in his pitiless stripping of human nature down to its naked core. As already observed, the satirical use of the body dressed and stripped naked is so extreme, precisely because Peter's use of clothes is so arrogant and extravagant.

Nothing reveals more clearly the earthly nature of the human body than death itself, and the third way of stripping man naked, in order to lay bare his frailty and earthly nature, is precisely to put him to death. Swift has different ways of doing so. In *The Last Speech and Dying Words of Ebenezor Elliston*, a man is about to be executed; in *The Bickerstaff Papers*, Partridge dies of a mysterious illness; in "A Satirical Elegy on the Death of a late Famous General", Marlborough has just died, "From all his ill-got honours flung, / Turn'd to that dirt from whence he sprung" (SPW, p. 229); "Verses on the Death of Dr Swift" shows the Dean passing away amidst the indifference of his acquaintances; and in *A Modest Proposal*, infant flesh is devoured.

Inflicted or incurred, death has always brought out the futility of certain human endeavours, the cruelty of men towards one another, and the character of a human society more often bent on self-destruction than on self-improvement. In the mock ballad of *Ebenezor Elliston* and the burlesque "death-bed scene" in *The Bickerstaff Papers*, death is the moment at which to confess the truth after a lifetime of crimes or lies. The former work shows truth emerging from a body not unlike that of the hack in *A Tale*, a body ravaged by lewdness, the pox, drink and scuffles (PW vol. ix, pp. 40 - 41). The latter work presents it as the expression of a body weakened by an inexplicable distemper. "I saw him accidentally once or twice about ten Days before he died," the anonymous gentleman who reports Partridge's death writes, and observed he began very much to droop and languish, although I hear his Friends did not seem to apprehend him in any Danger. About two or three Days ago he grew ill; was confined first to his Chamber, and in a few Hours after to his Bed. . .

(PW vol. ii, p. 153)

Approaching their last hour, both characters and alleged writers experience a belated outburst of moral conscience. The fact that these confessions are uttered by wasted organisms serves to reflect back on the lives of the two individuals, and reminds the reader of man's common lot of shared imperfection and sinfulness. There is a clear suggestion that they get the death that they deserve. Different is, of course, the case of "Verses on the Death of Dr Swift". In the first place, it concerns a worthy Dean, and then it focuses on the reactions of his contemporaries to his demise. There too, nevertheless, the fictions of the body form part of the satirical strategy. The account of the Dean's last months is told in such a way as to rid the writer of all illusion as to the esteem in which he is held by his acquaintances, friends and former admirers, at the same time as he becomes less and less physically present to them. Disillusion grows as physical weakness increases, and there is more than a hint in this parallel development that a man is quickly forgotten when he ceases to be present. The report of his last illness is prefixed with a vignette which introduces the motif of the dying body:

> Dear honest Ned is in the Gout,
> Lies rackt with Pain, and you without:
> How patiently you hear him groan!
> How glad the Case is not your own!   (SPW, p. 497)

And as the old man is wasting away, his friends report:

> " He hardly drinks a Pint of Wine;
> "And that, I doubt, is no good Sign.
> "His Stomach too begins to fail . . ."   (ibid., p. 499)

The first instance of the devouring of human flesh has been traced to *A Tale*. There, however, its consumption has been seen to be metaphorical and sacramental, an image of the way a writer communicates his experience. *Gulliver's Travels* flirts with it in the voyages to Brobdingnag and Houyhnhnmland. However, it is with *A Modest Proposal* that the anthropophagous inclination of man becomes, by means of a recognizable folktale motif, a central image of his cruelty and callousness, and of his dark impulses to make others suffer, whilst he relishes the spectacle. The purported author of *A Tale* ends up turning away from the horrible sight of the woman flayed alive. The projector of the *Proposal*, displaying a complacency that not even a cannibal would feel, muses on the different ways of preparing young flesh for the table:

. . . a young healthy Child, well nursed, is, at a Year old, a most delicious, nourishing, and wholesome Food; whether *Stewed*, *Roasted*, *Baked*, or *Boiled*; and, I make no doubt, that it will equally serve in a *Fricasie*, or *Ragoust*.

(PW vol. xii, p. 111)

Worse still, he suggests that their skins, "artificially dressed", be used to "make admirable *Gloves for Ladies*, and *Summer Boots for fine Gentlemen*" (ibid., p. 112) The fiction of the body partly devoured and partly utilized to adorn the rich shows the exploitation of the poor to be a kind of licenced criminality and cannibalism, such as was thought to exist only among the most primitive savages.

Swift makes clever use of the attitude of his time towards nakedness and the human anatomy. As a satirical device, the stripping naked and putting to death of the human body enable him to offer striking images of man's consciousness of his imperfect being. Reversing the Christian argument that one should pay more attention to one's spiritual than to one's physical nature, the satirist insists on the fact that it is not useless to remind people that they are also made of flesh. If an excessive interest in clothes leads man to forget his double nature, or if it causes him to spiritualize his animal being by idealizing its shape or scorning the ethical function of clothing, it is evident that stripping him naked is first of all a corrective measure. It denudes men and women of that by means of which they try to assert differences of rank, wealth, and power, or to acquire a false sense of security and protection. It deprives them of that "extension of the bodily self" which makes them feel important and proud.[51] Finally, beyond physical nakedness, it reveals another nakedness in human nature, which might be called moral. As he undresses man and has him dissected by his brethren, the satirist lays bare some of his most cruel instincts. The pleasure that he seems to take in reviling man's physical nature has often been considered as a reaction on his part which psychologists have described as characteristic of the prudish type of

51 J.C. Flügel, op. cit., p. 34; see also pp. 36 - 37.

man.[52] However, it is once again difficult to distinguish between what is purely satirical and what is personal. It is not at all impossible to imagine that, as a man, Swift did not find the human body loathsome and that he was even able to admire it on occasions, like anyone else. Does not Gulliver suggest that it is only the difference in size that makes the Brobdingnagian maids of honour look so little appetizing to him? It is perhaps more correct to say that Swift does not object to nakedness *per se*, but only to the lack of modesty that he assumes to be inseparable from an unbalanced attitude to the two sides of our nature.

More than the fictions of the body dressed, those of the body stripped naked run counter modern sensitiveness and beliefs. As already said, nakedness today has become a dress, which it was not for the satirist's contemporaries. In current post-Nietzscheian philosophies, it is not that which must be unveiled, but an envelope which must be torn to enable man to tune in to the pulse of anonymous cosmic life, to the flux of prepersonal forces and desires: it must dissolve, so that man can escape from himself.[53] When Swift peels off layer after layer of clothes, skins and organs, pursuing the process until the body is either a corpse or a mere collection of organs, he does exactly the opposite. The ritual of undressing does not aim at giving man a new identity or at freeing him from his condition. It reinforces his sense of individuality, fundamental loneliness, frailty and nakedness. Man has always felt ill-at-ease in his skin, but Swift's fictions of the body stripped naked intend to make him feel still more deeply ill-at-ease, by reminding him insistently that neither covering nor dissolving of the skin will ever enable him to escape from his condition. Among so many aspects of Swift's satires which continue to strike the reader, his presentation of nakedness is perhaps unique in that it sounds more unacceptable today than it once did.

The fictions of the body dressed deal with the superficialities of life, with the social manifestations of certain weaknesses, with appearances and with arrogance: with human life on show, which was becoming the subject-matter of the new genre, the novel. These fictions are usually associated in Swift's work with the comedy-of-manner components of the framed fictions, or with the deceits of conspiracy stories: *Polite Conversation, A Hue and Cry* and *The Humble Petition*. The fictions of the body stripped naked, dissected, devoured or killed probe deeper into

52 Ibid., pp. 96 - 97.
53 Jean Brun, op. cit., pp. 77, 78, 87, 105.

the psychology of man, of his unadmitted impulses, appetites and fears. They set in motion in the hearts of the readers discordant harmonies and play with the various effects of attraction and repulsion, fascination and horror. This second type of fictions of the body is the most disturbing, as is shown by the multifarious reactions aroused by them amongst readers and critics of many different generations. The two-hundred-year-old critical debate on the merits of Swift's writing, which has divided the literary fraternity between those who admire and love him and those who despise him, has nearly always centred, consciously or unconsciously, around this aspect.

IV

The fictions of the body dressed, or stripped naked, dissected and killed, are, for Swift, satirical ways of exploring the essence of man's humanity. The third category of fictions of the body can be said to deal with accidence rather than essence: with the body's social behaviour and with the way men communicate with one another without words in certain circumstances.[54] It draws attention to further aspects of man's physical nature and still other shortcomings resulting from his being made of flesh. It is simply more concerned with the details of everyday life, with social relationships and ordinary events, and less with human nature. In these instances, the satirist draws his inspiration from the art of posturing and from that of the contortionists. The body is shown in various postures and performing certain acts.

The fictions of the body in action cannot be mentioned without referring to Swift's interest in, and utilization of, the popular shows of his time, just as it is impossible to discuss the fictions of the body dressed without alluding to eighteenth-century fashions. Swift seems to have been fond of contortionists, posture-masters and rope-dancers; of prize fighting and fencing matches; of exhibitions of giants, pigmies, madmen, and exotic animals; of harlequinades, waxworks and conjurers' tricks; and of moving picture shows. This taste for popular entertainments is

---

54 Communicating by means of the body, its clothes and gestures is a prominent theme in the *Travels*, as anyone might expect in an account of newly discovered peoples. Françoise Lapraz-Severino offers a thorough analysis of its development in *Relativité et Communication dans les "Voyages de Gulliver"*, pp. 401 - 452.

particularly evident in the first two books of *Gulliver's Travels*. It has been said of Book i that the "whole Lilliputian regime . . . rests on the exercise of posturing: court ceremony is made up of elaborate physical contortions, the strict protocol and graceful pointlessness of which clash with the intrinsic turpitude of the obsequious placeman taking part."[55] As for "A Voyage to Brobdingnag", it has been suggested that the way in which Gulliver behaves, and the box in which he lives and is carried around the kingdom, are reminiscent of the fate of animals exhibited at fairs.[56] Swift's use of what a recent study calls his "puppetry",[57] is not restricted to these two voyages. It features in the last two books of the *Travels* as well, and in many other works: in *A Tale of a Tub, The Mechanical Operation of the Spirit, Polite Conversation* and *Directions to Servants*. There is only to think of the behaviour of the characters portrayed in these pieces, or of the harlequinade of the somnambulant Laputans to be convinced that they are reminiscent of puppets in a puppet show.[58]

Besides examples of posturing, contorting, acrobatics, fencing, exhibiting of giants, savages, pigmies, animals and various freaks of nature – the *lusi naturae*, as Swift calls them –, conjuring tricks, moving picture shows, and salestalk such as was heard at fairs, which all belong to the same category of cheap entertainments offered by travelling groups of acrobats, mountebanks and other professional or non-professional entertainers, there are also, in Swift's works, the closely related military parades and executions, episodes worthy of moving picture shows, like the flying island in Book iii, and visits to interesting institutions, like that to the Academy of Lagado, which resembles those prized entertainments of Londoners, the guided tours of Bedlam, the celebrated madhouse, or of Gresham College, the college of physicians situated not far away,

---

55 Pat Rogers, *Literature and Popular Culture*, p. 77.
56 Aline Mackenzie Taylor, "Sights and Monsters and Gulliver's *Voyage to Brobdingnag*", *Tulane Studies in English* 7: 29 - 82 (1957).
57 John Traugott, "The Yahoo in the Doll's House: *Gulliver's Travels* the Children's Classic"(*English Satire and the Satiric Tradition*, ed. Claude Rawson, Oxford, Blackwell, 1984, p.140). The author indicates another possible source of inspiration for the *Travels*: the child's fantasy in playing with dolls and toy soldiers.
58 In *Jonathan Swift: A Critical Biography* p. 86), John Middleton Murry associates the three brothers in *A Tale* with the puppet show, and John M. Bullitt (op. cit., pp. 170 - 181) devotes a chapter to the subject of "Puppet Symbol."

which offered its experiments to visitors.[59] Special mention must finally be made of "A Voyage to the Houyhnhnms". In the fourth book of his travel account, Gulliver describes a race of ur-savages, the like of which would again have delighted any visitor at a fair, and intelligent horses, a kind of prefiguration of today's cartoon animals, which must have reminded readers of fables. Besides, the Houyhnhnms and Yahoos recall animals trained in the precursors of circuses and exhibited in the first menageries.[60] To all this must be added the fact that Gulliver's behaviour is a further source of amusement when he learns to whinny in order to communicate with the horses (ibid., p. 234), imitates their gait (ibid., p. 279),[61] or kisses the hoof that his master Houyhnhnm raises to his mouth (ibid., p. 282).

If the fictions of the body posing and acting have been studied from an historical angle, little has been said, on the other hand, of their meaning-fulness, and of their importance as a fictional component. Like clothing, poses and gestures convey various messages. They feature prominently in social and religious rituals, which are ways of imposing some sort of order on the chaos of experience. They are designed to produce certain meaningful effects, which sometimes require the use of clothes. The way a priest holds his hands or a minister walks out of a room can be as significant as what they say in certain circumstances. In Swift's satires, the body's postures and movements are not only regularly associated with entertainments, they are even more frequently suggestive of empty, or gratuitous, rituals. Something must finally be said of a number of human activities by which man tries to transform his surroundings in order to change himself, or at least to escape from his condition. They are precisely the activities that interest the satirist. At any rate, there is usually something strongly mock-ritualistic or mechanical in the body's poses, gestures and activities, which reveals a lack of self-control on the part of its owner, or an ignorance of his true nature. Postures display the

59 Marjorie Nicolson, "The Scientific Background of Swift's "Voyage to Laputa", *Science and Imagination*, Ithaca, Cornell University Press, 1956, pp. 110 - 154.
60 According to OED, it was about this time that the menagerie appeared. The first mention of the word has been traced back to 1712.
61 In "Paradise Gained by Horace, Lost by Gulliver", *English Satire and the Satiric Tradition* (p. 163), William S. Anderson comments: Gulliver "has obviously failed to distinguish the relatively praiseworthy rationality of the Houyhnhnms, which he can and should imitate within human limits, from the equine form in which it here exists, a form that he cannot, and yet foolishly tries to, imitate."

body resting, contortions display it gesticulating or performing an action, and activities show man pursuing unproductive experiments.

At rest, it arouses curiosity, especially when it looks different or unusual: every reader remembers the inert mass of Gulliver's body that the Lilliputians find lying stretched out on their shore; the towering body of the same Gulliver, between whose spread legs the Lilliputian army is ordered to march; the tiny Gulliver proudly displaying to the giant figure of a little Brobdingnagian girl the short sword with which he has killed a giant rat nearly as big as himself. Such visions have been a source of inspiration for generations of illustrators of the *Travels*. No less of a spectacle are the postures of the Yahoos. The descriptions given of them stress their deformity, and their resemblance to nimble baboons or mandrills, yet with habits that are still more disgusting. The point is not to debate whether Yahoos are monkeys or hominids – they can be said to look like the former, but their social organization seems to be similar to that of the latter –, but rather to indicate that their behaviour recalls that of the favourite animals of public street shows and, perhaps, menageries, and that their posturing is akin to that of human bodies:[62]

They had no Tails, nor any Hair at all on their Buttocks, except about the *Anus*; which, I presume Nature had placed there to defend them as they sat on the Ground; for this Posture they used, as well as lying down, and often stood on their hind Feet.

(Ibid., p. 223)

Cumbersome or insignificant, proud in its bearing or deformed and soiled, the body at rest is in turn admired, studied and loathed. It is also a constant source of embarrassment to its owner, being either too unwieldy or too frail, too attractive or too repulsive. It is repeatedly an obstacle, and hence diverts upon itself the attention that should belong to the other aspect of man's nature, comprising his mind, his soul and his intelligence. It is presented in a way which defamiliarizes the human anatomy. Magnified as though by looking at it through a telescope, or diminished as though by holding the telescope the other way round, made impressive by what it wears, decayed beyond expression by age or illness, it is either an unattractive or a pitiful object to contemplate. Postures and poses are usually void of meaning and convey little more than the fact that man's

---

62 See Thomas Sheridan, *Life of Swift* [1784], *Swift: The Critical Heritage*, pp. 234-235.

physical nature holds a central place in his everyday life, and in social contacts in particular.

The body is more often presented gesticulating or performing than resting. It carries out its contortions with panache, although with dubious taste. They arouse amazement, which in turn gives rise to suspicion. In *A Tale* and *The Mechanical Operation*, the portrayals of dissenters, of enthusiastic, supposedly inspired, preachers and of their congregations, range between the playfully childish and the preposterous. The vile picture painted of the Aeolists in the former is not without analogy with the description of the Yahoos in their worst behaviour. Differently keyed, and yet similar, are the feats and pranks of servants in the *Directions to Servants*, and the fluttering about, the affecting of manners, the flaunting of fans, the dropping of handkerchiefs and the exhibitions of snuffboxes in *Polite Conversation*. Here is an example of the way footmen should handle dishes and plates when they serve at table, according to the *Directions*:

As to that absurd Practice of letting the Back of the Plate lye leaning on the Hollow of your Hand, which some Ladies recommend, it is universally exploded, being liable to so many Accidents. Others again, are so refined, that they hold their Plate directly under the left Arm-pit, which is the best Situation for keeping it warm; but this may be dangerous in the Article of taking away a Dish, where your Plate may happen to fall upon some of the Company's Heads. I confess myself to have objected against all these Ways, which I have frequently tried; and therefore I recommend a Fourth, which is to stick your Plate up to the Rim inclusive, in the left Side between your Waistcoat and your Shirt . . .   (PW vol. xiii, pp. 34 -35)

Such clowning is sure to destroy the decorous ritual of a great dinner. The previous chapter has described how the dialogues of the handbook on the art of conversation are given the overall pattern of an inverted comedy, and how they reverse the usual relationship between words and gestures. This in itself already reveals the prominence of the gestural comedy which accompanies the words of the characters even where, owing to the dramatic nature of the dialogues, this gestural comedy is merely hinted at: it is a matter in which the reader must make use of his own imagination. Wagstaff's introduction provides the necessary directions to this effect, so that the reader cannot fail to see the importance of mime.

Once again, it is in *Gulliver's Travels* that the physicality of the body's contortions is underlined most forcefully. Swift frequently puts the emphasis on the physical exertions of his characters: in the rope-dancing which enables the king of Lilliput to choose his ministers; in the jumping or crawling under a stick which is the basis for the endowing of merit by the same king; in Gulliver's various demonstrations of his skills to Brobdingnagian audiences – he performs "monkey-tricks" on the table of a Brobdingnagian inn (PW vol. xi, pp. 97 - 98),[63] sails in a miniature boat in a bowl (ibid., pp. 120 - 121), and plays an English tune on a gigantic spinet:

A Fancy came into my Head, that I would entertain the King and Queen with an *English* Tune upon this Instrument. But this appeared extremely difficult: For, the Spinet was near sixty Foot long, each Key being almost a Foot wide, so that, with my Arms extended, I could not reach to above five Keys; . . . Before the Spinet, a Bench was placed about four Foot below the Keys, and I was put upon the Bench. I ran sideling upon it that way and this, as fast as I could, banging the proper Keys with my two Sticks; and made a shift to play a Jigg to the great Satisfaction of both their Majesties: But, it was the most violent Exercise I ever underwent, and yet I could not strike above sixteen Keys, nor, consequently, play the Bass and Treble together, as other Artists do; which was a great Disadvantage to my Performance.

(Ibid., pp. 126 - 127)

These are well-known instances. Not so well known are the Laputans' feat of inclining their heads to one side, with one eye turned inward and the other looking up at the zenith, their habit of being aroused from their speculations by the boxes that a special caste of servants administer on their ears (ibid., p. 159), or that of the two academicians at Lagado who carry upon their backs whatever object is needed to communicate, because they want to dispense with words altogether (ibid., pp. 185 - 186): this is, by the way, a trick still used in comic sketches. The restless behaviour of the Yahoos must also be mentioned in this connection:

They climbed high Trees, as nimbly as a Squirrel, for they had strong extended Claws before and behind, terminating in sharp Points, and hooked. They would often spring, and bound, and leap with prodigious Agility. (Ibid., p. 223)

Gulliver reports that he regularly watched them, and they were forever digging up roots, searching for carrion meat or shining stones, swimming and climbing trees.

---

63 A.M. Taylor, op. cit., p. 31.

The body gesticulating, or performing its contortions, is a familiar image, yet it never fails to arouse curiosity. In this respect, the contortions comprise a collection of curios worthy of a waxwork collection. On the other hand, they usually seem, at best, without purpose – they are inadequate. The skills required to walk along a tightrope, or jump over a stick, are irrelevant to those necessary in the management of public affairs. The Yahoos' imitation of human manners is purely physical and meaningless, and so is the Aeolists' ritual: the rhythmical swaying of their bodies induces physical trances, not spiritual elevation. By displaying the manners of a gentleman in a context where they are irrelevant, namely on the table of an inn, Gulliver does not convince the Brobdingnagians that he is human: instead they take him for a clever little animal or piece of clock-work. The characters of *Polite Conversation* also behave like clock-work figures. The contortions of the body show it to be less than human: more some strange piece of queer mechanism than a living organism. Its performances are gratuitous and disconnected gestures, instead of forming part of meaningful rituals.

In *Gulliver's Travels* the connection between ritual and gestures is made most explicitly. The Lilliputian army marching beneath the arch of Gulliver's spread legs is celebrating a ritual of victory. Life on the flying island of Laputa and at the court of Luggnagg is strictly fixed but seems pointless too, as do the postures and contortions of those who dwell in these places. Only among the Houyhnhnms does one have the impression that the social ritual is in full harmony with the nature of the institutions and the general philosophy of the ruling race. The way the clever horses greet each other or their manner of dealing with the affairs of the country are the direct expression of their moral and civic values:

> . . . another Horse came up; who applying himself to the first in a very formal Manner, they gently struck each others Right Hoof before, neighing several times by Turns, and varying the Sound, which seemed to be almost articulate. They went some Paces off, as if it were to confer together, walking Side by Side, backward and forward, like Persons deliberating upon some Affair of Weight . . .   (ibid., p. 225)

That they behave somewhat pompously is, one feels, congruent with their philosophy. Besides, people did behave decorously in the eighteenth century. On the other hand, the Yahoos live in herds, and herds have no ritual regulating and disciplining their life. They only know the laws of their appetites and passions. They live without "ceremony", as

W.B. Yeats would have said: they live naturally, as people will have it today. Whenever there is no ceremony, or the rituals are out of order and meaningless, there is, Swift suggests, a failure of civilization.

"A Voyage to Laputa, Balnibarbi, Luggnagg, Glubbdubdrib and Japan" is of all Swift's satires the text that deals most fully with man's technical activities, as opposed to rituals. The flying island is a superb image symbolizing man's effort not to remain glued to the earth, but to shake off his earthly nature by extending his technological domination over his surroundings. The penalty for this is known: the Laputans become inhuman. No less interesting are the unsuccessful attempts of the academicians at Lagado to reverse the course of nature. They experiment in order to convert excrements back into food (ibid., pp. 179 - 180), to make spiders do the work of silk-worms (ibid., pp. 180 - 181), and to find out whether virtues or vices are a better basis for the taxation of a subject or citizen in the state (ibid., pp. 189 - 190). Even the Struldbruggs, who are endowed, by nature itself, with a quality that many wish to possess to escape from their condition, are unable to take advantage of their immortality. All man's attempts to transform the world in order to change himself prove erratic or dangerous.

Whenever any physical performance is involved – and even some of the activities at the academy of Lagado deserve to be labelled as such –, "display" is the key word, as was "disclosure" in the cases of the body being stripped naked. Sometimes the display is deliberately exhibition-istic. If they do not have a social or religious significance and are not sanctioned by any ritual, displays of manners, of one's skills, or simply of one's person, usually aim, like clothes, at impressing others, at holding their attention and at imposing on them. It is always an egocentric gesture. It serves to make oneself conspicuous. But what do unnecessary contortions and eccentric activities make an individual conspicuous for if not for his physique or soullessness. They represent moments of vain assertion of one's superiority, of mere agitation or of empty performance. By becoming the source of too great an interest, or through being handled improperly, the body ends up blocking the view, obscuring man's true humanity and reducing him to something subhuman: a trained monkey, a clock-work figure or a puppet. The more strongly they convey the impression that the body is a crazy piece of mechanism, the more vividly they also suggest that man is something very different, though this may not always appear clearly from his behaviour.

Long before the tale of the three coats begins and the first image of dissection appears, and as though to lead up to the theme of the frailty of human flesh, *A Tale* gives three examples of man's theatrical and hollow exhibitionism: in preachers, in convicts going to the gallows and in mountebanks. Each has his own "oratorical machine", according to Swift, in order to make a spectacle of himself, as well as to impress others. Each performs for the pleasure of onlookers. When crowds gather to attend the execution of culprits, they do so, not to hear them deliver their "last speech" and confession, but rather to watch them climbing up the ladder "by slow Degrees, [until] Fate is sure to turn them off before they can reach within many Steps of the Top" (PW vol. i, p. 38). That Swift chooses to apply the description metaphorically to certain poets and their art detracts in no way from its representation of a body playing up to an audience. More obvious still is the way Swift capitalizes on display in *Polite Conversation*. In the introduction that he provides for his compendium of clichés, Wagstaff shows that he wants the potential users of his handbook to learn the proper gestures which correspond to his repartees. For the ladies, these consist of "those hundreds of Graces and Motions, and Airs, the whole military Management of the Fan, the Contorsions of every muscular Motion in the Face" (PW vol. iv, p. 112). In a sense, what he recommends is that each person in society play up to the audience of the other persons present, as they play up to him.

In his fictions of the body posturing and performing, Swift then makes it clear that people cannot be divided into actors and spectators. What has just been said about *Polite Conversation* shows that everyone is a spectator of everyone else, and at the same time a performer in relation to them. Swift's imagination constantly recurred to this idea throughout his life. The purported author of *A Tale of a Tub*, discussing the attitude of his fellow hacks towards the product of their fraternity as a whole, comes up with an unexpected anecdote concerning the spectators at a street show, which already stresses the same confusion of rôles between spectators and actors. The anecdote, one of these typical and delightful Hogarthian vignettes that enliven his framing discourses, seems irrelevant in its immediate context, until one realizes that it is the first explicit indication that the fictions of the human body will be one of the central satirical motifs in the book. To ensure that the reader will not miss its importance, the anecdote is printed in italics and contains two of the key words of the fictions ("carcass" and "guts"), together with an expression that refers to the volume of the body ("compass"):

A Mountebank in Leicester-Fields, *had drawn a huge Assembly about him. Among the rest, a fat unweildy Fellow, half stifled in the Press, would be every fit crying out, Lord! what a filthy Crowd is here? Pray, good People, give way a little, Bless me! what a Devil has rak'd this Rabble together: Z—ds. what squeezing is this! Honest Friend, remove your Elbow. At last, a Weaver that stood next him could hold no longer: A Plague confound you (said he) for an over-grown Sloven; and who (in the Devil's Name) I wonder, helps to make up the Crowd half so much as your self? Don't you consider (with a Pox) that you take up more room with that Carkass than any five here? Is not the Place as free for us as for you? Bring your own Guts to a reasonable Compass (and be d—n'd) and then I'll engage we shall have room enough for us all.* (PW vol. i, p. 28)

The theme of the spectator turned actor, sometimes against his will, is pursued systematically in three books out of four of *Gulliver's Travels*. In them, the visitor and his hosts are continually studying each other. It is quite right to describe Lilliputian court life and protocol as a spectacle for Gulliver and the reader, and to say that Gulliver becomes an object of curiosity for the Brobdingnagians. Yet the rôles are often reversed: differences in size make the spectacle reciprocal. Aspects of the body and gestures are mutual sources of interest for creatures big and small. The skirmishes fought on the handkerchief of the "Man-Mountain" entertain Gulliver. In return, the gigantic visitor never ceases to be an object of curiosity and admiration for the Lilliputians, for his body is always on display to them. In Brobdingnag, Gulliver is exhibited in the way that a dwarf, or an animal trained to imitate human behaviour, would have been shown to British audiences, both educated and common. For his part, Gulliver never loses interest in the huge bodies of the giants, which he seldom sees in their complete form – they are too big for that –, but whose parts are constantly and impressively displayed to his eyes. A tumour, a wart and the nipple on a woman's breast, these successively attract his attention and call for a careful description by him. In "A Voyage to the Houyhnhnms", finally, Gulliver is accorded the position of a visitor to a menagerie, a man interested in zoology, who is struck by the contrast between the beauty of the horses and the ugliness of the baboon-like hominids, which moreover he finds, contrary to expectations, to be more difficult to train than ordinary monkeys, until, that is, the situation is reversed once more, so that the horses themselves become the zoologists, who start comparing the human visitor with the Yahoos (ibid., pp. 229 - 230). A case can even be made for the Yahoos' curiosity towards Gulliver. Whereas the horses study the human visitor rationally and base their judgment on what they observe and what he tells them, the hominids try to imitate him in an attempt to understand who he is. Their unintelligent response is purely physical: the result of sensory impressions. When Gulliver, whose interest in the Yahoos has been awakened by his master Houyhnhnm's remarks about them, begins to study their way of life, he notices that they have "some Imagination": "they would approach as near as they durst," he adds," and imitate my Actions after the Manner of Monkeys, but ever with great Signs of Hatred . . ." (ibid., p. 265). In the absence of any paratextual indication of what the fiction of Book iv is exactly referring to and satirizes, there seems no better support for the contention that Houyhnhnms and Yahoos respectively represent the Shaftesburian and Lockean views of man than this inverted menagerie situation found in the middle of an animal fable. It presents a human being confronted with the animal embodiment of two opposed philosophies, who despairs of ever being able to live up to the demanding standards of true rationality proposed by one and makes a fool of himself by blindly adopting the coarse sensualism of the other.

If everyone is a spectator of everyone else, every actor is also likely to become someone else's clown. This is particularly the case whenever there is a failure or absence of social ritual. In consequence, Swift's fictions seem implicitly to plead for an unaffected behaviour and for gestures disciplined by the restraining influence of meaningful social ritual, as his fictions of the body dressed do for the wearing of decent but plain clothes. Extravagant or artificial manners or gestures are more likely to betray his animality, or just his lack of humanity, than to show his true nature.

What is intriguing here is that, at the core of the satirist's fictions, is found an image which presents the same characteristics of reversibility that was noted between purported authors and their readers in the framing fictions. It strongly suggests that one of the subsidiary techniques used by Swift to achieve the desired satirical effects and make the reader feel as personally concerned as possible is that of the exchange of rôles. No rôle is stable and permanent. The satires – and singularly the fictions of postures and body contortions – give the impression that any individual may at any moment find himself cast into the very rôle that he has once watched others play with distaste or amusement.

The fictions of the body considered here have often lost their original referents: the specific shows of Swift's time. However, their entertainment value remains intact. As the motif of body postures and contortions always gives pride of place to the image of the human anatomy as well as to what it accomplishes, the body itself is so vividly portrayed that the reader has always found it easy to enjoy the display without any special assistance from the historian. Where there is a body, there is a show, and the show is entertaining. Its light-hearted character links it to that other aspect of the fictions of the body, the pageant of the body dressed and the spectacle of human folly. On the other hand, the pleasure that the reader takes in the displays of vanity and weaknesses is not unmixed because, at the same time, postures and contortions bring back his attention to the inadequacy of the human body. On this point the link is rather with the motif of the body stripped naked. As much as nakedness, body postures and contortions ultimately underline the fact that the body acts as a clog in man's everyday spiritual and intellectual life, and that it is the source of his psychological frailty or the channel through which this frailty is made manifest, because he exerts insufficient control over it. Consequently, it should neither be made too much of nor too little; more important still, perhaps, it should be accepted for what it is – which is precisely what the Laputans fail to do. Swift's invention of the Laputans, which has often been decried, is, in this respect, as central to the development of the body and clothes motif and to Swift's satirical universe as the Lilliputians, the Brobdingnagians, and the Yahoos. Although they are concerned with accidence rather than essence, and although their character is altogether different from that of the fictions of the body dressed and stripped naked or killed, the postures and contortions of the body fit beautifully into the brilliant and varied pageant of its metamorphoses. They complete the Hogarthian sequences of little tableaux that constitute the third fictional patterns of the satires. There is no solution of continuity between their figurative message and that of the other components. On the contrary, they contribute something quite specific with their vision of the body as symbol of man's imperfect life. They make the human body itself the picaresque hero of the satires.

V

The fictions of the body lend piquancy to the framed fictions, and even occasionally to the framing discourses as well, by means of their Hogarthian vignettes. In the framed narratives and dramatic scenes inspired by folktales, in the conspiracy stories and comedies of manners, the human anatomy figures prominently. Bodies and clothes can be said to give life to what are otherwise mere general patterns: they are the actors.[64] What are the Peters, Jacks, Dismals, Lilliputian rope-dancing ministers, and Laputans with their flappers, but bodies with suits of clothes? Even the purported authors in the satirical fictions, the Gullivers and Wagstaffs, assume the characters of bodies and suits of clothes, when they themselves become the subject of their own discourses, and describe themselves parading their clothes, flaunting their good manners, and making postures and contortions out of their anatomies. Or, when they are not actors in their own stories but are, nevertherless, identifiable figures like the hack in *A Tale*, the clergyman in *Meditation upon a Broomstick* or the footmen in *The Humble Petition of the Footmen of Dublin*, the purported authors betray enough sympathy for the people they are writing about and appear concerned enough with man as a body dressed, posing and gesticulating in their tales, to become associated in some implicit way with their one-sided representation of human nature. The author of *Polite Conversation* cannot but be a posturing and contorting body, whilst that of *A Modest Proposal* is surely a potential anthropophagous body. As for Gulliver, his body is inspected by his different hosts in every aspect. *Gulliver's Travels* gives the issue of the place held by the body in man's life its most forceful expression. In what remains one of the most controversial pages of the great satirist, Gulliver's Houyhnhnm master discusses the imperfections of the human body. To have an animal do this in the middle of an animal fable or tale is such an unheard of occurrence that this topic has been one of the most strongly objected to by readers of Swift:

He then began to find fault with other Parts of my Body; the Flatness of my Face, the Prominence of my Nose, mine Eyes placed directly in Front, so that I could not look on either Side without turning my Head: That I was not able to feed my self, without lifting one of my fore Feet to my Mouth: And therefore Nature had placed those Joints to answer that Necessity. He knew not what could be the Use of these several Clefts and Divisions in my Feet behind; that these were too soft to bear the Hardness and Sharpness of Stones without a Covering made from the Skin of some other

64 In "Des outils pour écrire le corps" (*Panoplie du corps, Traverses* 14 - 15: 12, 1979), Michel de Certeau writes that every story is a discourse articulated by bodies. If such is the case, Swift can be said to have, according to his custom, given an extreme development to a common narrative device, in order to turn it into a satirical device.

Brute; that my whole Body wanted a Fence against Heat and Cold, which I was forced to put on and off every Day with Tediousness and Trouble.

(PW vol. xi, pp. 242 - 243)

Now, considering the ambiguous and, most of the time, reversible relationship established between the enunciator on the one hand and the reader on the other, the latter cannot in these cases escape from the impression that the satire is addressing him as a body, too, even if he dissociates himself from the purported authors, when they prove all too blind and biased to be trusted. In so far as the parody of contemporary journalistic or polemical writing serves to take the reader to task for various moral and intellectual shortcomings, this same recipient can now be said to be taken to task also as a human body and a being of flesh, all its weaknesses and imperfections exposed. To the extent that the body provides the show, it is a source of amused detachment: but to the extent that the body is deprived of the glamour pertaining to entertainments and is, or becomes, a reflection of the reader's via the purported author, it can be apprehended as coming uncannily close to an unpleasant experience. The pattern of anaesthesia followed by deferred recognition, noted on the other two structural levels of the fictions, or else due to their loose combination with gaps between them, leads to the discovery of a human body that is different from one's experience – defamiliarized, and yet all too well-known.

As a fictional device, the body has been seen to be a rich source of invention. Whether dressed, stripped naked, dissected, devoured, experimented on, killed, posturing, gesticulating or performing all kinds of contortions, it is always clearly depicted. A recent study finds the physical imagery gross.[65] This grossness is that of caricature. There is always something extreme and somewhat coarse in caricature. On this point, the satirist's art is not unlike that of the cartoonist. As Swift's characters are beings that are at every moment just what they look, scenes, both narrated and dramatized, are usually organized around a body or group of bodies providing the show. In varying degrees of extravagance, suits of clothes and disguises enclose physical anatomies which, in turn, conceal clock-work organs or digestive systems that are disgusting to a greater or lesser extent. Dressed, undressed or dissected, posing or acting, the body is above all spectacular, in the etymological sense of the

---

65 Brian Tippett, *"Gulliver's Travels"* (The Critics Debate), Basingstoke, Macmillan, 1989, p. 21.

185

word.[66] An English peer disguised as a chimney-sweep, Lord Peter adding layer upon layer of ornaments to his inherited coat; the beau dissected; an ageing prostitute, the "beautiful young nymph", undressing before going to bed; Gulliver crossing the channel that separates Blefuscu from Lilliput and dragging a whole fleet of tiny ships behind him; the Yahoos nimbly climbing up a tree to urinate and defecate upon Gulliver's head, Marlborough stripped to his ass's ears and dirty hands, all these belong to a world seen in terms of a show and entertainment, artificial like that of the stage, a circus or a menagerie. By placing the body or the clothes in the foreground, rather than their "wearer", Swift depersonalizes his narrative or drama just sufficiently to make it appear to be of no real consequence. Nothing could be further from the way characters are portrayed in the novel.

Of the art of the cartoonist, Swift's handling of the fictions of the body in the framed narratives and dramatic scenes evidences another trait. He has already been seen to utilize the method of the caricaturist in the Hogarthian vignettes of the framing discourses, underlining a few features here, distorting others there, in order to make them more expressive. When he transposes the all too familiar human anatomy into the more or less fanciful fictional worlds of folktales, fables, conspiracy stories and comedies, when he combines the real and the imaginary, he goes one step further and creates a different type of vignettes. At this stage, the satirist exhibits, in an extreme form, what could be called, paraphrasing Paul Ricoeur, the competence to produce new illogical species by means of metaphoric or metonymic associations, in spite of the resistence of the usual categories of language and literature. This assimilation through associations lends the vignettes of the body which form the core of the framed fictions the partly un-natural character of tropes, while retaining the dramatic nature of the Hogarthian vignettes. On the palm of the giant king's hand, Gulliver does become an impotent

66 In *The Tremulous Body: Essays in Subjection* (London, Methuen, 1984), Francis Barker detects a shift in the literary representations of the body between the seventeenth and the eighteenth century. He describes it as a shift from the spectacular body present in public life to the private body of bourgeois subjectivity hidden in the text and sees in the transition a sign of a change from public to private sensibility. It would be very tempting to enlist Swift in support of this thesis on the basis of what is said in this chapter. But it must be remembered that, for satirists and caricaturists, the body has always been a public target and, consequently, spectacular.

and grovelling insect. The metamorphoses of the body are not odd because they are identifiable as the products of an eighteenth-century imagination inspired by current fashions, medical research and popular entertainments: they are so because the satirist can be said to have availed himself to the full of the fact that no discourse can name the body as the ultimate verification that gives foundation to a narrative without alienating this body at the same time. He, or the purported authors of his parodies, are themselves "*Monster-mongers* and . . . *Retailers of strange Sights*" as he puts it in *A Tale of Tub* (PW vol. i, p. 81). Dismal, Jack, Mr Neverout and Gulliver are neither the precursors of Fielding's Tom Jones, nor of Beckett's Vladimir and Estragon, nor of Ionesco's Mr and Mrs Martin.[67] As bodies and suits of clothes they are similar to puppets – a cross between flesh-and-blood Robinson Crusoe and wooden Pinocchio[68] – and the kith and kin of characters in fables and folktales.

The creatures invented by the caricaturist are never absolutely true to life, although they point clearly to real people as his target. Their actions are always preposterous. But it is a quality of imagination peculiar to Swift himself, and his personal philosophy, which make him represent them in a form that recalls the puppet show. If for Shakespeare the world is a stage, for the satirist

> *The World consists of Puppet-shows*
> Where petulant, conceited Fellows
> Perform the part of *Punchinelloes*;

and where the Punchinelloes

> . . . Wrigle, Fidge, and make a Rout
> Put all [their] Brother Puppets out,
> Run on in one perpetual Round,
> To Teize, Perplex, Disturb, Confound,
> Intrude with Monkey grin, and clatter
> To interrupt all serious Matter . . .
>> ("Mad Mullinix and Timothy", SPW, p. 342)

---

67 C.J. Rawson, op. cit., pp. 94, 70 - 71, 96.
68 *Pinocchio* is a later creation: 1880. What is interesting, however, is that the book was written about the time when Victorian editors discovered that Gulliver had all the qualities of a hero for children.

The tricks devised by Peter to deceive his brothers as well as credulous listeners are farcical caricatures of certain Catholic practices; the clowning in *Polite Conversation* and *Directions to Servants* is an empty imitation of good manners; and Gulliver's panegyric of his country before the king of Brobdingnag, his reviling of English life to his Houyhnhnm master, and his tirade against man as "a Lump of Deformity, and Diseases both in Body and Mind, smitten with Pride" (PW vol. xi, p. 296) at the end of his account, ought to be read in the same spirit as the proud and vindictive tirades of characters in a "Punch and Judy" show, which usually follow a flurry of blows, only to incite another volley upon their authors' heads.

Individually, each group of images and motifs analyzed above is linked to a specific train of associations. When every pose, gesture or accident that befalls the body becomes a suggestive nuance and fresh satirical innuendo, an exhaustive survey of the ideas thrown up by these fictions is, of course, out of the question. Furthermore, every reader will respond differently, according to his own experience. What is important is to grasp the drift of the satirist's imagery, to recognize the outline of the mental picture he is creating, and to understand the way it functions within the confines of the text. For this, a brief recapitulation will suffice.

The fiction of the body dressed lays the stress upon the assumption of a social status and rôle. Dress has a social function, but not just in the sense implied by the Houyhnhnm, when he tells Gulliver that he thinks "it not unwise in us to *cover* our Bodies, and by that Invention, conceal many of our Deformities from each other, which would else be hardly supportable" (ibid., p. 260). Clothes are used to establish an advantage, to make an impression on others, to attract or deceive, or in response to pressures to conform. They identify people and place them according to group, social class or religious denomination. Clothes also symbolize man's excessive concern with appearances, the pride he takes in what is merely a surface, sometimes to conceal an inner emptiness or hidden corruption; or, on the contrary, as with the Laputans, they connote man's ignorance of his mixed nature. In fact Swift's satirical fictions dealing with clothes, and in particular *A Tale, Polite Conversation* and *The Humble Petition*, show that the horse's criticism is wide of the mark. On the other hand, all the satires agree as to what clothes should ideally be: a plain but decent covering, granted to all, affording protection against the inclemencies of the weather, and inconspicuous so as not to attract attention to itself.

With the postures and contortions of the body, there is a shift from social to personal concerns. Man's acrobatics are both assertive and exhibitionistic: they evince an unhealthy interest in his physical nature *per se*. On the one hand, they engender self-satisfaction or at least a sort of complacency, and, on the other, pleasure in the display of purely physical and non-intelligent skill. Between the monkey feats of the Yahoos, those of Gulliver in front of a Brobdingnagian audience at an inn or at court, and those of the Lilliputians performing on Gulliver's handkerchief, the difference is not in kind or spirit, but in skill of showmanship – no matter what Gulliver himself may think. He does not realize that exhibiting good manners will only convince the giants that he is a clever piece of clock-work, and not that he is a thinking being. Undue concern for the body eventually encourages a natural inclination towards satisfying its appetites, or towards slovenliness. In the description he gives to the clever horses of the state of the English nation, Gulliver is led to say something about doctors, diseases, and the way people feed in order to sustain their bodies. As in the Houyhnhnm's verdict quoted above on the inadequacies of the human anatomy, the interest in the body is shown, in this passage, to extend beyond its figuration in the framework of the narrative fiction to become the subject of the characters' own conversations with each other:

I told him, we fed on a Thousand Things which operated contrary to each other; that we eat when we were not hungry, and drank without the Provocation of Thirst: That we sat whole Nights drinking strong Liquors without eating a Bit; which disposed us to Sloth, enflamed our Bodies, and precipitated or prevented Digestion. That, prostitute Female *Yahoos* acquired a certain Malady, which bred Rottenness in the Bones of those, who fell into their Embraces: That this and many other Diseases, were propagated from Father to Son; so that great Numbers come into the World with complicated Maladies upon them: That, it would be endless to give him a Catalogue of all Diseases incident to human Bodies; for they could not be fewer than five or six Hundred, spread over every Limb, and Joynt: In short, every Part, external and intestine, having Diseases appropriated to each.   (Ibid., p. 253)

Such discussions are of capital importance, since they provide the link between the satire on human nature developed through the fictions of the body on the one hand and the social and political satire found in the discursive references to institutions or in the story on the other. In a narrative the body always becomes a "social body" in that it plays a rôle in a social environment and interacts, as demonstrated above, with other bodies. As semeiotics puts it, "the individual gives up the autonomy of his body in order to become a fully integrated 'member' of the institutional body."[69] This is precisely what happens to the body posing and contorting. Each time Gulliver enters a new world, he experiences this loss of autonomy and becomes a body performing before and for others. By having the social implications of the body's behaviour discussed by the body posing and contorting itself, the satirist turns what could have remained a purely narrative requirement into an explicit theme, which enables him to extend the range of the satirical reflexion and to show that man's physical infirmity is at the bottom of the corruption of institutions.

As for the fictions of the body stripped naked, dissected and devoured, they help to bring out what is wrong with the other two concerns: with social appearances, and with what Swift considers to be the bent of man's physical nature. They persistently unveil what *A Tale* calls "the carcass": the imperfections of the flesh, especially those due to intemperate habits or a lack of cleanliness, as the above quotation suggests. *A Modest Proposal* reminds us that infancy and adolescence are appealing stages, and Swift was in all likelihood no less sensitive to their charm than anybody else. But the rest of his work has opted to insist on the fact that this charm is soon lost, and it is not, in any case, the privilege of everyone. His satirical fictions offer some of the cruellest depictions of human physical decay. Written at a time when life expectancy was suddenly soaring from thirty to forty years,[70] the description of the Struldbruggs without doubt remains one of the most memorable images of decrepitude in literary history:

At Ninety they lose their Teeth and Hair; they have at that Age no Distinction of Taste, but eat and drink whatever they can get, without Relish or Appetite. The Diseases they were subject to, still continue without encreasing or diminishing. In talking they forget the common Appellation of Things, and the Names of Persons, even of those who are their nearest Friends and Relations. For the same Reason they never can amuse themselves with reading, because their Memory will not serve to

---

69 Ivàn Almeida, op. cit., p. 10.
70 Pierre Chaunu, *L'historien dans tous ses états*, Paris, Perrin, 1984, pp. 181 - 182.

carry them from the Beginning of a Sentence to the End; and by this Defect they are deprived of the only Entertainment whereof they might otherwise be capable.

(PW vol xi, p. 213)

The fictions of the body stripped naked, not content with exposing the carcass and its animal appetites, place the emphasis on man's mortality. The motif comes as near to expressing the churchman's theological conception of man's fallen nature as he dared to go outside ecclesiastical occasions,[71] and the fact is of indubitable interest.

How far Swift's notion of the body still is from the "sensitized body"[72] and delicate nervous system of mid-century sentimental literature is obvious. Whether directly or indirectly, Swift's fictions are indebted to Descartes' and Hobbes's conceptions of man as a complex machine, as well as, more generally, to the medical discourse of the first half of the century, that of a Hermann Boerhaave, Bernard Mandeville and George Cheyne.[73] They present the picture of a being that can be broken up into a number of components: first into a soul and an animal body, and then the body itself into smaller mechanical units. Descartes had dared to invent his fiction of the man-machine because it was implausible,[74] and Swift can be said to have utilized it with an even clearer conscience than was possible for the philosopher, as his purpose was not serious but satirical description. His human body can be taken to pieces and put together again but, disarticulated or complete, it is never more than an image of

---

71 Roland M. Frye, "Swift's Yahoo and the Christian Symbol for Sin", *Journal of the History of Ideas* 15: 201 - 217 (1954).

72 John Mullan, *Sentiment and Sociability: The Language of Feeling in the Eighteenth Century*, Oxford, Clarendon, 1988, p. 228.

73 Hermann Boerhaave, *Aphorisms* (London, 1715); Bernard Mandeville, *A Treatise of the Hypochondriack and Hysterick Passions* (London, 1711); George Cheyne, *The Natural Method of Cureing the Diseases of the Body and the Disorders of the Mind depending on the Body* (London, 1742). On the general aspect of the medical discourse that interests us here, see Claude Bruneteau, "La Maladie anglaise", *Le Corps et l'âme en Grande-Bretagne au XVIIIe siècle*, pp. 11 - 23. One striking difference between the medical discourse summed up in Bruneteau's study and Swift's own discourse is that the former tends to insist on the way the state of health of a person can affect his mind and soul, whereas the latter prefers to demonstrate that the corruptions of the mind affect the body's health and history.

74 Rudolf Zur Lippe, "Une Unité problématique: Eléments pour une histoire des conceptions du corps", *Etudes de Lettres* 2: 31 (1983).

essential imperfection, of the loss of man's original unity of being, or of that unity of being that will always elude him, and, in so far as the fictions of the body form narrative sequences, of an imperfect existence. In his fictions, the satirist brilliantly synthesizes the image that early eighteenth-century philosophy and medical science were trying to give of man, whilst picking holes in the implications of their conception of human nature. Indeed, for him, the body is never the whole being. If drawing attention to it is an effective satirical strategy, the satirical vision is never complete: it is synecdochic, the representation of a part for the whole. Satire is not philosophy, and Swift's intention is not to propose an ontological definition of human nature. He only deals with a limited aspect of man: his physical nature and flesh, seen as a cause of imperfection. In this respect, the fact that, at the end of the *Travels*, Gulliver rejects human company, including that of his wife, on account of their smell, may be more explicit than has been assumed: an indication that his misanthropy is due to his temporary incapacity to realize that he is more than a body, or here an anatomy, dressed.

To say that the fictions of the body's metamorphoses are synecdochic and that they do not make an ontological statement about the nature of man does not mean, however, that they lack depth. For one thing, they produce the same type of generalizing symbolism as metaphors. Furthermore, the synecdoche, which momentarily erases the distinction between the body and the soul, does not function alone. If it did, it would merely achieve the kind of stylistic oversimplification which helps to underline caricatural traits. In fact, it combines with what has been regarded as precisely another basic strategy of caricature. Caricature has recourse to a compensatory move, one which comes within the province, not of language, but of experience, namely that of observing people, and which achieves a somewhat contrary and complementary effect.[75] As already suggested, the eye of the caricaturist observing people abolishes the reality-versus-appearance duality and depicts the body as "a complex of symptoms".[76] By focusing on what he sees as the epitome of man's frailty, the satirist makes the reader see the soul in the body, and the reality in the appearance: he reveals the true body that exists beyond

75 Michel Jouve, "Corps difformes et âmes perverses: quelques réflexions sur la pratique de la caricature", *Le Corps et l'âme en Grande-Bretagne au XVIIIe siècle*, pp. 111 - 117. This essay deals with what is called above the art of the cartoonist but it makes interesting connections with that of satire.
76 Ibid., p. 112.

selfspun illusions and is an expression of the state of health of man's mind. There is something Pascalian about the double synecdochic and caricatural process. The metamorphoses of the body make it clear that man's physical nature is an essential feature of his being, which he cannot ignore. They portray man as a being who is lonely and ill-at-ease in his body and who, in Jean Brun's beautiful simile, feels that his skin clings to him like a Nessus tunic.[77] A prisoner of his humanity, man never stops wishing to escape his condition and, precisely, Swift's Peters, Jacks, Wottons, Wagstaffs, Ellistons, beautiful young nymphs, Gullivers, Lilliputians and Laputans, all the purported authors and characters of his important satires, never cease to try to remodel humanity and invent new forms of being and existence, or to admire and envy those who seem to them to have been able to achieve this purpose. Only the Houyhnhnms are satisfied with their lot and accept their bodies and its death with serenity. The satirist demonstrates that all attempts to do otherwise are vain. Clothes, acting rôles or technological inventions cannot cure man of his frailty. They change neither his nature nor his condition. Man's body is his limits, his skin the frontier between the self and the world, and both frustrate his efforts to shake off the reality that he wants to change. In whatever size, shape or costume, assuming whatever poses they like, making whatever contortions they can, individuals cannot break the spatio-temporal frame of their body.

On their own, the fictions of the body dressed or of the body posturing and contorting, reveal the satirist in the festive mood of a comic writer. Those of the body stripped naked, on the other hand, express his sense of the despicable depravity of man. Situated, as they are, at the core of the satires, the fictions of the body mark the ultimate development of Swift's satirical strategy, consisting in debunking false claims and ideas. The process, which begins with the identification of the fake as fake, starts off by undermining the confidence of the reader in the value of the purported author's rhetoric in his text. In the second stage, with the narrative and dramatic patterns reversed, surprise turns to mistrust of man's optimism, and a deeper consciousness of the unpleasantness of life. The belittling process of satire is completed when the fictions conclude by reducing man not, as has been suggested, to the status of a beast,[78] but to that of a body, a carcass, a "Lump of Deformity", or a suit

77 Op. cit., p. 8.
78 R.C. Elliott, *The Power of Satire: Magic, Ritual, Art*, Princeton, Princeton University Press, 1960, p. 219.

of clothes: this is what his "puppetry" consists of. After belittling the authors and their writings, Swift's satires make use of the fictions of the body to do the same to man himself. When he reduces his characters to mere suits of clothes, clock-work organisms, posturing clowns and acrobats, he is humbling them by making fun of them.

In Swift's satirical fictions, it is dangerous to underestimate the detachment of the satirist. In his *Anthologie de l'humour noir*, André Breton quotes from a comment to the effect that Swift is remarkable among humorists in "provoking laughter without sharing in it."[79] Breton adds that the Anglo-Irish satirist is always "impassive and as cold as ice."[80] Such remarks are worth further reflexion. It is important to remember that, structurally, Swift's bodies, suits of clothes and puppets are not Breughelian figures populating his imagination: for they are twice removed from their author-creator. Firstly, they are presented as figments of the imagination of the various purported authors of the framing discourses which contain the tales or comic scenes; and secondly, the alleged authors have themselves been described as drawing their identities as much from the gaps in structure of the satirical fictions, as from any information given about them explicitly. They are hollow figures, mere impersonators, and so the puppets of the shows are seen to be somewhat similar to the product of a ventriloquist's art. Furthermore, because all the rôles are interchangeable, the fictions of the satirist reflect the world of the reader as a recipient of the message, never that of the true author as creator. Swift is not a Joycean novelist: he offers his fictions as though they were anybody's and everybody's representations.

---

79 *Anthologie de l'humour noir*, Paris, Pauvert, 1966, pp. 20. John M. Bullitt speaks of Swift's "detached gaiety" (op. cit., p. 163). It seems important to stress the point at a moment when a reconsideration of the importance of Swift's more personal writings has tended to underline the vulnerability of the man.

80 André Breton, op. cit., p. 19.

Chapter 4

Fictional Patterns, Laughter, Meaning

The previous chapters have perhaps given the impression that Swift's satires are like nuts, which must be cracked open in order for the reader to get the bitter-sweet kernel. It is, of course, in the first place the approach itself which suggests this image, but the simile is not totally unapt as a way of describing the configuration of the fictional patterns within the satires. These patterns have been seen to be extremely varied, ranging from the mimetic to the isomorphic, and from the seemingly realistic to the avowedly fantastic. Each has been said to fulfil a precise function according to its character. There remains to consider the effect achieved by their in many cases complex combination. A first remark to make concerns the pervasive and fundamental rôle that these fictional components play in Swift's art of satire. Now, there has never been any doubt in anyone's mind that Gulliver's story, the tale of the three brothers, Peter, Martin and Jack, or the will and testament of Ebenezor Elliston are pieces of fiction. But, by documenting the case, one is led to realize that the fictions are not just the way in which the satires are dressed, and the irony made palatable: they are "the focusing component which rules, determines, and transforms the remaining components" like structure, style, imagery, themes and motifs, as well as the nature of the satire: in other words, they are truly what the Russian formalists and the structuralists call the *dominant*.[1]

Coming as it does from a man who clearly set reason above imagination, this heavy reliance on fiction can appear a little surprising. It is true that rational ages have their fictions like other ages. The Enlightenment, which saw the emergence of the novel, was no exception. Then, Swift's fictions are usually made to reveal their unreasonable character. So it is not so much the fact that he uses all sorts of fictional devices which is interesting, as the way in which he handles them. In this respect, his work can even be said to belong to the early manifestations of a shift in literary trends towards, not a rejection of fiction in the name of reason,

1 Ladislav Matejka, "The Formal Method and Linguistics", *Readings in Russian Poetics* p. 289.

but, precisely, the more critical manipulation of traditions and conventions which later led a man like the historian Jules Michelet to think of the eighteenth century as an "essentially literary age". Once more, the comparison with the early novelists illustrates the point. The fact that Swift's utilization of fiction is not altogether dissimilar to that of the initiators of the new genre has been underscored. Like theirs, his fictions are offered as allegedly authentic documents to a public more hungry for news and polemics than tales, whilst their contents are at times, like theirs again, as extravagant as one could wish. Real as it is, the kinship must however not conceal significant differences. For his satirical fictions, Swift has drawn from a far greater and more varied range of sources than the early novelists. He has a much surer sense of literary structure than they have: with Aphra Behn and Defoe, framing – in the sense defined by this study – is mostly a matter of titles, or of a few stray remarks inserted haphazardly in a realistic romance, in order to testify to its authenticity. Only in Swift does framing achieve full status as a formal framework and a precise structural device or systematic discourse, which establishes with care, by means of references to other writings of the same order, the intention of the author with regard to his readers. He can also be said to have turned it into a more subtle means of anchoring a fiction in circumstantial reality. Finally his adaptation of numerous types of discourses to unsuitable ends lends his work this self-conscious quality which was something new at the time.

Among the various patterns by means of which his satires construct their reference to social reality and the world of everyday experience, there are then first the framing fictions of purportedly serious polemical or journalistic pieces offered as a mimetic representations of literary activities. There are the fantastic folktales, the fictitious conspiracy stories or the comic fragments, which, individually or combined, assume the status of fanciful descriptive representations of all aspects of human life. And there are the "Punch and Judy" fictions of the body, which focus on man's social attitudes and behaviour in a world of inter-personal subjectivity and communication. All three fictional types bear the hallmark of a formal inventiveness without bounds and an exuberant imagination, which have delighted generations of readers. This much is obvious, but as soon as one asks how such very different fictional patterns are made to work towards a common end and constitute the basis of the satirical meaning, there is good reason to be baffled. Faced with the complexity of the heterogeneous combination, the student of literature who approaches the work with classical expectations of form is likely to feel most deeply this confusion. Even granting that satire is more an attitude than a form and that, consequently, neither unity of design and nor harmony of execution are primary expectations,[2] he is hardly prepared for the yoking together of more numerous and disparate components than is normally the case. To put it in simple terms, satire is usually content to combine one form or formal pattern with an inadequate subject matter, and not two or three, each of which reshapes it to some extent in its own way. At the same time nothing is done to hide the joins in the construction. On the contrary, they are allowed to remain glaringly obvious. It is indeed something of a mystery why Swift's detractors have not seized upon precisely these disparate fictional structures, in order to run him down. The lack of response on this point is all the more intriguing when one considers that the baroque quality given by the mixture of fictions to his satires ought to have appeared particularly unpalatable, if not to their first readers, at least to those who followed and belonged to an age reputed to have revered elegance, balance, symmetry and purity of form. It would seem, then, that whatever it is that disturbs readers in Swift's work, it has little to do with the heterogeneous character of his satirical fictions.

In other words, the study of Swift's use of fiction in his satires poses, in a different way and more generally, a problem that has featured prominently in this century's discussions of *A Tale of a Tub* and *Gulliver's Travels*, namely the question of whether they are coherent as works, and, beyond that, the broader question of whether coherence and singularity of purpose are needed in a satire, in order for it to achieve its special critical effect through ridicule. In so far as the structure and aesthetics of satire are concerned, Swift's output is clearly an extreme case, as well as being a test case, and it may not be amiss to begin this last chapter by considering what light the preceding analysis of the satirist's fictions sheds on this important issue.

The first point to note is that, whatever their additional complexity, Swift's satires are organized like all other satires. The central dichotomy that exists between framing devices or fictions and the framed fictions also serves to articulate a subject, in the form of an isomorphic but fanciful representation of circumstantial reality, and an inadequate form, as in

---

2 W.B. Carnochan, *Lemuel Gulliver's Mirror for Man*, Berkeley, University of California, 1968, p. 25.

Pope's contemporary mock epic. The only differences are its specific nature and the character of the divisive tension. The division could be described as a rupture. Whereas other satirists employ irrelevant formal patterns to mould the satirical material, thus giving it the general appearance of a coherent whole, Swift goes in for abrupt shifts of expressional mode. These shifts, amounting to ruptures, occur whenever a preface, first part, title page or form of publication prove unsuited to the contents of the work itself, and whenever untimely digressions interrupt the course of the central narrative, or tales and anecdotes interrupt the flow of the main discourse. They always create gaps, as said above. In the longer works, each part remains distinct, rather than fusing with the others: hence this impression of components yoked together. As the need arises, the satirist can even move back and forth between the fanciful picture of human reality, which exploits to the full the public's craving for tales, sensational stories or comedies in the framed fictions, and the framing of polemical and journalistic discussion, which would seem to require factual references and informed accounts. The particularity of this structure is that the main components have opposite orientations: one is looking out of the text towards circumstantial reality, whilst the other looks inward towards subjective outlook, in the form of fantasying. Therefore, although the reader finds in Swift's satires the same conjunction of incompatible components with diverging aims to alert him to the intended satire, he also perceives at once that its character is different from that of traditional satire, and there is no doubt in his mind that Swift's satires appear all the more striking precisely because of this difference.

Even more unusual is the second aspect of Swift's use of fictions. Different expressional modes produce different levels of fiction and, consequently, different satirical universes and, with their divisions into distinct parts, his satires may be said to constitute odd assortments of widely different satirical visions. Between voyages Gulliver lives in eighteenth-century England, at times he is in fairyland, and at others he is to be found in a world of omnipresent conspiracies. The digressions in A Tale also allude to scenes from Swift's own lifetime, as do all of the framing discourses, whereas Peter, Jack and Martin live in a folktale universe of simplified relationships and concrete objects possessing symbolical value. It is occasionally difficult to dismiss from one's mind the knowledge that the framing discourses present purportedly real people playing an active rôle in real contemporary activities, whilst the framed fictions contain more or less imaginary characters, who at times can even become nothing more than puppets, as is the case in the fictions of the body. As if to make things more complicated still, the same character can change from being a flesh and blood person addressing his contemporaries one moment, to a folktale figure living in an imaginary world the next, to a sort of wooden Pinocchio with no more than a stage existence straight afterwards. Gulliver is such a character, and the lack of consistency in his portrayal has justifiably puzzled critics, although, strangely enough, not so, to anything like the same extent, the lack of consistency of this traveller's manifold universe. The way a travel account, various fairy tales and fables, conspiracy stories, a long auscultation of the body and frivolous self-exhibitions of the same, combining as they do, manage to produce the *Travels* is bordering on the miraculous, and similarly the jumbling together of some mad digressions, a folktale and the story of dressmaker's dummies to form "a tale of a tub". In the care of a clumsier hand, this assemblage of heterogeneous visions would surely fall apart: but here it does not and, as already observed, it has even survived the scrutiny of critics with high formal expectations. The only possible way of explaining the reader's ready acceptance of the fictional discrepancies present in the text would seem to be that, far from dissociating the fiction from the world by lending the former an air of gratuitous artificiality, the central satirical rupture draws attention to the link between life and its representation by its very abruptness; and that, once the central satirical division has firmly established the said link between the outside world which is being criticized and the text which criticizes it by denying that any link exists, any degree of fantasy is possible: verisimilitude may be forgotten. The satirist enjoys a practically boundless freedom for invention. The universe he creates can even be one of perfect disbelief. By dint of their greater frequency, the secondary fictional discrepancies further contribute to this effect by reinforcing the satirical bias. The more heterogeneous the vision, the greater the opportunity for providing unsettling clashes and situations which might distance the reader, and the more preposterously satirical the representation itself becomes. Each fresh change in the fictional framework modifies the nature of the satirical distortions, alerting the reader anew to the importance of distortion as an interpretative phenomenon. It is idle to speculate as to whether this can be carried out convincingly, since Swift has certainly been very successful in doing so.

The third point highlighted by the present analysis of Swift's fictions is precisely the way the satirist underlines rather than masks the joins in his fictional compositions, in order to heighten the satirical effect by making it more expressive. That the effect is not due to mere carelessness, but is deliberate, receives confirmation from another structural feature, of which relatively little has been said so far: the balanced ordering of parts and other patterns of regularity found in longer works. The fairly regular alternating of narrative sections and discursive digressions in *A Tale*, and the intricate balancing of Book i against Book ii, or the respective couplings of Books i and iii, and Books ii and iv, in the *Travels* have usually been regarded as non-negligible factors of coherence. The same functions have been attributed to the recurrent themes and motifs in both works: the theme of madness in the former, in turn illustrated by overdressing, reacting against it, writing in a modern way, and aberrant religious behaviour; and in the latter the motif of basic human requirements for food, clothing and shelter that Gulliver has to satisfy, whatever the situation in which he finds himself. In minor works, like *A Tritical Essay* or *An Examination of Certain Abuses*, the regularity is related to the recurrence of similar folklore allusions. However, with respect to the composition of heterogeneous fictions, these organizing features assume an altogether different function from that of ensuring coherence and continuity. One thing to note about them is that the very type of rhythmical and geometrical coherence, lent by them to the works in question, is totally external to the fictions themselves. It is artificially imposed and has little or nothing to do with the way they develop and are combined. At no point can these patterns of regularity be said to harmonize the fictions, or bridge the gaps between them by concealing their disparate characters and making the action of the narrative or drama progress. On the contrary, in so far as they introduce parallels and oppositions, they emphasize the abruptness of the breaks, gaps and incompatibilities of the fictions. It is the sudden and close juxtaposition of, together with the stark contrast between, the "Digression concerning Madness", the preceding description of the Aeolists' practices and the following episode of the last stage of Jack's destructive folly that bring their respective satirical natures into full relief. The same is true of "A Voyage to Lilliput" and "A Voyage to Brobdingnag". What applies to the main dichotomy also goes for the minor discrepancies resulting from the combining of folktales with conspiracy stories, fragments of comedy of manners and fictions of the body.

By thus foregrounding the joins in his satirical fictions, Swift pushes to the fore the very features that sollicit a satirical interpretation on the part of the reader. As the structural ruptures, fictional gaps and other discrepancies stand out, they favour parallels and contrasts and turn the structural disharmonies into a source of multiple ironies: dramatic, psychological and fantastic, besides verbal. It is the obviousness of the ruptures that causes the flight into fantasy of the framed fictions to mock the affected seriousness of the framing devices and the stances of their alleged authors: in *A Modest Proposal*, the wide gap between the folktale flavour and the nature of the proposal shows that the proposal itself is tainted with the impractical idealism of the folktale's "all's-well-that-ends-well".[3] It is again the obviousness of the gaps that, conversely, causes the nature of an essay or project to turn the happy overtones from folktales into unpleasant experiences or even nightmares, as can be verified, in the same proposal, when the callousness of the projector's attitude and the cruelty of his "modest proposal" show the ogres to triumph over their victims, and pessimism over optimism. The same relationship, which exists between the framing devices and the framed fictions, also holds true for the interaction between either one of them and the fictions of the body. Within the structure of the satires, the fictions of the body are not ordinary isomorphic portrayals of the actual attitudes and behaviours of man: they are imaginative ways of exploring the practical implications of errors of appreciation. In *A Modest Proposal* once again, the fictions of the body dehumanize the human actors just sufficiently to give them the appearance of puppets. This has two effects: on the one hand, the proposal becomes an act of self-dramatization on the part of a projector who is no more than a gesturing clown; on the other hand, the dehumanization makes the proposal sound less immediately threatening for the intended victims of the Irish ogres, because it is too preposterous to be put into practice. As a result of the shifting viewpoints, the reader can contemplate with amused horror man's "comedy of great vices and tragedy of little failings", as though it were a vivid show. This has been one of the central ideas of the preceding chapter.

3 Carole Fabricant (op. cit., pp. 15, 17) also draws attention to Swift's preference for ruptures and unpolished forms and connects it with a refusal to idealize, and a fascination with transience, destruction and chaos, which explains his propensity towards satire.

The deliberate subverting of coherence noted here, from the conjunction of modes of expression usually considered as incompatible and of irreconcilable types of fictions, down to the underlining of the hiatuses between them, are in fact verbal extensions of the techniques of caricature, with its predilection for abrupt juxtapositions. Like caricature, satire strikes one by the very incongruity of its representations. It is to a large extent the extreme to which Swift pushes this art of caricature that distinguishes his satires from those of other satirists.

In so far as it foregrounds the process of satirical interpretation, Swift's strategy links up with one of the central themes of his work, which has been identified as the erroneous evaluation by people of their own, and others' situations, actions, and beliefs, as a result of either overestimation, underestimation, prejudices, misconceptions, or obsessions. All are types and degrees of blindness, embodied in literary kinds of fictions or rhetoric. Swift's satires set them against one another by means of his abrupt combinations, in order to expose various errors of judgment. Hence Swift, a writer who, with a consumate sense of literary form and skill in manipulating language and the language of fictions, so often announces new developments in literature, such as the comic novel, the erotic novel or the philosophical tale, would not have claimed paternity of any of them: on the contrary, he would have been the first to warn readers against the lies they spread.

The observations made here on the strategic importance of the ruptures and dissonances in Swift's satirical fictions furthermore shed light on the reading process involved by the unusual configuration. Because they are composed of distinct parts, separated by ruptures, and distinguished from each other by inter-fictional discrepancies, Swift's satires are apprehended as dynamic processes and as sequences of fictions. At this point, the verbal art of caricature parts company with that of the pictorial caricaturist. The time factor intervenes, and the recourse to static critical tropes, like those of framing and framed constituents, should not obscure this central characteristic. In the first place, the satirical effect is not meant to be perceived in the same way at every stage. As pointed out before, the reader is not supposed to realize at once that what he is reading is a hoax and a satire. The framing discourses are specifically selected to take him in; the ruptures and other fictional gaps are intended to surprise him, and to prepare him for the discovery that the voice of the purported author does not, in fact, command the authority, objectivity or even respect that are naturally deemed inseparable from authorship. This experience is repeated with every reading. Then the nature and quality of the satirical representation changes, as the text shifts from one type of fiction to another. This automatically influences the reader's response. The parodic aping of contemporary practices, which creates the illusion that the literary and journalistic debate of the time is a ludicrous game, appeals to him in a different way from the representation of social activity as an inverted folktale, as a comedy, or, more significantly still, as a puppet show. As each new fictional component comes into operation, the reader is confronted with a new type and degree of satirical transposition. The three degrees distinguished in this study could tentatively be summed up as making these activities look, in turn, disingenuous or silly in the framing fictions, belittling, harmful, culpable, or even vicious in the framed fictions, and soulless, unreasonable and unfeeling with the fictions of the body. This is, of course, a gross oversimplification, but it will serve to show that the satirical essence is not always the same. It varies in intensity and quality, inspiring every imaginable nuance of scorn.

There are two suggestive illustrations in *Gulliver's Travels* of what the delayed recognition of the satirical meaning, due to the interweaving of different fictional patterns, entails. They are the king of Brobdingnag's and the Houyhnhnm's well-known condemnations of men as "little odious Vermin" (PW vol. xi, p. 132) and "a Sort of Animals to whose Share . . . some small Pittance of *Reason* had fallen, whereof we made no other Use than by its Assistance to aggravate our *natural* Corruptions" (ibid., p. 259). Taken out of their contexts, they sound like straightforward utterances and, for that reason, they have often been found offensive. To explain their severity, it has been felt necessary to invoke a fast developing feeling of misanthropy on the part of the author. However, they are not, to use Baxtin's formulation, Swift's "unmediated, intentional utterance . . . focused on its referential object", mankind.[4] They sound at first like tentative statements made by characters in the course of a conversation. In both cases, the conversations are exchanges of views between a traveller from a remote country and a sedentary host, and the words quoted express the opinions that the hosts have formed of Europe after listening to the traveller's summary and, by his own admission, imperfect descriptions of his native land. They do not express

4 Mixail Baxtin, "Discourse Typology in Prose", *Readings in Russian Poetics*, p. 180.

so much their knowledge of Europe as their sense of cultural differences. As such, they can be dismissed as partly unfounded or grotesquely distorting. This is how they should be interpreted in so far as they belong to the traveller's account introduced by the framing discourse. Besides their being traveller and hosts in a travel account, Gulliver, the king of Brobdingnag and the Houyhnhnm are also fairytale characters: the king is a giant confronted with a tiny replica of himself, and the Houyhnhnm a rational animal who has never seen a human being or, at least, a more highly developed representative of the human species than a Yahoo. In this second context, the statements take on an additional colouring, because a sense of enormous physical differences makes the lack of understanding more inevitable than in the case of travellers and hosts. Physical differences, now added to cultural ones, further relativize the import of the statements, which thus lose their cutting edge. A first kind of irony lurks in this relativization: after all, one condemnation is that of an imperfectly informed giant, who understandably feels somewhat scornful towards what he sees as a diminutive replica of himself, and the other that of a self-satisfied horse whose judgment is influenced by his experience. If they are unjust, allowances must be made for all that separates the protagonists and their views. Yet they are not untrue either, considering the evidence reported by Gulliver himself.

Thereupon the fairy tale, however, takes a sharp turn for the worse, and the reversal of its pattern begins. It also becomes obvious, with the increasing weight of the fictions of the body, that, personally, Gulliver is little better than a gesticulating Pinocchio figure, which one can dress and undress at leisure. Worse still: in one case, immediately after the interview with the king, Gulliver, tiny as he is, conspires against the security of the Brobdingnagian kingdom; in the second case, his increasing fascination with the abhorred Yahoos, and his fear of passing for one, after his interviews with the horse, progressively convince him that he is a Yahoo indeed. In both instances, then, after the event, the giant king's and the Houyhnhnm's verdicts on man, whose truth had sounded so relative a moment before, seem all of a sudden to be verified, and by whom? by Gulliver himself. Has Swift then delayed the full recognition of the import of these condemnations in order to make them sound more final? Again, the textual strategy is more subtle: the two statements have not really become truer, because Gulliver has by then started to make such a fool of himself that his behaviour can no longer incriminate all mankind, but only himself. This, of course, his hosts do not know, as they can only judge man from what they see of Gulliver. But the reader is not in the same position, and besides Swift has prepared him for this new slight correction of the import of their words by manipulating the fictional patterns in consequence. From the moment Gulliver reveals the full extent of his wickedness at the court of Brobdingnag, he is no longer presented as weak man confronted with a threatening giant, but as a nasty imp disturbing the social stability of an ordinary human society; the king of Brobdingnag is no longer a ogre-like giant, but man grappling with a subhuman doll, a dangerous little Tom-Tit-Tot: he is a responsible monarch, who considers "that whoever could make two Ears of Corn, or two Blades of Grass to grow upon a Spot of Ground where only one grew before; would deserve better of Mankind, and do more essential Service to his Country, than the whole Race of Politicians put together" (PW vol. xi, pp. 135 - 136). Among the Houyhnhnms also, Gulliver behaves in such a way that he can no longer be considered as a representative human being: he loses his self-respect too much for that, when he becomes obsessed with his physical nature. There is another kind of irony here, of a type opposite to the first: at the beginning, the two judgments passed on man had appeared questionable because their enunciators had been misled by their informant, and by their different physical natures and personal experiences; then the same statements had come to sound unexpectedly true; at the end, they prove again doubtful because they only fit one man, who has lost his human bearings and has become a special case.

It turns out that the king of Brobdingnag's and the Houyhnhnm's judgments are sometimes more and sometimes less true, according to which fictional pattern happens to predominate and influence the reader's understanding at a certain moment during the reading process, and according to the stage reached by the development of the action; but neither is true *per se* and once for all. Through his fake travel book, Swift is making a profound statement on the way reasonable creatures form opinions about one another. The press and travel accounts proceed in the same way, and it is from these that readers take their cue. As these two illustrations furthermore demonstrate, one's understanding of the import of a comment or episode is always liable to change, because life validates opinions one day and invalidates them the next.

The fictions give the satires their dynamic character and their satirical twist, and it is a failure to appreciate their strategic rôle that has occasionally caused readers to be misled.[5] Not that a thorough under-standing of the imaginative patterns dispels all ambiguity as to what Swift precisely thought – as opposed to meant – as a person. By relativ-izing the pronouncements of his mouthpieces, the satirical twist may even be said to add to their ambiguity, in making them sound half-serious and half-jocular, at once true and untrue, because they are suggested and withdrawn simultaneously. Swift's irony is not one of counter-statements: it is one of tantalizingly unpleasant suggestions.

The satirical effect results from the conjunction of disparate compo-nents, each retaining its singularity, and from the discordances they produce with each other. But do the glaring divergences exclude possible common denominators? What has been said so far relating to the problem of the satires' coherence of conception has tended to answer this question in the negative, yet, in all fairness, it must be admitted that, even with the fictions, the use of structural discordances does not exclude the possibility of secret harmonies, or other factors of coherence subtending them, although they remain secondary.[6] On this last point, the analyst treads on less certain ground, however, as any connections that may exist can only lie buried at a deep level of intuitive suggestions. Consequently, the following comments are offered tentatively, and they do not pretend to be exhaustive.

One common denominator that has been repeatedly observed is the popular nature of the fictions, popular both in the sense of being fashion-able at the time, and in "not seeking to appeal to refined and classical taste". It is a cunning trait, more rare in literary satire than in cartoons – which have long accustomed us to pictures of heads of states disguised as cowboys or of unscrupulous businessmen disguised as big, bad wolves visited by Little Red Riding Hoods. As a factor of satirical distor-tion, this popular quality, which more often than not takes an attractive form in Swift, has the significant advantage of proposing vivid represen-tations of the moral implications of unsound ideas and devious courses of actions.

Another factor of coherence, far less obvious, concerns the impression that each individual is a prisoner of his own subjectivity. The shift from

5 I develop this point in "Misreading Contexts: Sir Walter Scott on *Gulliver's Travels*".
6 The great error of many studies is to have made too much of these factors of co-herence.

the discussion of contemporary affairs, or the description of the state of the world, in the framing discourses to the imaginative and fanciful tales of the framed constituents has been seen to indicate the purported author's, and the reader's, inability to escape from the trap of self-centered and blind subjectivity. In fact, it becomes increasingly clear that, even at the moment when they think they are most objective and most attentive to the outside world, the purported authors succumb to the temptation of self-dramatization or fantasizing, which is also a form of subjectivity in itself, and which Swift ridicules in the trope of the literary game.

In opposition to this movement, which shows the self imprisoned in the subjectivity of its representations, and the discourse trapped in the mesh of its obsessions or merely of its standard patterns, there stands a contrary movement, which may be considered as a third unifying factor. It is itself closely linked to the first, the popular inspiration pervading the satires. The folktale, conspiracy and comedy-of-manner elements or patterns pursue the metaphor of the game in their narrative representations of human activities, transposing it from the mimetic to the isomorphic narrative, descriptive or metaphoric mode. The choice of ministers and the breaking of eggs in Lilliput (PW vol.xi, pp. 38 - 39, 49 - 50), the lawsuits described by Gulliver in "A Voyage to the Houyhnhnms" (ibid., pp. 248 - 250), the disguise of Dismal in *A Hue and Cry* (PW vol. vi, p. 139), the transformations of the brothers' inherited coats and the way they misinterpret their father's will in *A Tale* (PW vol. i, pp. 49 - 55) are all games of a sort. Like the latter example from *A Tale*, the conversations between Colonel Atwit, Miss Noble, Lady Smart and Mr Neverout, and the folklore lucubrations of *An Examination of Certain Abuses* are, more precisely, verbal games. The fanciful transpositions of the narrative and dramatic framed fictions endow human activities or gestures with a degree of gratuitousness. To the extent that they remove all sense of urgency from the problems alluded to and make the reader forget – at least up to a certain point – the sad or infuriating practical implications of such activities and gestures, the transpositions convey the impression that life is a game. There are few fictions from which this suggestion is totally absent. The fictions of the body themselves become material for the game when they develop into exhibitions of the anatomy or its attire, shows, entertainments and masquerades.

Altogether more diffuse is the link that may be discerned between the fictions of the body and the framing discourses. The body has already been seen to be a link between, on the one hand, the folktales, conspiracy stories and comedies of manner, and, on the other, the fictions of the body, the latter developing germs present in the former through their interest in the body itself or in disguises. There also seems to exist a metaphorical connection between the portrayal of the body in the framed fictions, and what the framing says. The clowning of soulless and mechanical bodies seems an apt image for empty minds, lack of intelligence and blindness, which characterize the purported authors of some pieces by means of the vagrancies of their discourses. Gesticulating bodies and tailor's dummies inevitably remind the reader of the ventriloquism of the framing discourses – and of their putative authors. The family resemblance between the puppets of the body show, and the figures of fun in the literary and journalistic game, is perhaps the most subtle of the hidden links between the disparate fictions.

The preceding analysis has also shown that, however disparate the combination of fictions is, and however considerable the effects of ruptures look, they are never completely unmotivated, nor structurally unjustified. The fact that the purported author of the digressions is only the editor of the story of the three brothers accounts for the widely different natures of the two components in *A Tale*. As for the fictions of the body, they have been seen to develop what is already a motif in the story of the brothers. An evolution can nevertheless be detected in the work of the satirist. The early works, *A Tale, The Battle of the Books*, or *A Tritical Essay*, are, though tactically unattackable, the most irregular. With the years the integration of the various constituents tends to become more faultless, and the articulations between the parts less abrupt, though they are never seamless, so that it is difficult to accept as final the verdict of those who, like Samuel Johnson and Ricardo Quintana, consider that the early works are the best. They are more flamboyant, but less convincing, than the later pieces.

Finally, it must be remembered that each new fiction, as it is brought into play, functions as a deflatory factor for the preceding one, lowering the reader's estimation of the matter discussed, or of the purported author's approach to it. When the serious framing discourse shifts to folktale, sensational secret history or comedy, the sense of entertainment increases as the assumption of seriousness is shattered. But when these narrative or dramatic patterns turn into puppet shows, light-heartedness destroys the last traces of pretence and pretension.

The main burden of expressing satirical intention falls to the fictions and, more precisely, to their odd combination. With Swift, the result is a more complex use of disparate fictions than is usually the case . They are forcibly yoked together, in order to bring out the absurdities in each other's representations of man's and society's activities. Ruptures, fictional discrepancies and effects of discordances are called upon to play a significant rôle. They develop their effect in the temporal dimension of the reading process. Swift's practice represents a departure from the norm of a fusion of incompatible components in a unified structure. It flirts with incoherence, but at the same time achieves a satirical pitch unknown among other satirists. As most adverse criticism has shown, Swift possesses to a supreme degree the art of making people feel ill-at-ease, while being capable of charming them with his impersonations, stories and comedies, and his handling of fiction largely contributes to this ambivalent effect.

II

The preceding remarks have gathered the threads of the central analysis as a preliminary to taking it one step further. It is indeed impossible to conclude this study of Swift's satirical fictions without touching upon the topic of the use these make of laughter. One does not automatically associate Swift with laughter, and the adjective "Swiftian" usually connotes a caustic kind of irony. Or it is said that laughter is for him a way of venting his "anger and indignation."[7] As everyone knows, laughter is a complex phenomenon and a response to widely different impressions. The study of his fictions, this dominant in his satirical output, demonstrates that the reader is first of all confronted with the creativeness of a mind endowed with an acute sense of the comic, before he becomes aware of an underlying indignation. Mention has just been made of the techniques of caricature that he utilizes, and the link between caricature and laughter is well-known. Besides, Swift's satires do not all express anger. Indignation is felt in places, in the virulence of the caricature in some passages of *A Tale* and *Gulliver's Travels*, and in *A Modest Proposal*, but

7 David Nokes, p. 17.

certainly not in *The Bickerstaff Papers*, *Polite Conversation*, *A Hue and Cry* or *Certain Abuses*. On the other hand, comic features have been identified in every aspect of his satires. From the example of the Laputan dreamer walking into lampposts to the hoaxes at the expense of an astrologer or criminal, and from the instances of swindlers swindled to the examples of inverted folktales, the occasions of laughter are numerous. Swift constantly relies on the comic to underline or qualify his satiric effects. It helps to squeeze the ridiculous out of certain attitudes or situations. The comic does not always play that rôle in other satires, nor, when it does, does it always do so as consistently.

The nature of Swift's comic is that of the classical age: that of French comedy and its roughly contemporary English adaptations, and there is no better guide to his ways of "fabricating" it than Henri Bergson's celebrated study, *Laughter*,[8] which is to a large extent based on an examination of the classical comedy of the same period. For it must not be forgotten that the causes of laughter – in contradistinction to its physical expression – and its social manifestations are subject to change, as is everything else in the life of a society and culture. If there is any difference between the laughter aroused by the comedies of the age and that aroused by satire, it is usually one in quality rather than kind. Swift's comic mostly belongs to the type known as burlesque, a type closely akin to caricature, which usually treats a foolish gesture, action, speech or piece of writing as serious or makes a serious one seem foolish. Now, it is not surprising that burlesque should hold a central place in his work, as it did in that of many eighteenth-century writers. It is a kind of comic whose analytical structure is of the same nature as that of the reigning conception of discourse as "representation" and "spreading out" of the observable, which the author of *A Tale of a Tub* has been seen to share with his age.[9]

The peculiarity of his burlesque is that it is more ambivalent than other kinds, because it works both ways at the same time. This is a new instance of the reversability of his satirical strategies. On the one hand

8 Henri Bergson, *Laughter*, reprinted in *Comedy*, ed. Wylie Sypher, Baltimore, Johns Hopkins University Press, 1956. All references are to this edition.
9 The word "burlesque" is used here in a more general sense than it was in the eighteenth-century distinction between "burlesque" and "travesty". This essentially stylistic and formal distinction does not apply in the case of Swift, who only occasionally utilized the extremes of "high" and "low" styles to satirical effects and whose burlesque is as often human as literary.

the farcical metamorphoses of the body and the metamorphic transpositions or reconstructions of contemporary reality by means of fanciful or literary patterns presents serious issues in an amusing way, and on the other hand these amusing and fanciful reconstructions are offered most seriously to the public as attested facts or maturely weighed opinions by their alleged authors or the type of publication that contains them.

Most conspicuous among Swift's comic procedures are the simple comic effects and common instances of ridicule. This is hardly surprising, when it is remembered that one of the significant features of the satires mentioned above is the popular nature of their fictions. This popular quality, which results from the deliberate choice of favourite contemporary writing forms, the recalling of tales likely to appeal to an unsophisticated public, and the evocation of a universe of almost childish entertainments, is unquestionably that which gives Swift's work a characteristic unity of tone. The nature of the comic brings it into even greater relief.

To assess the nature and function of the comic in Swift's satires, it will be convenient to retrace our steps. For him, the body is an inexhaustible source of comic and human burlesque, on occasions somewhat grating, but more often deliciously farcical, a fact which is frequently overlooked. His fascination with the poses, gesturing and metamorphoses of the human body has made it abundantly clear that he delights in reducing the "human form divine" to the level of a biological mechanism, a tailor's dummy or even an empty suit of clothes. Now, it is well-known that an overriding concern with the body, with this embarrassing mortal envelope for man's spiritual being, is conducive to laughter. When the *Travels* repeatedly draw attention to the demands of Gulliver's body, demands which he has to satisfy in whatever circumstances he finds himself – and some of them are pretty awkward –, or when coats become more important than their wearers in *A Tale of a Tub*, or when the nymphs of the poems and the "beaux" and "belles" of the aforementioned *Tale* proceed with their unsavoury strip-tease, the materiality of the body and its artificial covering become so insistently present to the imagination that the thinking side of man, his mind and soul, appears to have been stifled, or forcefully imprisoned without any chance of escape. Fixed in their materiality, the body and the clothes become absurd.

Other human figures, or occasionally the same ones, have been observed to pose and contort their anatomies in more or less grotesque manners. They are preachers and their congregations, orators and their listeners, entertainers and their audiences, or the characters peopling the social comedy of everyday life. They have been shown to behave mechanically, in a way that turns them into puppets with movable joints, and jumping jacks. To the Brobdingnagian countrymen, Gulliver appears to be little more than a well-oiled mechanical toy, and the spirit he puts into his performances does nothing to convince them to the contrary. The characters in the mock comedy of *Polite Conversation* also give the impression that they act and talk as though under the effect of released springs.

The notion of puppets with movable joints becomes inescapable when, in the cases of strip-teases and dissections, the satirist carries the comic of disarticulation to extremes, and the body, separated from its covering, is itself taken to pieces. The previous chapter described the synecdochic nature of Swift's representations of man. Now the practice consisting in diverting the reader's attention "to the physical in a person when it is the moral that is in question"[10] is precisely a common comic strategy. The synecdoche can even be said to be the basis of Swift's human burlesque. The satirist, who utilizes it systematically, spares the reader no detail in his descriptions of the characters' gestures, when these gestures betray an aspect of their frailties "unknown to, or at least apart from, the whole of [their] personality."[11] On the other hand, he omits to give a full account of their actions and, above all, of the way they might be deeply affected by their experience as individuals. If anything, Swift is more ruthless than other comic writers in his use of the body and clothes as comic synecdoches.

Another comic device, connected with the fictions of the body, is the use of disguise. Disguises are by no means always comic: in folktales, and even more in conspiracy stories, this is seldom the case. Yet Guy Fawkes Day and Carnivals show how easy it is with masks and disguises to pass from the serious to the comic, and vice versa. With Swift, there is not the slightest hesitation. Disguises turn all conspiracy stories into masquerades and farces. In the first place it must be remembered that, for him, clothes are in general disguises of a sort, in so far as they conceal man's frail or decrepit physical nature. In this respect, Corinna, the "beautiful young nymph", Chloe or Celia in the poems, and Gulliver, are brethren of the same mold. Peter, Martin and Jack's extravagant additions

10 Henry Bergson, p. 135.
11 Ibid., p. 153.

to their plain coats turn the latter into carnival attire. The erosion of a distinction between dress and disguise is what makes the former comic. As for the stories featuring real or assumed disguises, like *A New Journey to Paris*, *A Hue and Cry*, or *An Examination of Certain Abuses*, their comic character is directly linked to their use of extravagant, inefficient, or assumed but non-existent, concealment. Lastly, the connection between disguises and masks has been noted, and the unmasking of villainy usually marks the triumph of comedy over tragedy.

A fourth comic device, omnipresent in the fictions of the body, is that defined as the substitution of regulations and automatic procedures for the laws of nature.[12] The meaningless court ritual of Lilliput, with its rope-dancing and leaping over sticks (PW vol. xi, pp. 38 - 39), is one instance of custom solidifying into meaningless repetition. Through repetition, these gestures have acquired an impetus of their own, which becomes the justification of their perpetuation. Gulliver's descriptions to his master Houyhnhnm of the way wars and lawsuits, once started, never end offer other instances of this self-engendered impetus (ibid, pp. 245 - 247, 248 - 250). Part of the comic here resides in the fact that one loses sight of the true purpose and meaning of the action. In Bergson's words, *"the manner seek[s] to outdo the matter, the letter aim[s] at ousting the spirit"*,[13] so that performance becomes an end in itself; the more brilliantly it functions, the better. The same type of comic can be detected in the two "vignettes" of London life, "A Description of the Morning" and "A Description of a City Shower". The regular recurrence of dawn and showers kills both their magic and the mythological meaning of these two events: the sense of awe they ought to awaken is lost. In the former (SPW. p. 86), dawn no longer appears as the miraculous rebirth of purity and a new, innocent beginning. The scrubbing and washing of the early hours only temporarily erase the traces left by the sinful activities of the previous night. At the same time, these activities have become so habitual that the very thrill inspired by sinning is dulled. In the second poem (SPW, pp. 91 - 93), the flood following the heavy shower, far from representing a permanent cleansing of the city, merely means the temporary interruption of pleasurable activities, and exists as a momentary nuisance. It drains off refuse, only to allow it to accumulate again.

12 Ibid., pp. 90-91.
13 Ibid., p. 94.

With the fictions of the body, the reader is made to laugh as "we laugh at Sancho Panza tumbled into a bedquilt and tossed into the air like a football. [Or] we laugh at Baron Munchausen turned into a cannon-ball and travelling through space."[14] The comic of the body can be said to be the most conspicuous source of laughter in Swift's satires, although it is not the only one. The development of the framed fictions provides another.

Folktales may not be funny, but their inbred optimism relates them to the comic mode. With them, the idea that "all's well that ends well" is the rule, rather than the exception. Furthermore, stories of fathers' wills, brothers' rivalries, and dwarfs and giants afford opportunities for amusing scenes and encounters. It is obvious that a "hazel-nut child" falling into a bowl of cream, a gigantic ogre outsmarted by a boy or girl, or a human being outdone by an animal are figures that can easily be ridiculed, and Swift can always be counted upon to make the most of such openings. The conspiracy stories are another matter: they contain little that can be turned to good account, apart from their occasional use of disguises and the theme of unmasking – when, of course, as in comedy, the unmasking is that of a villain. The satirist must therefore supply comic elements from other sources. One important source is the portrayal of the typical villains of comedy, the so-called "blocking" characters: Dismal, the treacherous politician is such a character; the Earl of Wharton, the unscrupulous and dishonest free-thinker is another; and the king of Lilliput, the vain prince imbued with a sense of his importance and omnipotence, a third one. Swift does not conceive them as real characters, but as general types according to the typology of classical comedy. They are figures whose devious frames of mind is for ever fixed, and for whom the narratives of conspiracy are a means by which they can be presented in action and shown to be evil. As for the scenes related to the comedy of manners, these provide the satirist with the whole range of familiar, ready-made, comic features.

Yet another source of comedy in the framed narrative and dramatic fictions can be put down to the systematic upsetting of expectations. This can take two forms: on the one hand, several of these fictions are tales of swindlers swindled or overreachers defeated by themselves. In *A Tale*, Peter, at the pinnacle of his luxurious dressing, ends up being mistaken for his tattered brother, Jack (PW vol. i, p. 127). In *The Bickerstaff*

14 Ibid., pp. 97-98.

Papers, an astrologer's predictions turn against him and ruin him, instead of supporting him and his family. As against that, however, there is the way Swift transforms literary patterns into mock patterns, thereby defeating the expectations of the reader. Such mock patterns are a first instance of literary burlesque. When the mind sufficiently distances itself, there is always something amusing about reversals of patterns, and little does it matter if the winning side in a conflict is not the expected one, so long as it is the more likeable one. The satirist knows this well, even when he seems to have disregarded the rules of comedy. Where comedy idealizes the weak and blackens the powerful, in order to vindicate the former, Swift is at pains to adapt the colouring where necessary, as he does with the Lilliputians and the Brobdingnagians, so as to ensure that the reader rejoices at the escape, or victory, of the magnanimous giants, and at the discomfiture of the "pernicious Race of little odious Vermin", who are, in one case, the Lilliputians themselves and, in the other, a would-be representative of European man, Gulliver. Whereas broadside ballads idealize criminals, Ebenezor Elliston's *Last Speech and Dying Words* is a nasty swipe at a celebrated thief, and the reader is led to approve of his execution, and to applaud the veiled threat that his supposed confession represents for his former associates. Because they upset traditional expectations, Swift's mock patterns are not merely satirical, they are also comic, or they are satirical because they utilize comic devices. In so far as they do not aim at ridiculing the traditional patterns which they borrow from and invert – the folktale, conspiracy story and comic scene –, they can even be seen as an essentially comic device.

Like the framed fictions, the framing discourses develop their particular kind of comic devices. Here again, the genre of the discourse is not what is comic: the medium is chosen primarily because it is a convenient means of attracting attention. Besides, the news item, the letter, the essay, the proposal are the very forms that Swift uses with the utmost seriousness as a polemicist. In fact, calling parodies these fakes that form the wrapping of his satirical fictions may even be a misnomer, for each piece is exactly what it declares itself to be: a contribution to a debate in its own right, even if it proves to be a blotched job or/and a fake in the end. So the target of the satire, as already said, is usually the pen that wrote it, or the use some writers and readers make of the genre, but not the genre itself. The comic, where there is any, focuses on use and the user. This is, of course, as it should be in productions dating from the age of classical comedy, when writers were more convinced than ever that only what is human, whether man himself or his actions, could produce comic effects.

At this point it is necessary to return once more to the ruptures and other inconsistencies that have been brought into relief by the above description of the satires' structures. The discrepancy between what the fake pieces pretend to be, and what they turn out to contain, or between one kind of fiction and another, show them to be inconsistent, and these inconsistencies usually suggest an inconsequent human behaviour or an illogical argument. Now everyone knows that inconsistencies and illogicalities are a frequent source of laughter. The second chapter of the present study argued that the gaps between the framing discourses and the framed fictions endow the purported authors with whatever individuality they possess – whenever there is an identifiable purported author, that is –, and that this individuality proceeds from their failure to recognize their errors or misconceptions. The chapter came to the conclusion that their particular type of blindness is a shortcoming which gives them their individuality. It cuts them off from the collectivity of their readers, who are made to feel that they know better. This is again a common comic strategy, based on the fact that, "invisible to its actual owner, . . . the comic ever partakes of the unconscious".[15] Truly comic characters all present a similar blind side, which renders them laughable to their circle of acquaintances on the one hand, and to an audience or readership on the other. The central rupture and other discrepancies between the fictions, which embody this blindness, are that which triggers off the laughter, as one begins to perceive the inconsistency of the framing discourse. The blindness of the purported authors takes different forms, as has already been suggested. When they are fully individualized, like Wagstaff or Gulliver, it is the result of pride, vanity, poor education, partisanship, prejudice, limited intelligence, just as in the case of traditional comic characters - and, of course, the purported authors *are* stock comic figures of a sort.

The ruptures and discrepancies between the fictions are not the only source of comedy in the framing discourses. The rhetoric of the discourses is often another. The special character of Swift's literary burlesque appears here in its clearest form. Sometimes the prestige of a certain literary form leads a purported writer to use it mechanically. The

15 Ibid., p. 171

form is left to play itself out, irrespective of the nature or value of the message, or else it is repeated again and again. The succession of prefatory pieces and the digressions in *A Tale* conveys this impression: the purported hack cannot stop writing one after another. Sometimes the form is shown to be adapted inappropriately by its alleged author to any topic, as though it were a universal recipe. For this reason, *A Meditation upon a Broomstick* fails to meet what was an imperative requirement of serious writing in the eighteenth century: for the subject matter, the absurd trope of a broomstick which symbolizes man, is not in keeping with the elevated style and the solemn nature of the occasion, a religious and moral meditation. The fake uninspired essays, *A Tritical Essay* and *The Mechanical Operation of the Spirit*, in which the rigidity of the outline prevents, or rather, stifles the full fictional development of the folklore, conspiracy or comedy germ, also exhibit this type of comic feature. The form hangs loose upon the thin contents. Like inconsistent ways of behaving or illogical arguments, a rigid and mechanical application of fashionable formalism here serves to amuse. Laughter is provoked by the soullessness and emptiness of the performance. The piece and the writer are made to appear duds, for all their efforts and pretentions.

As a contrast to the cases where mechanical formalism predominates, there can be placed those instances where the discourse stumbles over "reality". Failing to keep a rein on his imagination or obsessions, the purported author ignores the purpose for which the form is an adequate medium, or rather, he seeks to bend the form to his own needs. His mind follows its own course and becomes inattentive to facts. In so doing, his vision distorts reality. The best illustration of this comic device has been seen to be *An Examination of Certain Abuses. Gulliver's Travels* is another example. The repetitive pattern in it is not of the same type as in *A Tale*: it is not mechanical and gratuitous, but obsessive. Not only does Gulliver tell, not one, not two, not three, but four fanciful voyages, but the ending gives a hint of further repetitions. The purported author's diatribe against man's vanity at the end of Book iv, which sounds as though it were coming from the mouth of Molière's misanthrope, recalls the sombre letter, signed by himself, which prefaces later editions. In so far as the ending brings the beginning back to mind, the reading process becomes circular and suggests the endless rehearsal of sailors' yarns. This may well have been intended to underline the presence of the grating comic, not only in the last pages, but throughout the travel account. In the *Travels*, the presence of this comic of repetition makes sense: it fits in with the portrayal of the narrator himself, who is a typical inattentive, comic figure, as is shown by the numerous inconsistencies he betrays in his behaviour and ideas, as he moves from one fairyland to another. In consequence, when at the end of his account he expresses his preference for the company of horses to that of his wife and family, the overall organization of the satire should put it beyond dispute that both the situation and the intensity of his horror of mankind are typical of the comic of the classical age. With purported authors getting carried away by their emotions or ideas, like Gulliver, the comic proceeds from a lack of sense of proportion and from an attempt on their part to bend reality to their own fixed ideas. Such an attempt is always doomed to failure, and laughter is inspired by the excess and the relief afforded by that failure.

A word must be added about the discourses where the purported author is not important. It should be pointed out that these are not completely devoid of comic either, but it results from mere incongruity of structure, from the combination of ill-assorted constituents: like the news item featuring a folklore character or a melodramatic conspirator, and a reportage on city life presented as a pastoral. As already noted, the gap between form and content draws attention to itself, and the comic touch is light. It brightens up the fiction, and at the same time underlines the satirical point. Rather than speak of a comic effect in this case, it may be preferable to speak of humour, as such pieces do not so much claim to be one thing whilst really being another, as affect to be that which they are not.

The general development of the framing discourses with their ruptures triggers off laughter during the process of reading; the stylistic expression of character and/or mechanic formalism prolongs it. There is another comic device, connected with the wrapping of the fictions in fashionable forms, which may be said to have a delayed effect. Individual pieces have been described as practical jokes played on particular individuals. More generally, Swift's satirical fictions give the impression of being spurious contributions to a large contemporary debate of ideas. They allude to other contemporary pieces or their authors by title and name. They mention the numerous writings on this or that subject. In doing so, they evoke the image of an irresistible, cumbersome accumulation of writings, supporting and contradicting one another, which is flooding the market. Each new piece, Swift's like everybody else's, implies that a new impetus is being given to the debate, in order to revive or accelerate it. This accumulation or acceleration, conveying as it does the impression of an unending process of repetition, with variations, contributes to making the debate seem like a game, and the game seem like another vast and amusing joke. Unfortunately, there is no shower here that can wash all the trash away, as there is in "Description of a City Shower".

One further factor needs to be mentioned, which is not comic in itself, but which is capable of producing, or at least underlining, comic effects. This factor is the use of repetitions and parallels in a work: recurrent words, gestures, situations and events found mainly, although not exclusively, in the more ample fictions. Not only do these recurrent features bring discrepancies and automatisms into relief, but they are also a necessary condition for the comic of repetition and unexpected reversals. One of the evident effects achieved by the alternance of folktale episodes and digressions in *A Tale*, by the collection of four journeys, and not three or two, in Gulliver's narrative, and by the accumulation of three acts of the same nature in *Polite Conversation* is, to quote Bergson again, to bring "a group of characters, act after act, into the most varied surroundings, so as to reproduce, under ever fresh circumstances, one and the same series of incidents or accidents more or less symmetrically identical."[16] The hack's compulsive desire to interrupt his narrative with digressions, Gulliver's compulsive departures away from home, and the characters' tedious repetitions of worn out phrases in every circumstance are instances of the comic often defined as that of a "Jack in the box", and Swift avails himself of the patterns of parallels and repetitions, in order to make use of it – although more discreetly than one would expect from such an incisive satirist. As a result, the overall effect is at least as comic as satiric: a fact well worth reflecting upon.

If there is relatively little disagreement on how comic effects are produced, analysts of the phenomenon of laughter since Bergson have found it more difficult to accept his contention that "laughter is really and truly a kind of social 'ragging'" of the victim:[17] a correction administered to a mal-adjusted person, "being intended to humiliate" and "make a painful impression on the person against whom it is directed."[18] What has been said so far suggests one reason for this dissatisfaction. To the

16 Ibid., p. 119
17 Ibid., p. 148
18 Ibid, p. 187

extent that Bergson emphasizes the fact that laughter is "an immediate corrective"[19], his explanation is truer of satire than of comedy proper. A discussion of the function of comedy within a satire makes it necessary to distinguish their nature and rôle more precisely, in order to understand what is added by the comic element to the satirical effect.

When Bergson describes man as an animal which laughs and "which is laughed at"[20], when he argues that the comic is mostly unconscious[21] and the result of a certain "automatism, *inelasticity*, habit that has been contracted and maintained", or of "some simple mechanical action in which [the] personality would be for ever absorbed"[22], he seems to be assuming, without expressly saying so, that laughter aims at producing a consciousness within the victim that will lead him to reform and adjust his ideas or conduct, according to the truth of experience and the exigencies of communal life. Consciousness must replace unconsciousness and lead to a change of attitude or behaviour. Satire may wish to attain that goal, but comedy does not. The purpose of laughter is not to rectify and produce reforms, for the essential reason that this would dry up the spring of comedy itself. The failings people laugh at may, at times, be inconvenient for society. They may even represent certain dangers, when the person exhibiting the symptoms is in a position of power – but laughter does not wish for the disappearance of that which makes it possible in the first place. Laughter is conservative. So it would be more accurate to say that the classical portrayal of character types, such as the miser, the misanthrope or the hypocrite, holds up to ridicule certain general weaknesses, in order to discourage, not their incorrigible victims, but other people from yielding to the same inclinations, or even from merely condoning their existence. Rather, it would seem to be the rôle of laughter to create a temporary alliance between those who share a good joke at the expense of a victim. Laughter excludes the victim from the group. At the same time, for those who laugh, it renders impossible the attitude or conduct or idea ridiculed, thus creating a bond of complicity between them.[23]

19 Ibid., p. 117
20 Ibid., p. 62.
21 Ibid., p. 71.
22 Ibid., p 76.
23 In a different approach to the problem, which stresses the painful emotions often aroused by laughter, rather than its "detached gaiety", Allan Ingram, following Freud, comes to a similar conclusion (op. cit., pp. 90, 116 - 117).

If this is the case, the comic side of Swift's satirical fictions cannot but modify the satirical effect, particularly in that which concerns its *ad hominem* attack and rebuke. Much ingenuity has been displayed in attempts to reconcile Swift's practice with the general theory of satire, to show that he usually contrives to trap the reader into identifying himself either with the blind purported author, or with some other figure of fun in the fiction. The argument, as it goes, is that the figure functioning as the satirical target within the fiction is a sufficiently generalized type for him to be seen as a mirror, in which the common reader can recognize himself. The reasoning has been employed in the analysis of *Gulliver's Travels* to gain results that are more interesting than convincing.[24] The study of Swift's fictional patterns and use of comic devices brings a somewhat different light to bear on the question of the chastening effect of his satires. After all, are there many readers who have ever identified themselves with Gulliver? Has not Gulliver always been that queer chap, that as-it-were "Hazelnut creature", to whom the funniest things happen? If there is an identification by the reader with the target of the ridicule, it surely cannot be left to such an uncontrollable phenomenon as a feeling of empathy: it must proceed along different lines.

As is demonstrated in the first chapter of the present study, the reader is hooked as a reader, whose tastes, passions and prejudices are flattered by a writer who apparently expresses them. This basic structural function of parody combines with the art of caricature. Swift's images of over-dressed bodies and anatomies stripped naked, posing and contorting, frequently appeal to the co-enunciatior's perverse instincts. The strip-tease or devouring of some characters and the performances of others titillate before they repulse. As he begins to perceive the general drift of the argument and becomes aware that he is being fooled and that his least noble instincts have been awakened, the reader dissociates himself from the purported author who is addressing him, and distances himself. It is here that the comic intervenes. Having made its first contribution by drawing the reader's attention to the deception, it then leads him, progressively or abruptly as is the case, to realize that the purported author is wrong, that his blindness is due to some unacceptable rigidity

<hr>

24 Robert Merle, "Les Desseins de Gulliver," *Revue de Paris* 66: 15 (1959); Samuel H. Monk, "The Pride of Lemuel Gulliver," *Sewanee Review* 63: 73 (1955); Hermann J. Real and Heinz J. Vienken, *Jonathan Swift: "Gulliver's Travels"*, pp. 78 - 79.

in his mind, and that he should no longer accept his rôle as co-enunciator. Once the reader has experienced the sting of undeception, which is truly satirical, the comic brings him the relief of laughter, a relief which is however not complete, as he who knows that he has been nearly or actually trapped never laughs as spontaneously as the strictly detached observer of a comic event. Laughter makes him feel that he is in league with those who cannot, or will not, accept the shortcomings and absurdities being ridiculed. Consequently, the comic does not so much correct a victim, as make those who laugh at him watchful as regards their own conduct, as well as that of others. It exerts a pressure that keeps them in the league of those who share the laugh. No one likes to be excluded from the group of those laughing, least of all those who feel a little guilty: laughter represents consciousness and knowledge on the part of a privileged group of initiates; it is a cohesive force within the group. Along with complicity, it creates a sort of consensus, which is as reassuring to the insiders as it seems threatening to outsiders. Reading *The Bickerstaff Papers* makes it an improbability that sensible readers will be taken in by almanac predictions in the future. Perusing *A Tale*, *The Battle of the Books* and *A Tritical Essay* discourages readers forever from taking seriously certain claims of the literature of the "Moderns". *A Modest Proposal* throws suspicion on similar proposals of final solutions, and on the motivations behind them. *An Examination of Certain Abuses* and *A Letter from the Pretender to a Whig Lord* force the reader to dissociate himself from blind partisanship or political dishonesty. Gulliver should have even rendered impossible any feeling of the white man's superiority, of the superiority of his social and political institutions, and of his civilization, among other things. That this early anti-colonial tract did not may have something to do with the fact that there was at first little cause to heed the warning contained in its message and that, later, when it was found embarrassing in the nineteenth century, it was drastically reduced to the status of a classic for children and the product of a deranged mind. It is also significant that nineteenth-century readers, of all readers, should have been the most impervious to the comic side of Swift's satirical fictions, and their strategy of dissociation through laughter.

To those who have felt that Swift's description of man's endless varieties of shortcomings comes closer to the cosmic and nihilistic laughter of a Beckett, than the social and psychological comic of a Molière, the reply can only be that, in his satires, laughter is repetitive, not cumulative. It ridicules precise objects but, however numerous these are, it does not harden into a prolonged peal of desperate laughter, which would, indeed, have been a sure sign of misanthropy: one of those contracted bad habits that classical comedy knew how to ridicule so well. As is made clear by the study of Swift's handling of fictional patterns, separately and in combination, and of his handling of the comic, the time factor of the reading process, frequently ignored by commentators, is of greater importance with him than with perhaps any other satirist. For him, satire is a strategy designed to sting a conscience which is enclined to embrace this or that attitude, and then to dissociate it from the evils thereby exposed, by amusing it with the contemplation of its ridicule. But it must be remembered that an acute sense of the comic does not automatically make a man an optimist. The greatest comic artists have probably been more often disillusioned with mankind than confident in its capacity to improve. Perhaps laughter, in its most refined artistic expressions, is a way of preventing things from getting worse, a protest on behalf of man's dignity, at the same time as being a means to relief: all things that pure satire is not, and does not do.

III

When Swift utilizes fictions to construct his references to reality, he creates verbal and mental representations of this reality. By means of various structural devices and laughter, he directs the reader's attention to the human ridicule portrayed in these verbal and mental representations, thus turning them into satire. In so far as narrative and dramatic fictions are ways of making sense of certain aspects of life which elude discursive explanation, they mean what they tell and resist conceptualization. As repeatedly noted, they can only be evaluated by means of description and comparison. Beyond this point, everything becomes context-bound interpretation: namely personal or collective appreciation, instead of comprehension. On the other hand, it is true that eighteenth-century imaginative writings in general, and Swift's fictions in particular, lend themselves to conceptualization better than those of other periods. They are analyzable into distinct ideas and judgments because their use of fictions is itself analytical. It is with a glance at this conceptual meaning of his satirical fictions that this study of the satirist will conclude.

Few writers have been so inexplicit about their own intentions or the way their works should be read, as Swift was. Moreover, the fact that his satires are complex fictions does not make it any easier for the literary historian to define this "conceptual meaning". In the specific case of *Gulliver's Travels*, there are, it is true, two pronouncements from the Dean of St Patrick. Both occur in letters to friends. They suggest that the real subject of the *Travels* is man as a biological species. Among other things, they say that man is not a reasonable animal (*animal rationale*) as the treatises of logic will have it, but merely an animal capable of reason (*rationis capax*).[25] The temptation to extrapolate from these occasional statements, which are no more than sallies, and to see in them a central concern of the satirist from the time of *A Tale of a Tub*, is great. They constitute, at the very least, an acceptable hypothesis, as madness, or the failure to be reasonable, to behave or think sensibly, is a contant preoccupation in *A Tale*, *The Bickerstaff Papers*, *An Examination of Certain Abuses*, "Strephon and Chloe", "Cassinus and Peter", and *A Modest Proposal*, as well as in *Gulliver's Travels*. The capacity for reason is, moreover, connected with social attitudes and moral standards – in particular, decency and honesty. Swift dislikes all displays of extravagance and manifestations of stupidity and duplicity, as *Polite Conversation*, *Mr C[olli]ns's Discourse*, *Ebenezor Elliston*, *The Injured Lady* and *A Letter from the Pretender to a Whig Lord* testify. But these are very general and abstract ideas, and his satires are dramatizations of the concrete debates of his time, and of their practical issues. As satires, they tell of the evils of the day, as they were experienced by individuals. Their subjects are a specific category of hack writers or projectors, a particular kind of debasement of the language, the use and abuse of astrology in almanacs, identifiable criminals, the peace negociations of 1711 - 1712, the rivalry between the political parties, the court of George I, the way the king chose his ministers, poverty in Ireland with reference to the responsibility of the landowners, endless lawsuits that ruin people who seek reparation, the aberrations of fashion, decrepitude, physical weakness and deformity. Sometimes they address specific issues in relation to identifiable events, sometimes they address a general trend. The present study of Swift's use of fictions, concerned as it is with the way they help the satirist construct his references to these aspects of life, and give them a satirical turn, cannot dream of

25 *Correspondence*, vol. iii, p. 103

returning to the vast problem of the historical references themselves. Besides, this is unnecessary as it is ground already well trodden. It will be content to point out in conclusion what is contributed to the interpretation of circumstantial reality by the transpositions, the fictionalization and the distortions imposed on it: what is entailed by the simple fact of choosing this or that fictional pattern, and how the fictional reconstruction of the reference serves to qualify the reader's understanding of the specific, concrete facts alluded to.

Drama and narrative are concerned with processes, causes and consequences, or manifestations of hidden forces. When he presents societies and their political institutions, be it in a realistic or a fanciful way, Swift does so, not only in order to size up their qualities and deficiences, as a strictly topical satire might be content to do. When one of his purported authors is made to betray a preposterous notion or blameworthy conduct, this is done not simply to expose him. In both cases, the fictions show the reasons why things go wrong, or why they are not as they should be. With Swift, the explanation given remains much the same from work to work. Whatever is wrong with society or its institutions, whatever is reprehensible in man's behaviour or foolish in his conduct, can be attributed to the imperfections of his human nature. The malfunctioning of institutions is an indictment against the men who run them. People misbehave because they yield to their passions. Swift's fictions, as dramatic and narrative patterns, are concerned with the motivations behind the need to compose a ballad, a pamphlet or a treatise; the motivations behind the need to betray, to dominate or to be duped. All the satirical parodies of current forms of discourse, with their identifiable putative authors, are written as the language gestures of people who reveal unsound or guilty motivations. In these cases, the motivations are usually similar to those of the puppet characters, about whom they write in what becomes the tale within the discourse, or the farce of the fictions of the body within the tale. This quest for guilty, or at least blameworthy, motivations is one of the strengths of Swift's fictional satires, just as it is one of the weaknesses of his work as an historian: it is what makes his *History of the Four Last Years of the Queen* so disappointing as an historical work.

With the few exceptions of the characters used as foils to human targets in the satires, the purported authors and the characters within the fictions are motivated by what could roughly be termed the passions considered to produce the seven deadly sins of old theology. This is no accident, of course. As the Dean put it, in his sermon "On the Trinity":

the *Reason* of every particular Man is weak and wavering, perpetually swayed and turned by his Interests, his Passions, and his Vices. (PW vol. ix, p. 166)

Much the same point is made in *Further Thoughts on Religion*, in terms that are even more vigorous. In the course of a comparison of humans with animals, Swift writes,

men degenerate every day, merely by the folly, the perverseness, the avarice, the tyranny, the pride, the treachery, or inhumanity of their own kind. (Ibid., p. 263)

The seat of these passions may be the mind or the body, but it is always through the body, the frailer part of human nature, that they find expression. For the satirist, the body does not only constitute the formal core of individual fictions, it is also at the heart of his exploration of man's nature, and of its figurative representation. He strips it naked, auscultates and dissects it to lay bare the springs of human weaknesses. The fictions of the body dressed, posing or contorting then show these weaknesses in action, as do the other fictional patterns, folktales, conspiracy stories, comedy of little vices, or that other comedy proposed by the framing discourses, the impersonation of the vanity of authorship.

Swift's inventory of human weaknesses, which varies according to circumstance, is not exactly that of St Thomas Aquinas' sins, evidently. It bears the mark of Swift's own time. The satirist is closer to his admired La Rochefoucauld than to earlier theologians. As the *Catholic Encyclopaedia* puts it, "Evolution has revolutionized morality, sin is no more." The notion of an offense against God has been replaced by the notion of doing wrong. In this respect, Swift's list of sins is modern. On the other hand, the sense of degeneration is ancient: closer to Milton's and Marlowe's than to the Anglican theology of his contemporaries. For Swift, whatever is wrong is still profoundly evil, and not just bad; and the root of all evil is self-love:

The Motives of the best Actions will not bear too strict an Enquiry. It is allowed, that the Cause of most Actions, good or bad, may be resolved into the Love of our selves: But the Self-Love of some Men inclines them to please others; and the Self-Love of others is wholly employed in pleasing themselves. This makes the great Distinction between Virtue and Vice. (*Thoughts on Various Subjects*, PW vol. iv, p. 243)

According to St Thomas and St Gregory, the chief deadly sin was pride, from which all other sins derived. For Swift, it is self-love, which is a kind of pride, or rather, as the author prefers to have it, a kind of vanity: vanity is self-love based on particularly empty claims. Whether as pride or as vanity, self-love also leads to greed, gluttony, lust, sloth, envy, and anger or violence.

Of all these sins, it is vanity that the satirist ridicules most frequently: in the exhibitionism of ambitious, yet foolish, purported authors; in the pomp of kings; or in various examples of coquetry. By contrast to its sibling form, pride, it is a social failing, and for that reason it interests Swift, since the satirist is primarily concerned with the attitude of man in society: with the body that has lost its autonomy to become part of the "social body". Vanity causes blindness and is usually dismissed with a smile. Greed, however, is a more sinister force, and here the satirist's conception is more traditional. His depiction of it demonstrates a recognition of the negative influence it is supposed to exert on man's character and on social life in general. As a form of voracious egoism, it leads to treachery, burglary and blackmail, which are the themes of one of the central fictions of the satirical work: the conspiracy story. Gluttony could harldy have meant the same thing to the well-fed population of eighteenth-century England as it had done in earlier periods of hardship, and it would have been a similarly remote notion to the upper classes in Ireland, as _A Modest Proposal_ makes clear. Yet a celebrated passage of _Gulliver's Travels_ is devoted to excessive indulgence in food and drink (PW vol. xi, pp. 251 - 254). The victims are the gentry and their offspring, and the consequence of their actions a weakening of their race, and the increasing incapacity of the nobility to keep its rank. Gluttony is intrinsically connected with lust, again presented in the most traditional manner. Sloth is no longer seen as leading to despair and suicide, however. For Swift, it breeds spleen, then already becoming the fashionable malady of the upper classes, which in turn breeds lust and gluttony. Together these engender ill-health. By them, people are turned into dupes to be exploited by astrologers, quack doctors, and such unscrupulous clergymen as Peter is in _A Tale_. These weaknesses mostly harm the bodies of those who are prone to them, but also end up sapping the morale of society, and corrupting it. It is interesting to note that libertinism, which was, historically, less than fifty years away, and was to become in literature a liberating force and, for the individual, a means of achieving personal and political liberty, was still regarded by Swift as precisely the opposite: as an obstacle to the responsible exercise of liberty within the community and as a cause of enslavement. It was in such terms that Christian theology had described the phenomenon.

With envy, the satirist comes back to the vices and sins that cause divisions. Born of frustration, envy finds expression in hypocrisy and other kinds of deceit. An active feeling when coupled with greed, it brings about thefts, conspiracies, and all kinds of political upheavals and social disorders, as the reader is reminded in *The Humble Petition of the Footmen of Dublin*. On the other hand, coupled with sloth, it gives rise to the comedy of man's little failings. Lastly, anger is presented as a component in most other sins, either in the form of a brutal assertion of these other sins, or else as a violent reaction against any obstacles encountered on the road to the gratification of an individual's appetites.

Swift does not limit his attention to what, for the sake of convenience here, has been called "the seven deadly sins" and their effects. His various fictions reveal him to be sensitive to minor, as well as major, failings. However, it is the seven deadly sins that he exposes with the greatest severity, and which he describes in comic terms which are most cruel. The prominent rôle they play in the development of the narrative or dramatic fictional patterns can be regarded as underlining the connection between the work of the satirist and a further aspect of his activities. In addition to highlighting the connection with his work as an historian, they also reveal a close link with his activities as a churchman: a link between the satirist on the one hand and the author of the sermons and Dean on the other, who also led by example. Indeed, it could hardly have been otherwise considering how seriously this seemingly worldly writer took his ecclesiastical duties, firstly as a vicar, and later in his rôle as Dean of Dublin's Anglican Cathedral. The connection is not too obvious in his writings, but it is worth making the point that the moralist's sense of man's infirmity has its foundations in his theological understanding of man's fallen nature, even though he seems to have exchanged the old notion of sinning against God for the more modern equivalent of a dereliction of duty to society. Indirectly he uses the seventeenth-century concept of the corrupt nature of man to attack the more optimistic eighteenth-century doctrines of Man. This is the basis for what he calls his special brand of "Misanthropy (though not Timons manner)"[26]. The root of his satirical spirit is religious, grounded in a deep sense of divine

---

26 *Correspondence*, ibid.

perfection. Its orientation is social and political. Because of the former, he has been better understood by those of a religious inclination, such as the founder of the Methodist Church[27], than by the more wordly Anglican churchmen like William Warburton, later Bishop of Gloucester, Jonathan Smedley, Dean of Clogher and James Humes, theologian and Fellow of Dulwich College, who all regarded Swift's picture of man as an affront to man's dignity.[28] Because of the social and political orientation of his reflexion, however, he was hailed by the avant-garde of the French Encyclopedists as a kindred spirit, and he has continued to be described as a revolutionary thinker.[29]

Swift's profound sense of man's unworthiness may, to many readers, have made him appear to be a man turned towards the past, but in one respect at least he belongs to the new century, the eighteenth, and not the seventeenth. Man's depravity arouses not his horror, but rather his impatience, and at the same time inspires his disbelief and amusement. Hence the pleasure he takes in deflating whoever and whatever needs to be brought back down to earth – where what is acceptable is judged according to the truly British standards of empirical reasonableness and practicality. Swift's satirical fictions are his way of combatting the trivialization of evil in an increasingly secular age.

27 John Wesley, *The Doctrine of Original Sin, According to Scripture, Reason, and Experience* [1756], excerpts of which are reprinted in *Jonathan Swift*, Penguin Critical Anthologies, pp. 72-76 John Wesley also used to read aloud Swift's description of the Yahoos to convince his congregation of the horror of sin.

28 Concerning William Warburton's and Jonathan Smedley's reactions, see Bertrand A. Goldgar, "A Contemporary Reaction to *Gulliver's Travels*", *The Scriblerian* 5: 1 - 4 (1972).

The argument put forward here is not new. It was already used in 1755 by Deane Swift and John Hawkesworth in their defence of *Gulliver's Travels* against its detractors (see *Swift: The Critical Heritage*, pp. 144 - 145, 154). What is worth noting however is that the study of Swift's fictions confirms the validity of their response as readers, whereas the response of the detractors is best accounted for by the evolution of the mentalities.

29 A.L.Rowse, *Jonathan Swift: Major Prophet*, London, Thames and Hudson, 1975. What precedes shows, however, that I disagree with Dr Rowse's description of Swift as an upright practical man rather than a truly religious one (pp. 118 - 121).

Conclusion

At the beginning of this study mention was made that critics had usually devoted more attention to those aspects of Swift's satires which require historical explanations, and are therefore of less immediate interest today, than to the more universal features of their fictions. This is of course understandable, but unfortunate in so far as the latter account for the fact that his masterpieces have aged less than is habitually the case with satires. The present inquiry suggests that, owing to the multiplicity of their fictional patterns, Swift's satires have found in themselves the necessary resources to renew their power to captivate successive generations of readers.

Investigating the more creative aspects of Swift's satirical work has also served to demonstrate how his epistemological assumptions about language and genres, which are those of his time, find concrete expression in a great variety of literary forms handled with consumate skill. The analysis has shown how the parodies of current discourses, the free imitation of dramatic and narrative plots borrowed from folktales, conspiracy stories or comedies, and the constant metamorphosing of the human body enable Swift to re-figure his experience of his time in fictional, at the same time as satirical, terms.

Clearly, the restriction of the analysis to these organizing features does not exhaust that of his fictions. What precedes has more than once hinted that other, non-structural, fictional features are evident in the satires, such as the above-mentioned presence of the Restoration and Augustan typologies of comic characters and situations. Beyond all these components, there is finally the vision itself, or rather the visions, as each refiguration of experience produces a vivid world of its own. Nevertheless, a number of conclusions can be drawn from the preceding investigation. With respect to the aims advanced in the introduction, the results stand within precise limits. In so far as the basic fictional patterns determine the way in which the satirical vision in each satire is presented, they above all concern aspects which have some direct connection with the reading experience. They can be briefly summed up under six headings: the importance of the fictional elements themselves within the economy of the satires; the special qualities that the satires owe to this fictional dominant; the nature of the connection that Swift's satires have with the literature of their time on the one hand and that which they have with satire in general, in other words with the genre, on the other; the ambivalent nature of the satirist's work, which has been in turn extolled and decried; and the different impact that his satires can have on readers.

What is striking about the imaginative qualities of Swift's satirical fictions taken as a whole, and what remains odd, is that they characterize the work of a man who is also, in many respects, a convinced representative of the Age of Reason, an age inclined to mistrust the human imagination, or at least to hold it in only moderate esteem. In fact, his satires are proofs that he never considered his advocacy of a better use of reason as irreconcilable with a defense of imagination. The second half of his most popular work can even be said to offer the best apology of its time for the power of the imagination, a fact little noted by commentators. In the *Travels*, Swift bluntly accuses the Laputans of lacking "Imagination, Fancy, and Invention" (PW vol. xi, p. 163), with what consequences their frenziedly abstract speculations show only too well. Book iv is not quite as explicit, it is true. Gulliver is simply shown to be so fascinated by the Houyhnhnms' rationalism that he overlooks their inability to accept that there exists a world beyond their island, which is different from their own. This is enough however to suggest that reason untempered by imagination makes for an uncomplicated world of cold relationships, and for an oversimplified view of that life which the rest of the travel account is at pains to represent in some of its rich variety. On closing the book, which reader does not retain the impression that the King of Brobdingnag, Glumdalclitch, Pedro de Mendez, the Portuguese captain who rescues Gulliver after his departure from Houyhnhnmland, and Gulliver himself on occasions, are superior to the utilitarian Lilliputians, the Brobdingnagian scientists, the Laputans or the rational horses because they have the gift of imaginative sympathy? On the basis of such evidence it would seem reasonable to conclude that, for Swift, it is not reason or the use of language alone that characterize man as a creature, but imagination as well: imagination which is all too often for him a main cause of blindness, selfishness and imperfection but can also at times help him to overcome these limitations. Swift's obstinate recourse to fictions throughout his career demonstrates this again and again. In this connection, what precedes can be read as an attempt to clarify how

232

he was able to reconcile the demands of rationality with the fantasy of a vivid and fertile imagination.

His satires repeatedly suggest that if anyone wishes to follow the paths of reason he should begin by relentlessly tracking down manifestations of unreason in the way he thinks, which can only be done if he learns to discipline his imaginary. It is for this reason that he borrows rather than invents his fictions. The imaginary exists. His creativeness consists in using available material. He knows how to exploit his rich sources, and his work betrays a cunning sense of the way in which they can be combined to produce unexpected representations of the world. His satires are cleverly contrived and are meant to look so. His fictional patterns and motifs, which oscillate between conformity with respect to their models and deviation from the tradition, have been seen to lend some piquancy to his more insipid satires. This piquancy may result from the clever use of the staging of a dramatic language gesture, the nostalgic flavour of folktales, the thrill of conspiracies, or the fun of comedies and masquerades. In addition to a similar surface attractiveness, the combination of the same fictional patterns and motifs lend the more profound satires, subtlety, depth, and this pith, for which the qualifier Swiftian has been coined. It is they that have contributed to the fascination and amusement of such different readers as Lady Mary Wortley Montagu, Walter Scott, William Hazlitt, André Breton, or Robert Graves who, more than two hundred years after John Dryden, replies to the latter that the author of *Gulliver's Travels*, not he, was with John Wolcott and Defoe one of the truly poetically gifted writers of their otherwise unpoetic age.[1] And has George Orwell, who is so critical of Swift's achievement, done so much better than his model in this difficult genre of the satirical fiction?[2] At their best, and in their own very special way – it is special because it uses fictions to warn readers against the deceits of fiction –, Swift's satires belong to that exclusive category of great English, German, Spanish or Russian fictional works which shake our confidence in man's rationality and probe deeper into the irrational, and at times dangerous, side of his nature.

The brilliant parodies of discourses, the inverted narrative and dramatic patterns or motifs and the fictions of the metamorphoses of the

1 "Politics and Poetry", *Epilogue* iii: 41 - 42 (1937).
2 "Politics v. Literature: An Examination of *Gulliver's Travels*", reprinted in *Jonathan Swift*, Penguin Critical Anthologies, pp. 342 - 361.

body are, of course, features which distinguish Swift's satires from those of other satirists. Yet their real significance lies elsewhere. In so far as their crucial function is concerned, it can be summed up as follows: their configuration operates both like an emplotment and a satirical ferment. Emplotments, whether of a dramatic or narrative nature, transform actions and events into self-explanatory stories. The difference in satirical emplotments is, as repeatedly observed, that the explanatory bias is accentuated. It is more patently interpretative than in other narratives, without however becoming either analytical or argumentative. The development remains fictional to the end. The various fictional patterns which, singly and together, constitute the emplotment, shape the satirical process and determine the changes of tone. Their configuration gives the satires the dynamic character both of an action and of delayed recognition. At every stage, finally, it brings the reader's attention back to man. Human nature, of which Swift presents an image halfway between the still religious English classical age of the end of the seventeenth century and the resolutely secular socio-political vision of the Enlightenment, is his main subject. The fictions of the journalistic and literary game, inverted folktales and comic situations, are primarily concerned with individuals and their responsibilities as members of society. It is on this partly humanist and partly protestant basis that are elaborated the sometimes more fragmentary and sometimes more comprehensive social and political visions proposed by the individual satires. The socio-political reflexion is derivative, because it is rooted in the criticism of human nature. To refuse to recognize the dominant function of the fictional patterns and of their configuration is in a sense to ignore what forms the central object of Swift's satires and what gives his work its typical Augustan quality.

Repeatedly too, the discussion of Swift's satires has come up against the ambiguity of some aspects of their meaning. The polysemic nature of narrative, dramatic and descriptive fictions, the combination of distinct modes and genres, the structural ruptures or reversals of patterns and, finally, the rôle of laughter as satirical leaven produce texts which evidence an openly ambivalent attitude towards various moral, social and political issues. At least, this is the impression left by many a satire. In this context, a remark made earlier takes on a particular significance. It was seen that Swift's fictions did not lend themselves to the conceptualization of their insights, and to a translation of their fictions into definite ideas, to the same extent as those of other eighteenth-century writers, and that his art was not one of counter-statements, like Pope's, Mandeville's, or Addison's. It is an art of disturbing suggestions, simultaneously offered and withdrawn. Once the satirist has "hooked" the reader and has him "fast", as a contemporary quoted earlier puts is, he modulates his effects to a climax of uncomfortable insinuations – of which "A Digression on Madness" and "A Voyage to the Houyhnhnms" are the most memorable illustrations. After that, he half reassures the reader with a less distressing comment, usually in a comic or at least major key, which however does not completely dispel the uneasiness. It is the art of a writer aware that his world is changing and no longer suffers the direct expression of certain deep convictions to which he remains attached. It lends his satirical fictions that special character which accounts for the peculiar hold they have over the reader's imagination.

It has also been noted that, whenever the configuration of Swift's satirical fictions is simple, either because it is essentially parodic or descriptively isomorphic, his representations of circumstantial reality bear an evident resemblance to the general image we have formed of the world of his time. They offer recognizable pictures of eighteenth-century life, as do the anecdotal and descriptive traits that pepper his non-fictional discourses. As the combination of various fictional patterns becomes more intricate and fanciful, particularly when it involves the use of folktales and of the metamorphoses of the body the representations prove less direct and the link with the actual historical referent less easy to establish with any degree of accuracy, so that they read more like fables. In either case, however, what emerges clearly is that, for all their realism or fancifulness, Swift's fictions reflect the sensitiveness of a whole period, as well as some of the more secret dreams and nightmares of man. Considering this, and the fact that our time has inherited so many of its views and problems from the age of Swift, it becomes difficult to accept the verdict of those who conclude that his satirical fictions are no longer of interest to anyone except eighteenth-century specialists and that they fail to appeal to the "modern critical imagination". In fact, paying proper attention to the fictional aspects of his satires may be the best way today to rescue his best work from the nursery and the den of scholarship to which the nineteenth century has confined it and where it lives an imperfect existence. At any rate, if his great satires do not attract all the attention they deserve, the blame should not be laid on the writer, as is commonly done. Since literary studies have become one of the human sciences, there has been a tendency to overstress the importance of sophistication in writing, and it is well-known that there is no lack of it in the works of the author of the *Travels*. The current interest in his complex satirical strategies has partly obscured the apparently more simple, and above all more attractive and universal, aspects of their presentation. As a result, what is often proposed is an impoverished reading of his satires. This is unfortunate, for the health and influence of a culture depends largely on the richness of its creative artists's insights and on the popularity of the works it considers as forming part of its tradition. A full appreciation of the suggestive power of Swift's writings can do much to restore the critical balance and revive the interest of a larger public. Readers who rediscover that the work opens a fascinating window on the psychological life of another age will also be the readier to accept it as one of the great monuments of human fantasy, woven out of the illusions and delusions of man, yet always transcending them.

Whether in their tactical sophistication or imaginative simplicity, Swift's satires have in any case more to captivate the modern reader than is often recognized in studies of his work. First of all, we are perhaps just emerging from two decades of exacerbated critical theorizing, and there seems to be a parallel between the present situation and Swift's own. His critical attitude towards criticism and theoretical abstractions in general, which finds expression in imaginative attacks on the weakness of human understanding, may well awaken echoes in the minds of those who have lost faith in the power of theories to enrich the reading experience. More technically – and it must not be forgotten that Swift is essentially concerned with the existential and experiential side of things –, the author of *A Tale* delights in manipulating points of views and can prove as daring in the matter as modern novelists. In his own way, Swift is as concerned with fiction-making and its illusionism as modern writers are. He makes and breaks patterns, of course not to convince readers that they are victims of predominant ideologies as is the fashion today, but more practically to bring them back to a little more common sense in the absence of unfailing reason. Magazines, and the popular press in general, continue to use some of the very strategies that Swift exposes in his satires: the reader's digest style, the we-understand-your-problem tone, or we-share-your-views attitude. Their serialized and shorter fictions, like his, have recourse to fairytale patterns, crime stories and scandalous chronicles to entertain their readers. Only the comedy of manners is, to a large extent, missing today, as are the columns on *savoir-vivre*. Moreover, psychiatry and anthropology have revived the interest in folktales and other eternal narrative and dramatic patterns, so that readers cannot but be alert to the satirist's handling of them. As for the fictions of the body, each century has its own, and ours are as insistent as ever. Our magazines are full of our own concern with our frail and cumbersome "carcasses". Season after season, their fashion pages tempt readers with chic garments designed to conceal decaying anatomies, their columns are devoted to hairdressing or new brands of make-up destined to caulk the lines on the face and repair the ravages of time, their medical pages endlessly discuss rejuvenating cures, slimming courses, or the advances of plastic surgery, all of them means of undoing the damage done by the gastronomy columns. The trouble with Swift's fables of man's mortality seems rather to be that, because they are classics, they do not find their way to the right category of readers; or, when they do, they fail to reach them in the proper situation and at the right moment. Although remote from ours, Swift's fictions are particularly apt in drawing attention to the biases in the values man lives by. Separately, the three fictional patterns of the framing discourses, framed tales and metamorphoses of the body have all that is necessary to interest readers today. Together they constitute an unsettling mirror of their illusions and anxieties. Finally, most disturbing of all perhaps for today's readers, they propose an exploration of, not the heart of man, but what Swift, unlike our age, considers as his unhallowed body.

The study of Swift's fictional devices does not revolutionize our understanding of his conception of man and life. There is no denying that this conception is often provocative and sombre. Yet a proper recognition of the crucial function played by the fictional patterns in the satires is an important qualification of the general appreciation of what has so often been called his misanthropy. It shows first of all that such different works as *A Tale of a Tub*, *The Bickerstaff Papers*, *A Hue and Cry after Dismal*, *Gulliver's Travels*, or *A Modest Proposal* cannot be reduced to a single common denominator, be it the wit for which Swift was celebrated by his contemporaries or that misanthropy he has since been accused of expressing. This type of reductionism does not do justice to the variety of the pieces considered in this study. On the contrary, it denies the satirist the very quality for which the eighteenth century found him unique: indeed, a systematic adaptation of the utterance to the recipient and the circumstances is one of the true marks of wit. The careful weighing of the various fictional components in each satire allows Swift to do precisely that. Why is it that the folktale motif of Hop

O' My Thumb and the ogre is so discreetly suggested in *A Modest Proposal*, if not to avoid giving the folklore fantasy too much prominence, when the horror and urgency of the social and economic situation require a starker use of realism, and even of surrealism, to shake the reader out of his complacency? Only the folktale's macabre overtones are heard in this case, and rightly so, as too conspicuous a fantasy ingredient could only have detracted from the horror. *Gulliver's Travels* is different. The satire is more general. It embraces the past, the present and even the future. It is not meant to sound the same urgent note, and the evils that it exposes range from the most serious to the lightest. For these reasons the fanciful folktale components, the adventure story and the puppetry of the fictions of the body are foregrounded, and, as seen above, even the denunciation of man as vermin by the King of Brobdingnag is given a more light-hearted and humorous perspective than would have been the case had it found its way into *A Modest Proposal*. This is not to say that the *Travels* are not also concerned with profound human problems. After all, the conspiracy motif is as insistent as the folktale ingredient, and Gulliver's earnest conversations with several of his hosts hold a central place in his memoirs. Grim criticism and fantasy achieve a precarious balance, unique in Swift's production. The *Travels* are *par excellence* a work that fits Bolingbroke's description of Swift's strength as a writer, when he writes to his friend that he is quite sure "to find, in two pages of [his] Bagatelles, more good sence, useful knowledg, and true Religion, than you can shew me in the works of nineteen in twenty of the profound Divines and Philosophers of the age."[3] When the subject is light and topical, however, as with the affair of the rivalry between the footmen and the bucks in *The Humble Petition of the Footmen of Dublin* or that of the Earl of Nottingham's villainous spying on a general of the English forces in *A Hue and Cry*, the fictions become pure fun, and one would be hard put to detect in them any sign of pessimistic attitude towards human nature. Swift has, to an eminent degree, the gift of adjusting the vigour of his attacks to the nature of the evils he exposes. The only work where he might be said to be at fault on this point is his first satire, *A Tale*. And so, before accusing this text or that of expressing only withering scorn or pessimism, it is necessary to take into account the factor of this adaptation of the means to a specific end, and there is no better way of doing so than by looking at the rôle played by the fictional

3 *Correspondence* vol ii, p. 416

elements in the work. Satire is a protean genre, and Swift avails himself of all its possibilities, from the most simply farcical to the most grating invention, as circumstances require.

No less important, the study of the fictions of the satirist warns against a confusion between the views of the man and those expressed by his work, here particularly his satires. The distinction is not always easy to make, but to fail to make it leads to unfortunate oversimplifications. It is now commonly accepted that different literary forms express distinct world views, but that their assumptions about the world are no safe guides to a writer's ideas and beliefs, as his choice of a mode of expression can be dictated by other than personal motives and, once adopted, a genre then imposes, to a large extent, its world view on him. Swift knew this, of course. With satire and, what is more, satire that never speaks in the writer's voice but utilizes a type of parody to mystify the reader by means of a radical distancing effect, one should be even more wary in assuming that a direct link can be readily identified. What has just been said about the variety of Swift's fictions forbids any hasty generalization, except of the most basic sort, like the fact that satire is , by definition, critical of the world and negative. But to say that it is critical is different from saying that it is pessimistic like tragedy or optimistic like comedy. It is neither. To conclude that, because Swift is critical about his world, he also hates mankind is a reader's inference, but not one that is warranted by the philosophy of the genre, and least of all by the nature of Swift's satirical fictions. Misanthropy is no inspiration for an ironist who, above all, delights in the things he criticizes. He is much attached to the shortcomings of man and society that inspire him: he feasts on them. Sometimes they draw pure laughter from him and sometimes laughter mixed with indignation. Each fiction has its own tonality. The question of whether Swift is misanthropic and pessimistic is ultimately of secondary importance and should not interfere with the reader's appreciation of the validity of his criticism.

Finally, due recognition of the nature and importance of the fictions of the satirist also helps to correct the impression often given by a cursory reading of the two or three main satires, and a few political pamphlets, that Swift's work is all in the same satiric strain. First of all, the turn of his stories or scenes, the wealth and selectivity of their details, the semeiotic range of their allusiveness, the physical thickness of the body actors that animate them and, above all, the combination of all these elements are to a large extent the source of a complexity unrivalled by his contemporaries and successors. Even Voltaire, the greatest of them, whose *Relation de la maladie, de la confession, de la mort et de l'apparition du Jésuite Berthier*, as well as his *Zadig, Candide* and *Micromégas*, are indebted to Swift in matters of literary invention, does not always attain the same vividness and incisiveness. By comparison, his tales sound more remote from everyday experience, and more cerebral. Much more than verbal irony and cunning rhetoric, the fictional components of the satires remain the true source of Swift's satirical power for readers today. To call him a satirist is to say little about his qualities as a writer. It is because he is a subtle parodist and an imaginative caricaturist that he is a satirist of genius. Another attractive characteristic of Swift's satirical fictions is their unpredictability. From the planning and staging of hoaxes and the impersonations of people and puppets to their punitive laughter, they never cease to surprise the reader. This quality, together with the fact that they are never longer than they should be, may not lend them the Faustian energy and exuberance of Rabelais, but exuberance is sometimes a little trying – at least his age thought so –, and there is room in life for other manifestations of creativity. In any case, Swift's satires display enough inventiveness, enough dry sense of humour, and even enough good humour when circumstances allow, to offset the forbidding and, to some, repulsive or galling aspects of his work. As generations of readers testify, the thrill of invention and laughter – *Shadenfreude* though it may be – is infectious, as is any expression of real creativity.

Index

207, 208, 215-9, 237

framed fiction, 35, 38, 39, 40, 42, 61, 66, 70, 73-124, 125, 132, 182, 183, 186, 197, 198-203, 207, 214-5, 216, 237

Fries, Udo, 43

Frye, Northrop, 44

Frye, Roland M., 191

Fussell, Paul, 116, 121, 128

game, 54-61, 65, 68, 82, 111, 124, 203, 207, 208, 219, 234

Gay, John, 76, 82, 128

Genette, Gérard, 26-7

genres (literary and journalistic), 14-5, 23, 26, 29-35, 38, 42, 44, 51-2, 66, 68, 69-70, 71, 73, 76, 82, 100, 107, 115, 122, 215, 231, 232, 234, 239; *advertisement,* 34, 40, 56, 65; *almanac,* 31, 56-7, 58, 106, 113, 147, 222, 224; *apology,* 34, 36; *broadside ballad,* 32, 33, 34, 35, 46, 76, 84, 90, 91, 215, 225; *conduct book,* 31, 35; *conte philosophique,* 72, 99, 202, 240; *death-bed scene,* 106-7, 110, 168; *dedication,* 36-8, 39, 56, 62, 97; *digression,* 34, 36, 38-9, 44, 59, 96, 97, 165, 198, 199, 200, 208, 217, 219; *elegy,* 33, 34, 57, 110, 113; *epistle,* 30, 35, 36, 37; *footnote,* 36, 39, 44; *foreword,* 34; *funeral oration,* 106; *half-sheet,* 41, 46, 57, 110; *handbook* (or *manual*), 31, 34, 38, 107, 176, 180; *introduction,* 29, 36, 37, 38, 39, 44, 107, 165; *lampoon,* 33, 34; *letter,* 25, 28, 32, 34, 36, 40, 56, 57, 58, 65, 70, 83, 100, 215, 217; *meditation,* 30, 217; *memoirs / memoir,* 28, 40, 44, 46, 47-53, 76, 101, 238; *mock epic,* 23, 30, 35, 81, 110, 198; *news item,* 32, 41, 42, 43, 46, 59, 81, 89, 100, 215, 218; *note,* 36-7, 59; *novel,* 27, 42, 44, 59, 61, 64, 70, 72, 75, 115, 123, 171, 186,

195, 196, 202; *pamphlet,* 33, 34, 42, 46, 59, 100, 225, 239; *pastoral,* 33, 110, 117, 218; *petition,* 33, 34, 59, 66, 100; *preface,* 37, 38, 44, 56, 59, 81, 97, 198, 217; *proposal,* 33, 34, 35, 59, 201, 215; *romance,* 28, 29, 48, 53, 70, 75, 76, 118, 196; *secret history,* 76, 101-2, 110, 114, 117, 125; *song,* 33, 34, 41; *travel book,* 23, 33, 35, 40-1, 44, 48-54, 56, 58, 59, 65, 66, 81, 86, 95, 96, 98, 163, 199, 204, 205, 217-8

Goffman, Ervin, 26

Goldgar, Bertrand A., 229

Goodman, Nelson, 21

Graves, Robert, 233

Grimm, Jacob and Wilhelm, 85, 86

Guthkelch, A.C. and D. Nichol Smith, 85

Hacking, Ian, 21

Hawkesworth, John, 229

Hazlitt, William, 233

Herder, Johann Gottfried, 12

hoax 45, 54, 56, 58, 70, 106, 107, 202, 210, 218, 240

Hobbes, Thomas, 116-7, 191

Hogarth, William, 62, 100, 132

Hopkins, Robert H., 117

Horace, 99

Huizinga, Johan, 68

Humes, James, 229

humour, 60, 74, 90, 96, 102, 123, 128, 194, 218, 238, 240

imitation (see *mimesis*)

Ingram, Allan, 55, 220

irony, 13, 14, 51, 76, 93, 137, 195, 201, 204, 205, 206, 209, 239, 240

Ionesco, Eugène, 187

Irving, H.W., 74

isomorphism, 23-4, 69, 74, 100, 121, 195, 197, 201, 207, 235

243